UNEVEN TIDES

UNEVEN TIDES
RISING INEQUALITY IN AMERICA

Edited by
Sheldon Danziger and
Peter Gottschalk

RUSSELL SAGE FOUNDATION NEW YORK

The Russell Sage Foundation

The Russell Sage Foundation, one of the oldest of America's general purpose foundations, was established in 1907 by Mrs. Margaret Olivia Sage for "the improvement of social and living conditions in the United States." The Foundation seeks to fulfill this mandate by fostering the development and dissemination of knowledge about the political, social, and economic problems of America.

The Board of Trustees is responsible for oversight and the general policies of the Foundation, while administrative direction of the program and staff is vested in the President, assisted by the officers and staff. The President bears final responsibility for the decision to publish a manuscript as a Russell Sage Foundation book. In reaching a judgment on the competence, accuracy, and objectivity of each study, the President is advised by the staff and selected expert readers. The conclusions and interpretations in Russell Sage Foundation publications are those of the authors and not of the Foundation, its Trustees, or its staff. Publication by the Foundation, therefore, does not imply endorsement of the contents of the study.

Library of Congress Cataloging-in-Publication Data

Uneven tides : rising inequality in America / [edited by] Sheldon Danziger, Peter Gottschalk.
p. cm.
Includes bibliographical references and index.
ISBN 0-87154-222-6
1. Income—United States. 2. Income distribution—United States. 3. Wages—United States. 4. Labor market—United States. 5. Tax incidence—United States. 6. United States—Economic conditions—1981– I. Danziger, Sheldon. II. Gottschalk, Peter, 1942– .
HC110.I5U47 1993
339.2'0973—dc20 92-14233
CIP

The paper used in this publication meets the minimum requirements of American National Standard for Information Sciences—Permanence of Paper for Printed Library Materials, ANSI Z39.48-1984.

RUSSELL SAGE FOUNDATION
112 East 64th Street, New York, New York 10021

10 9 8 7 6 5 4 3 2 1

To Our Children,
Jacob and Anna, and Julie

Contributors

Maria Cancian, Graduate Student, Department of Economics, University of Michigan

Sheldon Danziger, Professor of Social Work and Public Policy and Faculty Associate in Population Studies, University of Michigan

Richard B. Freeman, Professor of Economics, Harvard University, and Director, Labor Studies Program, National Bureau of Economic Research

Peter Gottschalk, Professor of Economics, Boston College, and Research Affiliate, Institute for Research on Poverty, University of Wisconsin—Madison

Edward M. Gramlich, Professor of Economics and Public Policy and Director, Institute of Public Policy Studies, University of Michigan

Michael W. Horrigan, Senior Economist, Bureau of Labor Statistics

Lynn A. Karoly, Associate Economist, Rand Corporation

Richard Kasten, Deputy Assistant Director, Tax Analysis Division, Congressional Budget Office

Ronald B. Mincy, Senior Research Associate, Urban Institute

Kevin M. Murphy, Professor of Business, University of Chicago, and Research Associate, National Bureau of Economic Research

Frank Sammartino, Analyst, Tax Analysis Division, Congressional Budget Office

Finis Welch, Professor of Economics, Texas A&M University, and President, Unicon Research Corporation

Contents

PART ONE

Background

1

Introduction

Sheldon Danziger / Peter Gottschalk

Conventional wisdom about income inequality in America is radically different in the early 1990s than it was ten to fifteen years ago. At that time, Alan Blinder (1980) began a review article on the distribution of economic well-being by noting that "the more things change, the more they remain the same." Blinder's central conclusion was " . . . when we . . . consider the *distribution* of economic welfare—economic equality, as it is commonly called—the central stylized fact is one of *constancy*. As measured in the official data, income inequality was just about the same in 1977 . . . as it was in 1947." (p. 416) Henry Aaron (1978) put it even more colorfully by stating that following changes in the income distribution "was like watching the grass grow." (p. 17)

Economists were puzzled as to why inequality of family income in the post–World War II era had been so stable, despite the rapid growth of government spending in general, and antipoverty spending in particular (Reynolds and Smolensky, 1977). Inequality, in contrast to poverty, was not much discussed in Congress or in the media. Economists writing in the late 1970s did not expect inequality to increase. Indeed, Robert Haveman (1977) concluded that

> If one were inclined to speculate, . . . it would not be unreasonable to forecast that, in 1985, analysts will attribute a modest reduction in income inequality during the 1975–1985 decade to some combination of (1) an overhauled and somewhat larger income support system, (2) a reformed federal revenue system resulting in increased effective tax rates on higher income recipients, (3) a

> significantly expanded public employment policy, and (4) a modest reduction of labor market rigidities, including a reduction in labor market discrimination against racial minorities. [p. 19]

Jeffrey Williamson and Peter Lindert (1980), using a model that had successfully replicated two centuries of United States inequality experience, also projected falling inequality for the 1980s:

> There are, it seems, three good reasons for expecting continued downward pressure on the pay advantages of the more skilled: Labor force growth will drop off and remain low throughout the 1980s; more balanced patterns of productivity growth are likely to be forthcoming in the wake of the jump in the relative price of the fuels; and the pattern of factor proportions has converged among sectors in a fashion that makes further leveling likely as average skill levels grow. [p. 289]

Peter Gottschalk (1981) was similarly optimistic about the trend in poverty. His projections, based on forecasts of the growth in mean earnings, earnings inequality, and the assumption that cash transfers would grow as fast as national income, were for a 1985 poverty rate of 9 percent.

We now know that these and other researchers did not foresee the slowdown in mean earnings, the rise in earnings inequality, the continuing high poverty rates, and the diminished governmental concern with poverty and inequality that characterized the 1980s. In fact, all four of Haveman's expected policy changes were reversed in the 1980s. The income support system is now somewhat smaller, effective tax rates on higher income recipients are lower, most public service employment programs have been eliminated, and much recent attention has been focused on persistent labor market discrimination (e.g., Kirschenman and Neckerman, 1991). After thirty years of relative constancy, a period that was ending when Blinder, Haveman, Williamson and Lindert, and Gottschalk were writing, we have experienced a decade of rising inequality of both earnings and family income.[1]

Economists, Congress, and the media are now focused on rising inequality and the growing gap in living standards between the rich and the poor. As Lynn Karoly demonstrates in her chapter, there is no doubt that inequality of earnings and family income have increased.[2] As a result, the old conven-

[1]See Karoly (Chapter 2) and Gramlich, Kasten, and Sammartino (Chapter 7) in this book for reviews of trends in inequality and the effects of government policies during the past decade.

[2]The only dissenting voices are Mayer and Jencks (1991), who use consumer expenditure, rather than income, measures of inequality. They find that inequality of expenditures did not increase between the early 1970s and mid-1980s. However, Cutler and Katz (1991), using the same consumer expenditure data for a different time period, show that inequality of expendi-

tional wisdom that "a rising tide lifts all boats" has been rejected. We now know that the 1980s was a decade of "uneven tides." Most small boats were docked where the tides were low, while the few large boats, docked in different harbors, rose with the uneven tides.

Although we know what happened in the 1980s, we do not know what will happen when the next economic recovery begins. The recent recession has probably led to an even higher level of inequality in 1992 than in 1989. But there is no simple explanation of the causes of the increased inequality of the 1980s. Will inequality continue to increase over the next decade as it has over the past decade? Why did inequality not fall during an almost eight-year economic recovery? What role have demographic factors played? Did changes in government programs and policies with regard to minimum wages, taxes, and income transfers contribute to rising inequality? These are some of the questions addressed by this volume.

While we have learned much about the trend in inequality from dozens of recent studies, the following statement, written in 1920 by Hugh Dalton, serves as an appropriate introduction to this volume:

> The question whether the inequality of income is increasing or decreasing in modern communities is one of the most important questions in economics. Many writers have attempted to answer it, but their answers do not generally carry much conviction. To determine whether, under modern conditions, inequality tends to increase or decrease, involves the enumeration of a large number of distinct and conflicting tendencies and the weighing and balancing of them one against the other. [Quoted in Brady, 1951, p. 4]

Recent research has taught us that Dalton was correct. There are no simple explanations. No single factor accounts for the many complex changes in the distribution of income. Rather than looking for a single "smoking gun," recent studies have tried to gauge the relative importance of alternative explanations. Those explanations that seem to be either inconsistent with the data or quantitatively too small to explain the rising inequality of the 1980s have been discarded. This volume continues in that spirit by bringing together original essays that explore several possible explanations for growth in inequality. Our objective is to fill in several gaps in our understanding of the causes of changes in inequality.

To place these studies in context, we first present a brief overview of the historical changes in inequality and the evolution of the conventional wisdom

---

tures did increase between 1980 and 1988. Thus, part of the Mayer-Jencks results reflect the earlier period they study. Since our concern is with the 1980s, the Cutler-Katz results are more relevant.

regarding the interpretation of these trends. We then briefly describe the chapters in this volume.

Historical Changes in Earnings and Family Income Inequality

In the most comprehensive review of long-run changes in income inequality, Williamson and Lindert (1980) place the post–World War II stability in inequality into historical perspective. After documenting the dramatic leveling of income differences between the Great Depression and the end of World War II (1929 to 1945), they conclude that

> the leveling ceased by 1950. By almost any yardstick, inequality has changed little since the late 1940s. If there has been any trend, it is toward slightly more inequality in pre-fisc income and toward slightly less inequality in post-fisc income. This stability has been extraordinary even by twentieth century standards. [p. 92]

Figure 1.1, however, shows that just as Williamson and Lindert were going to press, the "extraordinary" stability in family income inequality was breaking down. While the Gini coefficient for family income had declined by .013 points over three decades (from .378 in 1949 to .365 in 1979), it jumped by .036 points in the next decade (from .365 in 1979 to .401 in 1989).[3]

Another way to view this increased inequality is to compare families at different points in the distribution. Growth in mean family income was very rapid and widely shared between 1949 and 1969. The inflation-adjusted income of a family at the 20th percentile grew by 92 percent, while the income of a family at the 80th percentile grew by 82 percent. In contrast, mean income grew very little over the next two decades. Growth was substantial for families at the top of the distribution, while those at the bottom actually lost ground. In 1989, the real income of a family at the 20th percentile was 5 percent below the 1969 level, while that of a family at the 80th percentile was 19 percent higher.

Figure 1.1 shows inequality in family income rising almost continually after 1975. While the sharp increase in inequality between 1979 and 1983

[3]Levy (1987) has shown, and we agree, that the published Census data presented in Figure 1.1 overstate the trend toward inequality because they are based only on money income and exclude taxes paid and government noncash payments, such as Medicare and food stamps. However, accounting for noncash benefits and taxes would lead to an even greater increase in inequality during the 1980s, as public benefits to the poor and taxes on the wealthy were both cut.

Figure 1.1 Gini Coefficient of Family Income: 1947–1989

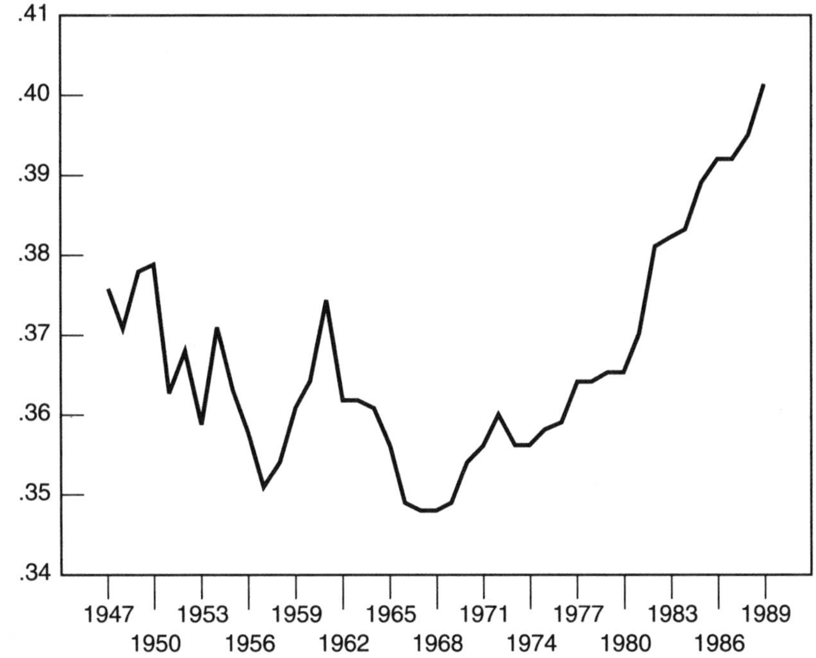

Source: U.S. Bureau of the Census (1990).

can be attributed to the recessions of the early 1980s, the continued increase during the ensuing recovery was counter to all expectations. The conventional wisdom (e.g., Blank and Blinder, 1986) holds that inequality is countercyclical. During recessions, employers retain the most experienced workers as demand declines. The newly hired and least-skilled, who have below-average earnings, are laid off and experience disproportionate income losses. Recoveries are characterized by increased employment of the least experienced. Such countercyclical swings in inequality have characterized most recoveries prior to the 1980s.

Blank and Blinder's (1986) prediction of the degree of inequality for 1989 demonstrates not only that the expansion of the 1980s had a counterintuitive impact on inequality, but also that inequality increased by a substantial amount. They estimated a model for the 1948–1983 period that describes how the income share received by each quintile of families had varied over the business cycle. Then they predicted what the income distribution would look like in 1989, given several scenarios. Their optimistic scenario, about which they said ". . . it is most unlikely for the economy to grow for seven

Table 1.1 Changes in the Distribution of Family Income: 1973–1989

	Share of Income Received by Each Quintile			1983–1989 Change in Income Share	
	1973 (1)	1983 (2)	1989 (3)	Prediction (4)	Actual (5)
Lowest Quintile	5.5%	4.7%	4.6%	+0.6%	−0.1%
Second	11.9	11.1	10.6	−0.2	−0.5
Third	17.5	17.1	16.5	+0.1	−0.6
Fourth	24.0	24.4	23.7	0.0	−0.7
Highest Quintile	41.1	42.7	44.6	−0.8	+1.9

Sources: For Columns (1), (2), and (4), Blank and Blinder (1986); for Columns (3) and (5), U.S. Bureau of the Census (1990).

years without a recession" (p. 206), used inflation and unemployment rates for 1989 that turned out to be quite similar to the actual 1989 values.

Columns 1–3 of Table 1.1 show the actual Census Bureau data on the income share received by each quintile of families in 1973, 1983, and 1989. As expected, inequality increased between 1973 and 1983, a period of falling real family income and increasing unemployment. Blank and Blinder's predicted changes in quintile shares for the 1983–1989 period are shown in Column 4, and the actual changes between 1983 and 1989 are shown in Column 5. Even though family income increased and inflation and unemployment declined between 1983 and 1989, inequality increased. The income share of the bottom 80 percent of families was lower in 1989 than in 1983 or 1973.

The 1989 income shares received by the lowest and the highest quintiles deviate the most from the Blank-Blinder predictions. The income share of the lowest quintile fell to 4.6 percent instead of rising to 5.3 percent and the share of the top quintile increased to 44.6 percent instead of falling to 41.9 percent. As the chapter by Edward Gramlich, Richard Kasten, and Frank Sammartino demonstrates, most of the income growth of this top quintile was actually concentrated among the top 1 and 5 percent of all persons.

The economic performance of the 1980s was atypical, and, in some ways, resembled the 1920s. While Williamson and Lindert considered the 1920s to be atypical, their description of it, which follows, sounds similar to patterns observed in the 1980s.

> This leveling was then undone in the 1920s, with higher-paid groups increasing their pay advantage over both the urban unskilled and farm labor. By 1929,

> the gaps between traditionally high-paid and low-paid jobs were almost as wide as in 1916, when the widest gaps in American history seem to have prevailed . . . The return to inequality in the 1920s was so great that . . . the real income gains for the top 7% of the nonfarm population alone matched the increase in real personal income, leaving no apparent net gain for the rest of the population. [p. 81]

By the late 1980s, there was widespread agreement in the public and academic press about the broad outlines of the distributional changes that had taken place. The causes of the change were, however, much less well understood. Research into the causes of changes in inequality were severely hampered by the dimensions of the problem—a complete explanation would involve nothing less than a full general equilibrium model of labor and capital markets with sufficient detail to capture the changes in labor markets institutions, demographics, and public policies that occurred during the 1970s and 1980s.

Rather than starting with a grand behavioral model, research in this area has tended to be exploratory and descriptive. By describing the dimensions of the problem and seeing whether potential explanations are consistent with the stylized facts, researchers have focused attention on a smaller number of potential hypotheses. The chapters in this book follow in this tradition by exploring specific changes in labor markets, demographic trends, and public policies that could have affected inequality.

Overview of Essays in this Volume

In Chapter 2, Karoly lays out the facts by answering the following questions: When did inequality begin to increase? What was the trend in the 1980s? Does the trend in inequality differ for individuals versus families, for men versus women, for blacks versus whites? Has inequality of family income (or individual earnings) grown due to decreases at the bottom or increases at the top of the distribution or both? Are the answers to these questions sensitive to the inequality measure used?

Karoly analyzes annual data on earnings and family income from the March 1964 through March 1990 Current Population Survey computer tapes. She examines a variety of income concepts and consumer units (family income, income of families and unrelated individuals, income adjusted by family size) and a variety of inequality measures (the relative income of percentiles, the variance of the logarithm of income). She concludes that inequality has been increasing by all measures. Furthermore, many of the time-series show that the relative economic status of families in the bottom of the distribution has been falling for almost two decades.

According to Karoly, the 1980s were unique in the extent of the relative gains of the rich. Although definitions of "classes" are arbitrary, she finds that the upper classes, as well as the lower classes, increased in the 1980s and that the middle class declined.

Labor Market Factors

The essays in Part II explore alternative explanations for changes in the distribution of earnings. Since labor market income accounts for about 70 percent of family income, changes in the distribution of earnings potentially offer the most important explanations for changes in the distribution of family income.

To put the essays on labor market changes in this volume into context, we briefly review the major findings from the rapidly growing literature on increased earnings inequality.[4] The puzzle that these studies attempt to unravel is why inequality between skill groups and within skill groups (e.g., the earnings of college-educated, white males, with one to five years' experience, working full-time year-round) increased during the late 1970s and 1980s. For example, in Chapter 3, Kevin Murphy and Finis Welch show that college graduates with one to five years of experience earned about 32 percent more than high-school graduates with similar experience in 1978. This college premium rose to 60 percent by 1989. Such large changes in such a short time span have seldom been experienced.

Research undertaken during the late 1970s and early 1980s focused primarily on supply-side factors to explain changes in both between- and within-skill class inequality (e.g., Murphy and Welch, 1988). For example, researchers explored the hypotheses that decreases in earnings among low-wage workers reflected labor supply responses to increased government transfer benefits, or that decreased wage rates of young workers reflected the excess supply of inexperienced workers as the baby boomers entered the labor market.

These and other supply-side explanations can explain, at most, only a small part of the recent increase in inequality. Although it could be argued that the baby boom depressed the relative wages of less-experienced workers during the 1970s, the fact that the earnings of young workers did not spring back when the baby boom was followed by the baby bust has eroded support for this supply-side explanation. Likewise, while increased income transfers could have induced labor force withdrawals and reduced the annual earnings

[4]For a review of all the recent studies, see Levy and Murnane (1991).

of less-skilled workers in the 1970s, the social welfare retrenchment of the 1980s should have had opposite effects. In fact, inequality of annual earnings grew the fastest during the period of most rapid retrenchment (Moffitt, 1990).

By the mid-1980s, researchers began to abandon supply-side explanations and to evaluate demand-side factors. This shift was partially prompted by the inability of supply-side explanations to explain the rising inequality. More important, however, was the fact that the earnings of more-skilled workers, particularly college graduates, were rising at the same time their numbers were also expanding. The simultaneous rise in prices and quantities implicated shifts in labor demand as the primary factor contributing to increased inequality.

Two demand-side factors have received the most attention—changes in industrial structure (fed largely by the globalization of markets and by changes in international competition) and changes in technology. According to the deindustrialization hypothesis (Bluestone and Harrison, 1982), increased international competition led U.S. companies to alter their patterns of employment and wage structures. The manufacturing base that had offered higher wage opportunities to less-educated workers shrank due to foreign competition in the markets for manufactured goods, as U.S. producers moved some factories to less-developed countries and reduced wages in their remaining U.S. plants. Meanwhile, the worldwide demand for highly educated American workers, and hence their earnings, increased. Their services could more easily be sold in international markets, where such skilled workers were relatively scarce. The result was a widening of skill differentials in the U.S. labor market.

This story is plausible, and also largely consistent with the time-series evidence. The increased inequality does partially reflect a growing skill premium, and it did occur at roughly the same time as the U.S. economy was increasing its role in international trade. The weakness in this explanation, however, is that it leaves largely unexplained the increased inequality *within* specific industries, especially in those industries that have little connection to international trade. While it is possible that wage differentials spread to all industries as a result of firms having to compete to keep their high-skilled workers, this requires large labor supply responses across industries. Furthermore, the bidding up of wages of skilled workers in these industries would lead them to become less skill intensive. Murphy and Welch (in Chapter 3) show that these patterns are not consistent with the facts. Gottschalk and Mary Joyce (1991) show that the pattern of greater skill intensity in the face of rising prices of skilled workers also occurred in a number of other industrialized countries in the 1980s.

An alternative demand-side explanation is that technologies have changed in such a way as to raise the productivity of educated workers relative to less-educated workers. The computer explosion and other examples abound, suggesting that the change in the skill differential reflects technologically driven increases in productivity. While the technology argument is plausible, it can only be tested indirectly since direct measures of technology are not readily available (see Bound and Johnson, 1989).

In Chapter 3, Murphy and Welch address the hypothesis that changes in earnings and wage inequality largely reflect changes in the industrial structure of employment. They ask whether the changes in the returns to skill and the skill mix reflect a disproportionate growth in industries that are skill-intensive and pay above-average differentials for skilled workers. If this were the case, then the data would at least be consistent with one part of the "deindustrialization" story.[5] They find that changes in the returns to skill and skill intensity resulted largely from changes *within* even narrowly defined industries. They conclude that even if the United States had maintained its manufacturing base and the relative size of the service sector had not grown, the distribution of earnings would still have become substantially less equal. They conclude that technological change, rather than changing industrial structure, is the primary factor contributing to inequality.

Changes in the institutional bases for wage setting offer another potential explanation for rising inequality. Unions, for example, have historically secured higher wages for their members, particularly in those manufacturing industries that have been most affected by changing patterns of international trade (e.g., automobiles and steel). The United States experienced a sharp decline during the 1980s in the percentage of the workforce covered by union contracts. This decline was concentrated in the private sector. Among blue-collar workers, union density fell from 39 percent in 1980 (the same as in 1970) to 24 percent in 1987.

In Chapter 4, Richard Freeman estimates the effect of declining unionization on earnings differentials between types of workers and on earnings inequality among male workers. He finds substantial effects. He estimates that about 20 percent of increased earnings inequality among employed men in the 1980s was associated with declining unionization. But increasing inequality was evident among unionized as well as nonunionized workers, suggesting that the primary cause of rising inequality lies elsewhere. When Freeman compares the U.S. experience to that of other industrialized na-

[5]The deindustrialization hypothesis encompasses other hypotheses, such as the hypothesis that changes in international competition were an important factor leading to changes in industrial structure and that the industries that grew were not only skill-intensive, but also the industries with high within-group inequality.

tions, he finds that inequality increased in many countries, but that increases tended to be smaller in those countries that were more highly unionized.

These labor market essays, and other studies that try to explain the rise in earnings inequality, all find large increases in wage inequality within finely defined groups. Murphy and Welch find increased inequality even after controlling for experience, education, and industry. Freeman finds inequality increasing even among unionized workers. He concludes that changes in unionization account for about 15 to 40 percent of the rise in the college premium, with the estimates falling in the lower range when he takes into account who is unionized.

What is the cause of this increased within-group inequality? One can argue by analogy that these increases must be due to increased demand for skills that have not been measured. If measured skills, such as experience and earnings, have higher rates of return in the 1980s than in the 1970s, it seems reasonable to assume that the same demand factors have raised the returns to unmeasured skills. The best procedure would be to measure these skills directly. While this may never be possible, Krueger (1991) does offer some evidence on one skill that is unmeasured in most studies—the skill associated with the use of computers. He finds that workers who use computers earn roughly 10 to 15 percent more than observationally similar workers who do not use them. Also, computer usage increased in most industries. Thus, this technological advance can explain part of the increased within-group inequality in many industries. It can, however, only explain part of the story, as computerization was of minimal significance in some sectors that experienced increased inequality.

Demographic Factors

The second major set of factors addressed in this volume consists of those demographic changes that influence family income inequality. Previous research in this area has focused on two demographic factors: the age and gender composition of families. First, changes in the age structure of family heads can potentially affect inequality, as younger and older families have below-average incomes. Karoly conducts a decomposition that partitions the increased inequality into one component due to the changing composition of the population and one to changes in within-group inequality. She finds that almost all of the increased inequality over the last twenty years is due to increased dispersion within age cohorts, and not to changes in the relative sizes of the cohorts.

The second commonly cited demographic change is the rapid growth in the proportion of all families headed by women without husbands present.

Since these households have much lower income than married-couple families, this demographic shift places more families in the lower tail of the distribution and is clearly poverty-increasing. However, previous research found that poverty rates were raised by no more than 0.1 percentage points per year because of demographic shifts (Gottschalk and Danziger, 1984). Similarly, Karoly finds that the increased inequality largely reflects rising inequality within family types, rather than the shift toward female-headed families.

Part III contains two chapters that examine the effects of recent changes in family size and family structure on income distribution. In Chapter 5, Gottschalk and Sheldon Danziger examine how changes in family size and family composition have contributed to rising child poverty and family income inequality over the last two decades. They find that the observed small changes in child poverty for blacks and whites since the late 1960s reflect large, but offsetting, demographic and economic changes. The trend toward female household headship has received considerable attention in the literature. However, several equally large, poverty-reducing demographic changes have received little attention. Gottschalk and Danziger find that decreases in the number of children per family and increases in maternal educational attainment have largely offset the poverty-increasing impact of increases in single parenthood.

In Chapter 6, Maria Cancian, Danziger, and Gottschalk examine how another important change in family structure—the increasing labor-force participation of married women—has affected the level and distribution of income among married-couple families. Wives' earnings have become increasingly important in raising mean income and in reducing inequality. In the past decade, wives' earnings accounted for more than two-thirds of the increase in the mean income of couples. Furthermore, income inequality among couples increased over the past twenty years and would have increased to an even greater extent were it not for the increased earnings of wives. Reductions in the dispersion of wives' earnings partially offset increases in the dispersion of husbands' earnings and the increased correlation in the earnings of spouses.

Public Policies

The third major area explored in this volume considers the effects of changes in public policies on the distribution of income. The late 1970s saw a reappraisal of the effects of the social welfare programs that had been enacted or expanded in the decade following the launching of the War on Poverty. This reappraisal was motivated, in part, by the economic stagnation—rising unemployment and inflation rates, falling real wages, rising real tax burdens—that characterized the years following the oil shock of 1973 and the subsequent recession.

The official perspective of the early 1980s, evident in the federal budgetary retrenchment in social spending, was quite different from that of previous decades. Antipoverty programs themselves were blamed for the fact that poverty failed to decline during the 1970s as it had during the 1950s and 1960s (Murray, 1984). The "Reagan experiment" assumed that if government avoided active interventions in a wide range of domestic policy areas, productivity and economic growth could be increased and prices, unemployment, and poverty could be reduced.

As a result, the 1980s were marked by historically large changes in tax and transfer policies. The effect of the rapid inflation of the 1970s was to erode the real value of many transfer benefits and push lower- and middle-income taxpayers into higher marginal brackets. Meanwhile the tax structure became more regressive, as social security taxes were raised and the progressivity of the income tax was diminished.

In Chapter 7, Gramlich, Kasten, and Sammartino examine the effect on family income inequality of changes in federal tax and income transfer policies. Like Karoly, they document that inequality in market incomes increased in the 1980s. They also incorporate Internal Revenue Service data, which have much better income information on the richest households than the CPS data that Karoly uses. They demonstrate that the income of the richest 1 percent of the population grew almost four times as fast as the mean income. Given the large increase in market inequality in the 1980s, government tax and transfer policies would have had to become more redistributive than they were in the 1970s just to keep post-tax, post-transfer inequality constant. Instead, tax and transfer policy changes became less effective in reducing market inequality. As a result, post-tax and transfer inequality increased by even more than market inequality. Between 1980 and 1990, the Gini coefficient of post-tax and post-transfer income increased by about 17 percent. About 60 percent of this increase can be attributed to increasing inequality of market income. The remainder reflects government's failure to maintain the redistributive effectiveness of the fisc.

The 1980s also differed from previous decades in that the Reagan administration opposed any increase in the minimum wage. Prior to the 1980s, the minimum wage was typically increased every few years. The minimum wage remained at $3.35 per hour between 1981 and 1990, falling as a percentage of the average wage to an historically low level. Michael Horrigan and Ronald Mincy, in Chapter 8, examine what would have happened to family income inequality had the minimum wage kept pace with inflation. They employ a simulation model and conclude that virtually none of the rising inequality of the 1980s can be attributed to the falling value of the real minimum wage. Such a change in the minimum wage would have reduced poverty (Mincy, 1990). However, it would not have affected inequality because minimum-wage workers are spread widely across the distribution of family income.

The chapters in this book were not intended to provide support for any particular agenda for reducing poverty or income inequality. Rather, they analyze the effects on inequality of recent changes in labor markets, demographic structure, and public policies. In general, most of these forces have been inequality-increasing and have contributed to the rejection of the pre-1980s conventional wisdom of a stable income distribution. They clearly document a new conventional wisdom—rising inequality in the 1980s. They also suggest that a return to the lower levels of inequality that characterized the post–World War II era is not likely to occur without dramatic changes in labor markets, demographic structure, or tax and transfer policies.

This volume was made possible by a grant from the Russell Sage Foundation. Eric Wanner, the president, provided intellectual leadership to the editors and contributors from the proposal stage to the final product. Madge Spitaleri provided administrative support and Lisa Nachtigall valuable assistance in the editorial process. We also thank the following conference participants for their helpful comments on prior drafts: McKinley Blackburn, Rebecca Blank, David Bloom, Gary Burtless, Larry Katz, Frank Levy, Robert Moffitt, Robert Plotnick, and James Smith.

References

Aaron, Henry. 1978. *Politics and the Professors: The Great Society in Perspective.* Washington, D.C.: Brookings Institution.

Blank, Rebecca, and Alan Blinder. 1986. "Macroeconomics, Income Distribution, and Poverty." In Danziger, Sheldon, and Daniel Weinberg, eds. *Fighting Poverty: What Works and What Doesn't.* Cambridge, MA: Harvard University Press.

Blinder, Alan. 1980. "The Level and Distribution of Economic Well-Being." In Feldstein, Martin, ed. *The American Economy in Transition.* Chicago: University of Chicago Press.

Bluestone, Barry, and Bennett Harrison. 1982. *The Deindustrialization of America.* New York: Basic Books.

Bound, John, and George Johnson. 1989. "Changes in the Structure of Wages During the 1980s: An Evaluation of Alternative Explanations." NBER Working Paper No. 2983.

Brady, Dorothy S. 1951. "Research on the Size Distribution of Income." In Conference on Research Income and Wealth, pp. 2–55. NBER, *Studies in Income and Wealth*, vol. 13. New York: National Bureau of Economic Research.

Cutler, David M., and Lawrence F. Katz. 1991. "Macroeconomic Performance and the Disadvantaged." Harvard University and NBER, mimeo.

Gottschalk, Peter, and Mary Joyce. 1991. "Changes in Earnings Inequality—An International Perspective." Boston College, mimeo.

Gottschalk, Peter, and Sheldon Danziger. 1984. "Macroeconomic Conditions, Income Transfers and Poverty." In Bawden, D. Lee, ed. *The Social Contract Revisited*. Washington, D.C.: Urban Institute Press.

Gottschalk, Peter, 1981. "Transfer Scenarios and Projections of Poverty into the 1980s." *Journal of Human Resources* 16 (1) (Winter): 41–59.

Haveman, Robert. 1977. "Introduction: Poverty and Social Policy in the 1960s and 1970s." In Haveman, Robert, ed. *A Decade of Federal Antipoverty Programs*. New York: Academic Press.

Kirschenman, Joleen, and Kathryn Neckerman. 1991. "'We'd Love to Hire Them, But...': The Meaning of Race for Employers." In Jencks, Christopher, and Paul Peterson, eds. *The Urban Underclass*. Washington, D.C.: Brookings Institution.

Krueger, Alan B. 1991. "How Computers Have Changed the Wage Structure: Evidence from Microdata, 1984–89." Princeton University and NBER, mimeo.

Lampman, Robert. 1973. "Measured Inequality of Income: What Does It Mean and What Can It Tell Us?" *The Annals of the American Academy of Political and Social Science* 409: 81–91.

Levy, Frank. 1987. *Dollars and Dreams: The Changing American Income Distribution*. New York: Russell Sage Foundation.

——— and Richard Murnane. 1991. "Earnings Level and Earnings Inequality: A Review of Recent Trends and Proposed Explanations." University of Maryland, mimeo.

Mayer, Susan, and Christopher Jencks. 1991. "Recent Trends in Economic Inequality in the United States: Income versus Expenditure versus Material Well-Being." University of Chicago, mimeo.

Mincy, Ronald. 1990. "Raising the Minimum Wage: The Effects on Family Poverty." *Monthly Labor Review* 113 (7):18–25.

Moffitt, Robert. 1990. "The Distribution of Earnings and the Welfare State." In Burtless, Gary, ed. *A Future of Lousy Jobs?* Washington, D.C.: Brookings Institution.

Murphy, Kevin, and Finis Welch. 1988. "The Structure of Wages." Los Angeles: Unicon Research Corporation.

Murray, Charles. 1984. *Losing Ground*. New York: Basic Books.

Reynolds, Morgan, and Eugene Smolensky. 1977. *Public Expenditures: Taxes and the Distribution of Income*. New York: Academic Press.

U.S. Bureau of the Census. 1990. *Money Income and Poverty Status in the United States: 1989*. Current Population Reports Series P-60, No. 168. Washington, D.C.: U.S. Government Printing Office.

Williamson, Jeffrey, and Peter Lindert. 1980. *American Inequality: A Macroeconomic History*. New York: Academic Press.

2

The Trend in Inequality Among Families, Individuals, and Workers in the United States: A Twenty-five Year Perspective

Lynn A. Karoly

In 1980, Alan Blinder outlined the conventional wisdom about the distribution of economic well-being in the United States. He said that the stylized fact concerning the distribution of income is one of constancy (Blinder, 1980, p. 416). Despite periods of growing and lessening inequality, he noted, inequality in 1977 remained at about the same level as it had been three decades earlier based on official Census Bureau statistics. Now, in the early 1990s, this conventional wisdom is being challenged. Numerous recent studies indicate that the distribution of income is becoming less equal, and that we are experiencing a shrinking middle class and a proliferation of low-wage jobs. The official Census Bureau statistics that revealed constancy for Blinder indicate that in 1989 the level of inequality had reached a post-war high (Bureau of the Census, 1989a, 1989b, 1990).

The contention that inequality is on the rise has generated controversy in both the popular press and the academic literature.[1] This debate takes place on two fronts. The first concerns the trend in income inequality among families or individuals; some analysts argue that the middle class is disappearing. For example, Bradbury (1986) finds that between 1973 and 1984, the percentage of families in the lower and upper classes increased while the percentage in the middle decreased. In contrast, Blackburn and Bloom (1986,

[1]Examples of articles appearing in the popular press include Kuttner (1983), Samuelson (1983), Steinberg (1983), Linden (1984), Thurow (1984), Wessel (1986), Perkins (1988), Wohlstetter (1988), and Lardner (1989). The numerous academic studies are discussed later in the chapter.

1987), using different definitions of the various income classes, report no change in the share of families in the lower class, but an increase in the upper-class share.

The second front concerns the theme of "good jobs versus bad jobs" and pertains to the distribution of earnings among workers. Harrison, Tilly, and Bluestone (1986a, 1986b) and Bluestone and Harrison (1986) marshaled evidence of growing polarization of annual wage and salary income among workers. Their results, showing a U-turn in inequality, were challenged by Kosters and Ross (1987) who argued, using another methodology, that the share of workers in the middle of the distribution has remained relatively stable, although the upper-class share has shown some increase.

In part, the evidence of growing inequality is disputed because of controversy over the appropriate way to evaluate changes in the distribution of income among families and the distribution of wages among workers. The methodological issues are basic questions, such as the appropriate way to measure inequality, the relevant unit of analysis, and the correct measure of income. Since there is no single answer, the recent studies of inequality often use different approaches, thereby making their results less comparable. In some cases, disagreement over the appropriate methodology has led to criticism that the measured increases in inequality are simply "statistical artifacts," derived from the implementation of improper methodologies.

In this chapter, I examine the trend in inequality in family income and individual earnings from 1963 to 1989. Rather than adopting one approach, results are compared using different methods of measuring inequality. Different definitions of the unit of analysis and the measure of income are employed as well. Within this framework, the chapter investigates three issues where previous studies have produced different results. First, if inequality has increased, when did the trend begin? For families or for workers, is the increase in inequality a recent phenomenon, coinciding with the Republican administrations of the 1980s, or does it date to an earlier period? Second, where in the distribution are the changes taking place? Has the rise in inequality been the result of increases in the incomes of the rich, or have the poor lost ground as well? Finally, what have been the experiences of different groups? Have different types of families or workers experienced the changes evident for all families or workers?

To set the stage, the next section of this chapter discusses the different ways of measuring inequality, and the third section briefly describes the data used in the analysis. In keeping with the current debate, the next two sections are organized around the two themes of inequality among families and individuals, and inequality among workers. Within each of these sections, the relevant methodological issues are discussed and the findings are presented. In each case, the results are also compared and contrasted with the findings of previous studies.

As discussed in the concluding section, this analysis demonstrates that the conventional wisdom of a stable income distribution does not hold over the last two decades, as inequality has increased both among families and individuals, and among workers. Although real median family income has shown positive growth since the 1960s, these gains were not equally shared by families throughout the income distribution. Families and individuals at the bottom of the income distribution have lost ground in relative terms since the late 1960s, while those at the top of the distribution have gained relative to the median in the last decade. Since 1979, the 10th percentile of the distribution actually declined in real terms, leaving the bottom 10 percent of families worse off than they were a decade earlier. These trends toward greater inequality are replicated for most groups of families characterized by their race/ethnicity, age, or headship type. Furthermore, the data through 1989 give no indication that inequality declined during the economic recovery of the 1980s. At best, inequality has stabilized in recent years at a higher level than that of the 1960s and 1970s.

Inequality has also been increasing in workers' earnings. Dispersion has risen in wages for both men and women workers since 1979. For men, the recent increases represent an acceleration of a trend dating back to the 1970s. The recent increases in inequality among women represent a reversal of an earlier downward trend. These changes in the wage structure are due to both relative gains at the top of the distribution and relative losses at the bottom. Men at the bottom of the wage distribution lost ground in absolute terms as well, with real wage declines since 1975. Even real median wages for men were no higher in 1989 than they had been a decade earlier. Inequality also increased over this period for most groups of workers within education and experience groups. Again, although the trend in inequality appears to have leveled off in the late 1980s, there does not appear to be a downturn in inequality as a result of the economic recovery.

Measuring the Trend in Inequality

In order to evaluate whether inequality is going up or down, one obvious methodological issue is how to measure changes in the distribution of income. A starting point is the substantial theoretical literature, which focuses on both objective measures of changes in the dispersion of a distribution and normative issues associated with comparing the level of welfare between income distributions (e.g., Atkinson, 1970; DasGupta, Sen, and Starrett,

1973; Rothschild and Stiglitz, 1973). Unfortunately, however, this literature does not offer a preferred method for evaluating the trend in inequality.

Instead, a variety of methods has been used in the recent studies. Some studies use summary measures of inequality to identify changes in the shape of the income distribution, evaluating changes in the dispersion or spread of the distribution. Others calculate class shares to reflect shifts in the location of the distribution to higher or lower income levels. In this analysis I will use a third method as well, and compare absolute and relative percentiles of the distribution. Before proceeding, it is worth considering the strengths and weaknesses of these three methods.

Summary Measures

Summary measures of inequality provide a convenient way to measure the shape of the income distribution.[2] Summary measures, such as the Gini coefficient, the coefficient of variation, or the variance of the logarithm of income, aggregate the income of individual units into a single number using an implicit weighting scheme. The weighting schemes, and the implicit social welfare function, vary across measures. For example, the variance of the logarithm of income is most sensitive to changes in the lower tail of the distribution, while the coefficient of variation is responsive to changes in the upper tail. Consequently, these measures of inequality will not necessarily rank two distributions in the same way, nor will the time-series pattern be identical for different measures.[3] Furthermore, summary measures can obscure the location in the distribution where the changes are occurring.

Class Shares

To identify the location of changes in the income distribution, several recent studies have calculated class shares, showing the percentage of the population that falls in the "lower class," the "middle class," and the "upper class." This methodology requires the researcher to define the income cutoffs that

[2]The most commonly used summary measures are all income homogeneous, i.e., they remain unchanged when all incomes are multiplied by a constant. If all units in the distribution experience the same rate of growth over time (e.g., due to inflation or real income growth), these measures remain unchanged.

[3]The sensitivity of the time trend in inequality to the summary measure is discussed in Karoly (1992). Summary measures are calculated for family inequality by Blackburn and Bloom (1986, 1987) and Levy (1987), and for earnings inequality by Henle and Ryscavage (1980); Dooley and Gottschalk (1982, 1984); Harrison, Tilly, and Bluestone (1986a, 1986b); Blackburn and Bloom (1987); Kosters and Ross (1988a); Bamezai (1989); Grubb and Wilson (1989); Juhn, Murphy, and Pierce (1989); and Burtless (1990).

divide the population into the various income classes. These income cutoffs have been defined as *absolute* cutoffs and *relative* cutoffs. Absolute cutoffs are calculated in the same way as the official poverty line: dollar cutoffs are chosen for a base year and then adjusted for inflation to determine the cutoffs in all other years. For example, Bradbury (1986) assigns families to the lower class (LC), middle class (MC), and upper class (UC) using cutoffs of $20,000 and $50,000 in 1984 dollars. Bluestone and Harrison (1986) also use absolute cutoffs to define earnings classes.[4] Absolute class cutoffs define an income interval with constant real purchasing power over time, implying that individuals or families are equally well-off over time if they maintain a constant real absolute standard of living.

Relative class cutoffs are usually defined as a percentage of the median of the current year distribution. Blackburn and Bloom (1985, 1986, 1987), for example, define the lower class (LC) as those with incomes less than 60 percent of the median, the lower middle class (LMC) as 60 to 100 percent of the median, the middle class (MC) as 100 to 160 percent of the median, the upper middle class (UMC) as 160 to 225 percent of the median, and the upper class (UC) as over 225 percent of the median. Kosters and Ross (1987, 1988a, 1988b) use cutoffs of 50 and 75 percent of the median to define the LC, and 150 to 200 percent of the median to define the UC. Based on relative class cutoffs, families or individuals are equally well-off as long as they maintain their position relative to the reference point, the median.

Although the class share approach is intuitively appealing, this methodology has a number of drawbacks. First, all methods of defining classes are arbitrary. There is no single definition of what constitutes the "middle class." Consequently, researchers have defined the middle class in many different ways, making their results difficult to compare. Second, findings based on absolute cutoffs are sensitive to the choice of the base year for defining the cutoffs and to the choice of deflator.[5] More importantly, changes in the percent of the population in various classes defined by absolute class cutoffs can reflect both changes in the *level* of the distribution as well as changes in the *shape* of the distribution. For example, even if the shape of the distribution remained unchanged, if there is real income growth, the percentage of the population in the lower class will decline while the percentage in the upper class will increase. Changes in class shares based on relative class cutoffs, however, will reflect only changes in the shape of the distribution.

[4]Bluestone and Harrison (1988), Kosters and Ross (1987, 1988b), Hilley (1988), and Bluestone (1989) also define constant dollar absolute cutoffs to evaluate the trend in earnings inequality, while Horrigan and Haugen (1988) define absolute cutoffs for their analysis of inequality among families.

[5]This point was demonstrated by Kosters and Ross (1987) in their sensitivity analysis of the Bluestone and Harrison (1986) study.

In addition, the class-based methodology, whether based on absolute or relative class cutoffs, does not capture changes in the distribution of income *within* the various income classes. For example, the percentage of the population falling below the lower-class cutoff may remain unchanged from one period to the next, yet the dispersion of income within that class may have increased. This limitation is critical given the way that income classes are often defined in practice. In many cases, they are defined nonsymmetrically, i.e., a different fraction of the population falls into the lower and upper classes.[6] For example, the relative class cutoffs defined by Blackburn and Bloom (1987) place about 30 percent of all families in the lower class but about 8 to 14 percent in the upper class. Consequently, their methodology is more sensitive to changes in the top tenth of the distribution and may miss changes in the bottom tenth. In fact, they find an increase over time in the upper class, but no trend in the lower class.

Percentiles

Another approach is to calculate percentiles of the distribution. At the 10th percentile in the distribution, for example, 10 percent of the population has income at or below that level. Absolute or relative percentiles of the distribution are the complement of absolute or relative class shares. The class-based methodology considers a fixed real absolute income cutoff or fixed relative cutoff and examines changes in the percentage of population in the class. The percentile approach holds the percentage of the population constant, and looks at changes over time in the real absolute income cutoff or the ratio of the percentile's income cutoff to the median. The trend in the real income percentile shows how the level of the distribution is changing at various points; the ratio of the percentile to the median shows how the shape of the distribution is changing. One advantage of using absolute or relative percentiles is that it is easy to examine changes in the distribution in a symmetric manner. However, the use of absolute or relative percentiles does not lend itself to direct comparisons of the status of various income classes. Instead, the trend in absolute or relative class shares must be inferred from the changes in the absolute or relative percentiles.

A number of researchers have used several of the above methods to test for the sensitivity of their results. For example, Horrigan and Haugen (1988) define the middle class using a variety of absolute class cutoffs and relative

[6]One exception is the analysis by Kosters and Ross (1987), which defined relative class cutoffs so that approximately one-third of the population of workers would fall into each of the low, middle, and high earnings categories.

class cutoffs. Others have reported results based on class shares and several summary measures (Blackburn and Bloom, 1987; Burtless, 1990; Moffitt, 1990). The approach in this chapter will be first to examine changes in the level and shape of the distribution as measured by the trend in the 10th, 25th, 50th, 75th, and 90th percentiles of the distribution. Results based on class shares and summary measures will also be provided to allow for comparisons with previous studies.

The Data

This analysis, like most recent studies of the trend in inequality among families and workers, relies on the March Annual Demographic File of the Current Population Survey (CPS), which provides detailed demographic and income information for individuals in about 50,000 to 60,000 households annually from 1964 to 1990.[7] The information about income received from various sources in the year prior to the survey allows estimates of the distribution of total family income and wage and salary income from 1963 to 1989 using various definitions of the unit of analysis and of the measure of income. However, a number of data limitations are associated with the CPS. These limitations, discussed more fully in Appendix 2A, introduce potential inconsistencies in the data that may make comparisons of income distributions over time less valid. The potential biases will be discussed in the context of the results presented in the following two sections.[8]

When measuring changes in the level of the distribution over time (e.g., the median or other percentiles), or when using absolute class cutoffs to compare income classes over time, it is necessary to correct for inflation using a price deflator. The results in this paper are based on the CPI-X, the Consumer Price Index that treats the measurement of housing costs

[7] Several researchers, such as Levy (1987) and Grubb and Wilson (1989), have relied upon the decennial Censuses for 1950, 1960, 1970, and 1980. In addition, Kosters and Ross (1988a), in their analysis of the distribution of labor income, used the May CPS from 1973 to 1978, and the Outgoing Rotation Group Earnings Supplements from the April, May, and June CPSs from 1979 to 1987, which provide information on usual weekly earnings and usual hourly wages.

[8] As discussed in Appendix 2A, one of the more significant changes affecting the comparability of the CPS data over time was the introduction of a new processing system with the March 1989 survey. Since the March 1988 data were re-released using the new system, it is possible to correct the time series for the discontinuity between the 1987 and 1988 income data. Thus, in all figures showing time trends in inequality, the trends are shown through 1989 after adjusting for the discontinuity produced by the new processing system. Other analyses, such as shift share, use 1987 as the end point, the last year for which the data are most comparable.

consistently over time.[9] Since a number of studies and the published Census Bureau reports use the official Consumer Price Index (CPI), some results will be presented using this deflator as well.

Inequality Among Families and Individuals

One recent focus of the debate over the trend in inequality is the distribution of economic well-being across families or individuals. While the War on Poverty highlighted the condition of the poor, the current debate concerns changes in the entire distribution, from the poor to the rich and the middle class in between. One of the first signs of growing inequality among families was the trend in the Gini coefficient and quintile shares calculated from the annual March CPS by the Census Bureau.[10] In the early 1980s, attention was called to a break in the historical pattern of stability. As shown in Figure 2.1, there is a clear U-turn in the time-series pattern, with the Gini coefficient reaching a minimum in 1967–1968 and a post-war peak in 1989.[11]

[9]Several of the studies relied upon the official Consumer Price Index (CPI), technically called the "CPI-U" (e.g., Bradbury, 1986; Bluestone and Harrison, 1986). As pointed out by Kosters and Ross (1987) in their critique of Bluestone and Harrison's (1986) JEC study, the official CPI-U overstates the rate of inflation during the 1970s due to the way that housing costs were calculated prior to 1983. In 1983, a new methodology was introduced into the CPI-U to include a rental equivalence measure for homeowner costs in the housing cost component of the index. The CPI-U-X1 replicates the new methodology for 1967 to 1982 and therefore provides a consistent price index over time. (For the 1963 to 1966 period, I have used the same inflation rate implied by the CPI-U.) The inflation rate based on the CPI-U-X1 is 165 percent over the sixteen-year period from 1967 to 1982, compared to 188 percent based on the CPI-U. The most recent studies have used the CPI-U-X1 (e.g., CBO, 1988; Horrigan and Haugen, 1988; Kosters and Ross, 1988a, 1988b; Hilley, 1988; Burtless, 1990). For simplicity, I refer to the two indices as the CPI and the CPI-X. The inflation rate based on the personal consumption expenditure (PCE) deflator used by Juhn, Murphy, and Pierce (1989) is similar to the CPI-U-X1.

[10]The quintile shares show the percentage of total income received by each fifth of the population, from the poorest fifth to the richest fifth. The Gini coefficient ranges from a value of zero (perfect equality) to one (perfect inequality). Graphically, the Gini coefficient is derived from the Lorenz curve. If income recipients are ranked from lowest to highest income, the Lorenz curve plots the cumulative percentage of recipient units against the cumulative percentage of income received by these recipients. The Gini coefficient measures the proportion of the total area below the line of perfect equality (the 45° line) that is between the Lorenz curve and the 45° line.

[11]The Census Bureau estimates that the standard error in the Gini coefficient reported in Figure 2.1 is 0.004 for 1958 data and 0.003 for 1970 data (Henle, 1972). Using the 1970 estimate, the change in the Gini coefficient from 1967 to 1989 is statistically significant. In contrast, the small decrease in the Gini coefficient between 1989 and 1990, from 0.401 to 0.396, would not be statistically significant.

Figure 2.1 Inequality Among Families 1947–1990: Census Bureau Data

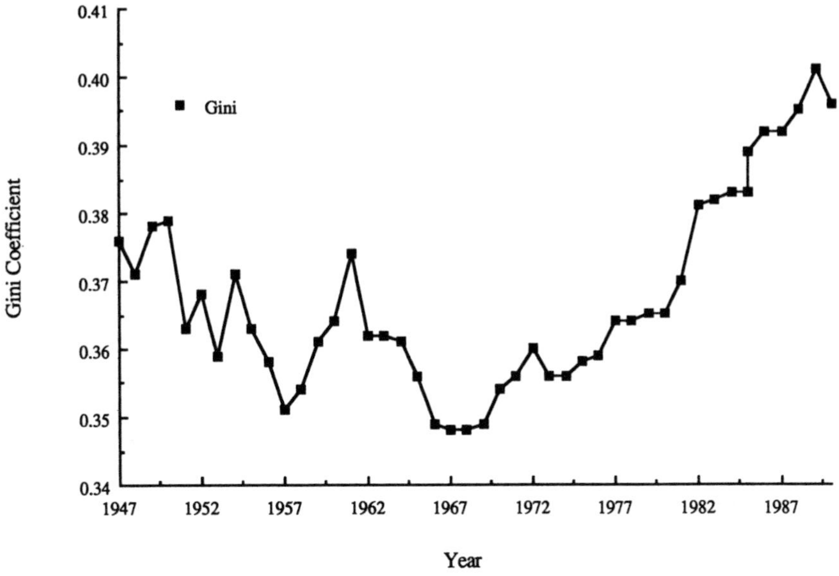

Source: U.S. Bureau of the Census, *Current Population Reports*, P-60 Series, various issues.

Data from the March 1990 CPS show that the poorest fifth received only 4.6 percent of total income in 1989, while the richest fifth received 44.6 percent, the highest share since the Census Bureau began tabulating the data (Bureau of the Census, 1990).

For a number of reasons, the data published by the Census Bureau are not entirely adequate for assessing the trend in economic well-being. As with any analysis of inequality, the choice of the unit of analysis and the definition of income are important conceptual issues. In the case of the Gini coefficient shown in Figure 2.1, the Census Bureau includes only families, defined as "a group of two or more persons . . . related by birth, marriage, or adoption and residing together . . ." (Bureau of the Census, 1989a). This definition excludes unrelated individuals, defined as persons living alone or with other unrelated persons,[12] a group that has grown from 20.2 percent

[12]The current Census Bureau definition of a family also excludes unrelated subfamilies (previously called "secondary families") from the count of families and excludes members of unrelated subfamilies from the count of family members. This change was implemented with the 1980 CPS.

of all "family units" in 1967 to 33.1 percent in 1987.[13] In addition, the Census Bureau data make no adjustment for the differences in family income relative to needs. A family of one and a family of four with $25,000 are treated as being equally well-off. The trend in Figure 2.1 thus does not account for the steady decline in average family size in the United States, from 3.1 persons per family in 1968 to 2.4 in 1989.

Conceptual Issues

Given the controversies produced by the recent studies of inequality, I begin with a discussion of the methodological issues involved in measuring inequality. The first consideration is the choice of the appropriate unit of analysis. Instead of focusing only upon "families" as defined by the Census Bureau, I also include unrelated individuals. The distribution of income differs when unrelated individuals are included, since they have lower incomes, on average, than families of two or more. Among the recent studies, Bradbury (1986) and Levy (1987) exclude unrelated individuals, while Blackburn and Bloom (1985, 1987) and the Congressional Budget Office (CBO, 1988) include them. For this analysis, results are presented and compared for the sample of families only and for the sample of families plus unrelated individuals.

Second, the measure of income must be defined. Most often, total annual income is chosen as the best indicator of differences in access to resources or purchasing power across individuals or families. Ideally, a comprehensive measure of income would be used: one that includes both cash income (e.g., wages and salaries, interest and dividends, social security payments) and income in-kind (e.g., government in-kind transfers, fringe benefits), one that accounts for taxes paid, and one that measures capital gains and imputed rents (Atkinson, 1983). Unfortunately, microlevel data over time that provide information on such a comprehensive measure of income are not available in the United States.[14] Instead, it is common practice for researchers,

[13] Similarly, unrelated individuals grew as a percentage of the total population, from 6.7 percent in 1967 to 13.6 percent in 1987.

[14] Although the CPS does not readily provide an estimate of comprehensive income, the distribution of income among families has been estimated for a measure of after-tax income that also includes in-kind payments. For example, the Census Bureau (1988) has produced income and poverty estimates using more comprehensive definitions of income. The Committee on Ways and Means study (1989) computes the distribution of income including noncash benefits (food and housing but not health and pensions) and accounting for taxes (federal payroll and income taxes) from 1979 to 1987. Levy (1987) provides estimates based on the Urban Institute's Transfer Income Model (TRIM2) for the distribution of income among families, corrected for taxes paid and nonmonetary benefits in 1979 and 1984. Pechman (1990) also provides estimates

as I do in this study, to use total annual money income as a proxy for a comprehensive measure of income.[15]

When comparing economic well-being across families, total income (whether measured comprehensively or not) does not account for differing needs across families at the same point in time or over time. Two alternative measures can be used to account for differences in resources relative to needs: income per capita or income per equivalent person. Unlike income per capita, which adjusts solely for differences in family size, income per equivalent person is based on "equivalency scales" that translate total family size into a measure of "equivalent" persons, adjusting for the age structure of the family and the economies of scale. A number of recent studies have used a measure of adjusted family income based on the equivalency scales implicit in United States poverty thresholds (Blackburn and Bloom, 1986, 1987; CBO, 1988; Committee on Ways and Means, 1989; Danziger, Gottschalk, and Smolensky, 1989).[16] As in those studies, adjusted family income here will be calculated as total family income divided by the family's poverty threshold.[17]

The distribution of income among families is measured by assigning a weight of one to each "family unit." Alternatively, the distribution of income among all persons can be calculated by assigning a weight to each family equal to the number of persons in that family.[18] In doing so, each person in the family is assigned the income level of his or her family. The distribution of income among individuals will differ from that among families by giving

---

of the impact of the tax system on the distribution of income among families. Generally, these analyses show that the distribution is more equal once taxes and in-kind transfers are accounted for, but that the trend in inequality during the 1980s is similar. This is because effective tax rates have declined over time for the upper-income groups, and government transfer payments have declined for the lower-income groups.

[15]The current debate has focused on the distribution of annual family income, the income concept measured in the CPS. Alternatively, differences in well-being can be compared based on lifetime income. Although the distribution of lifetime income provides a more comprehensive picture of differences in well-being by abstracting from income variation due to the life cycle, such an analysis is beyond the scope of this study.

[16]Equivalence scales have been calculated by a number of other researchers. A comparison by Lazear and Michael (1988) of several of these equivalency scales, including the one implicit in United States poverty lines, shows that the scales are not substantially different from each other.

[17]The official poverty line for each family provided on the CPS microdata files from 1968 to 1990 were inflated using the CPI. Following the method used in the studies by the CBO (1988) and the Committee on Ways and Means (1989), I have used the CPI-X to inflate the official poverty lines using the 1967 poverty lines as the base. This method assumes that the poverty lines in 1967 were the correct ones.

[18]See Danziger and Taussig (1979) for one of the earliest studies to use person weights to estimate the distribution of income among all individuals.

more weight to larger families. Consequently, the distribution of income among persons is a better measure of aggregate well-being since each person in the population is counted. In this analysis, the distribution of adjusted family income among persons will be calculated where each individual in the family is assigned his or her family's adjusted income. These results will be comparable to the studies by Blackburn and Bloom (1986, 1987) and the Committee on Ways and Means (1989).

Clearly, there are a number of different ways to approach an analysis of the distribution of economic well-being across families or individuals. To allow for comparisons with previous studies and to provide a broader picture of the trends in inequality, I present five different series: (1) for families only (excluding unrelated individuals) based on total family income and (2) adjusted family income; (3) for families plus unrelated individuals based on total family income and (4) adjusted family income; and (5) for all individuals based on adjusted family income.[19] Results based on total family income (FI) are presented for the period from 1963 to 1989. Data limitations reduce the period of analysis to 1967 to 1989 when adjusted family income (AFI) is the income measure.[20] Consequently, for purposes of comparison, the focus of the discussion covers the 1967 to 1989 period. This is also the period when the data are most comparable, as the 1963 to 1967 data suffer from several limitations (see Appendix 2A for a discussion).

Changes in the Level of Income Distribution

The trend in real median income is a commonly used indicator of changes in the level of economic well-being. Figure 2.2 shows how the trend in real median income varies with the definition of income and the unit of analysis.[21] To facilitate comparisons, each median income in Figure 2.2 has been indexed so that it equals 100 in 1967. Since adjusted family income is available only since 1967, this allows comparisons in the growth rates of all income measures over the same period.

Regardless of the unit of analysis or the income metric, the median family or individual was better off in real terms in 1989 compared to any year since

[19] The samples both of families and of families and unrelated individuals exclude related subfamilies, as the income of the subfamilies is included in the income of the primary family. Individuals living in group quarters are also excluded. Except as noted, the analysis will include families or individuals with negative and zero total incomes (about 1 percent of the sample).

[20] Unlike microdata files from later years, the CPS microdata files from 1964 to 1967 do not contain the appropriate poverty line for each family.

[21] The data reported in Figure 2.2 are tabulated in Table 2B.1 in Appendix 2B.

Figure 2.2 Real Median Income[1] for Families (F), Families and Unrelated Individuals (F&U), and All Individuals (I)

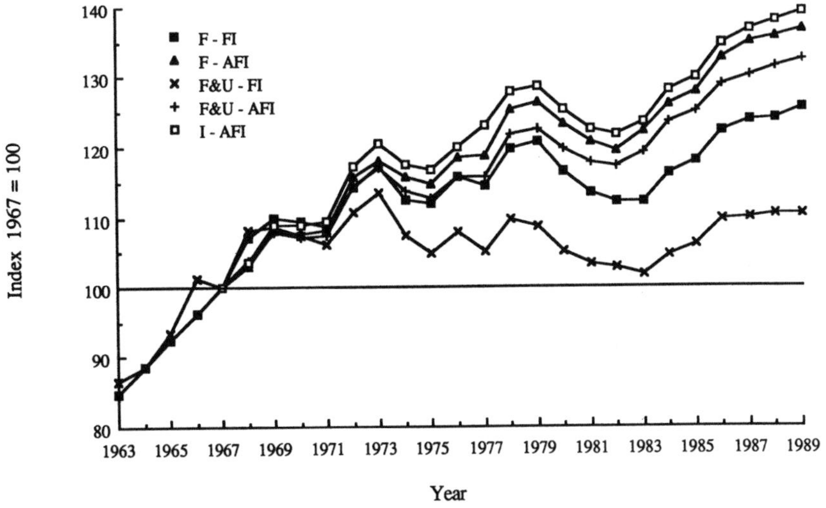

Source: Tabulations using CPS microdata from 1964 to 1990.

[1]The CPI-X is used to deflate family income (FI) and to adjust the poverty line for calculating adjusted family income (AFI).

1963. Furthermore, the growth in median income is always higher once an adjustment is made for changes in family size. For instance, among families and unrelated individuals, real median family income (FI) increased about 10 percent between 1967 and 1989 (from $20,515 to $22,615). For this same group, however, median adjusted family income (AFI) rises more than 30 percent, from 2.4 to 3.2 times the poverty line. The trend in median AFI across all individuals shows the greatest growth, almost 40 percent over the period. This long-run picture of real income growth, however, has been interrupted by several periods of stagnation, and even real income losses. All five measures of median income illustrate that the steady pattern of growth was interrupted by declines from 1973–1975 and again from 1978–1979 to 1982–1983. Although median incomes have grown in real terms since 1983, the rate of growth slowed from 1986 to 1989.

The trend in real median income does not necessarily reflect the experiences of families or individuals above and below the middle of the distribution. To illustrate these changes, Table 2.1 summarizes the percentage changes in the level of other percentiles, namely the 10th, 25th, 75th, and

Table 2.1 Percentage Change in Real Absolute Percentiles: Various Years

	Family Income (FI) Percentile					Adjusted Family Income[a] (AFI) Percentile				
Period	10th	25th	50th	75th	90th	10th	25th	50th	75th	90th
					A. Families[b]					
1967–1973	21.9	12.4	17.3	20.6	21.8	15.5	18.1	18.1	18.5	18.7
1973–1979	−1.2	0.2	3.5	5.0	6.2	0.7	4.9	7.2	8.1	6.4
1979–1987	−8.7	−1.4	2.4	7.7	10.1	−9.8	0.2	6.7	10.8	14.3
					B. Families and Unrelated Individuals[b]					
1967–1973	24.5	11.9	13.4	18.3	19.4	20.2	17.0	16.9	17.1	16.9
1973–1979	0.3	−2.1	−4.0	1.4	2.9	2.7	3.0	5.2	6.0	4.9
1979–1987	−6.4	−2.6	1.3	4.7	8.6	−6.1	0.1	6.2	10.4	14.4
					C. All Individuals[c]					
1967–1973						15.3	17.7	20.5	20.1	18.6
1973–1979						1.3	4.4	6.9	8.3	7.5
1979–1987						−10.2	−1.0	6.2	10.3	15.0

[a]Measured as total family income divided by the poverty line, where the 1967 poverty threshold is inflated using the CPI-X to calculate the poverty lines after 1967.
[b]Weighted by families.
[c]Weighted by persons in families.

90th percentiles, for various time periods.[22] In all cases, incomes at the 10th and 25th percentiles kept pace with or even exceeded growth at the other percentiles from 1967 to 1973. Between 1973 and 1979, however, real incomes at the bottom of the distribution failed to grow as fast as incomes at the top, and after 1979, they declined substantially for all five series. For instance, between 1979 and 1987, while real AFI for families and unrelated individuals at the 90th percentile grew 14.4 percent, real AFI declined 6.1 percent at the 10th percentile. Since 1979, inequality has clearly increased. Regardless of the unit of analysis or the income measure, families and individuals at the bottom of the distribution lost ground in real terms, while the ground gained by those above the median was greater the higher their level of income.

The Changing Shape of Income Distribution

The data in Table 2.1 provide an indication that the shape of the distribution has been changing at least since 1973 and more dramatically since 1979. Figures 2.3, 2.4, and 2.5 further illustrate the changing shape of the distribution by showing the trend in the ratio of the 10th, 25th, 75th, and 90th percentiles to the median for the same five income measures, again indexing the relative percentiles so that they equal 100 in 1967.[23] If the shape of the distribution remains unchanged, the ratio of any percentile to the median will be constant, and the index will equal 100 over the entire period. Variations in the relative percentiles indicate a change in the shape of the income distribution. For example, an upward trend in the 75th or 90th percentiles relative to the median is evidence of increasing dispersion in the upper tail of the income distribution. If the 10th or 25th percentile declines relative to the median, income dispersion is rising in the lower tail of the distribution.

The data in Figures 2.3, 2.4, and 2.5 leave little room for doubt that the distribution of income among families and individuals has become less equal. The general pattern indicates that, at least since 1979, incomes at the top of the distribution have grown much faster than the median, while incomes at the bottom have declined relative to the median. These trends in the relative percentiles can be translated into increases in the lower and upper classes and a corresponding decline in the middle class. Despite this general pattern, depending upon the unit of analysis and the measure of income, there are

[22] Again, the data for the full time period are presented in Table 2B.1. As discussed earlier and in Appendix 2A, changes in survey procedures make the data for 1988 and 1989 less comparable with data from earlier years. Consequently, 1987 is chosen as the end point for the comparisons in Table 2.1. The 1973 and 1979 break points coincide with the peaks in real median income.

[23] The data for Figures 2.3, 2.4, and 2.5 are tabulated in Table 2B.1.

Figure 2.3 Inequality Among Families
Percentiles Relative to Median Income

A. Total Family Income (FI)

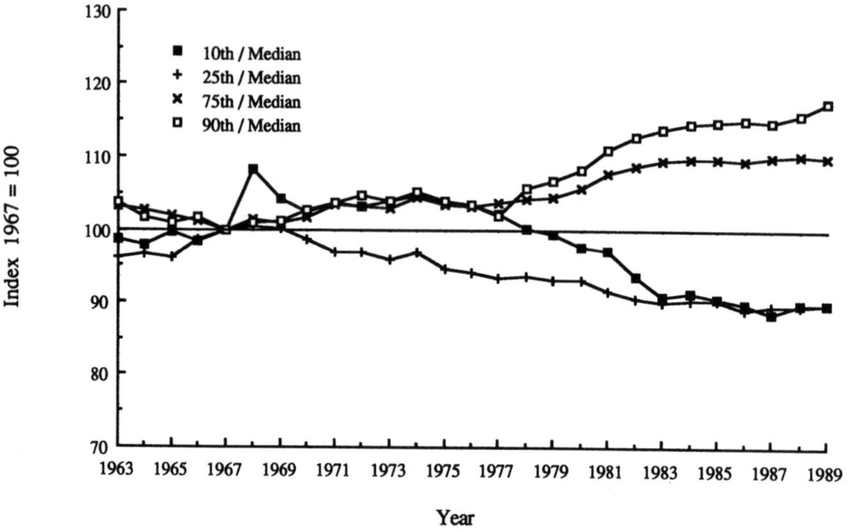

B. Adjusted Family Income (AFI)

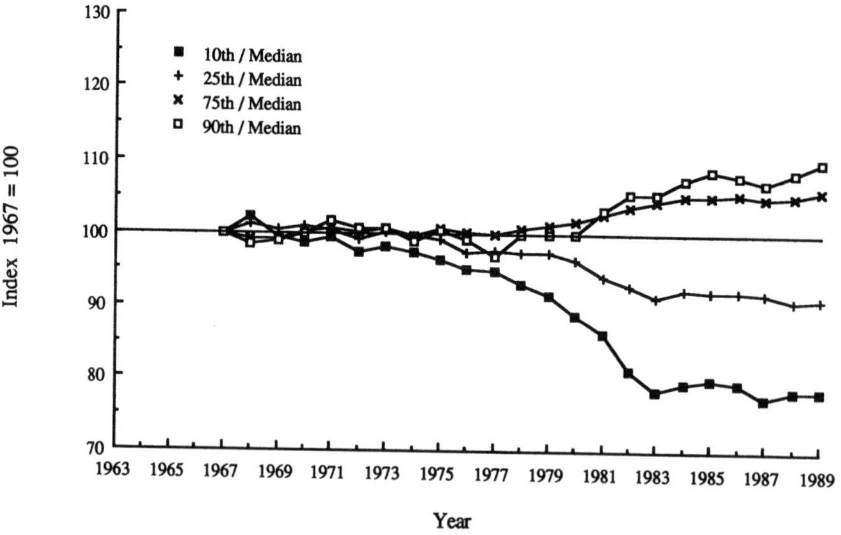

Source: Tabulations using CPS microdata from 1964 to 1990.

Figure 2.4 Inequality Among Families and Unrelated Individuals
Percentiles Relative to Median Income

A. Total Family Income (FI)

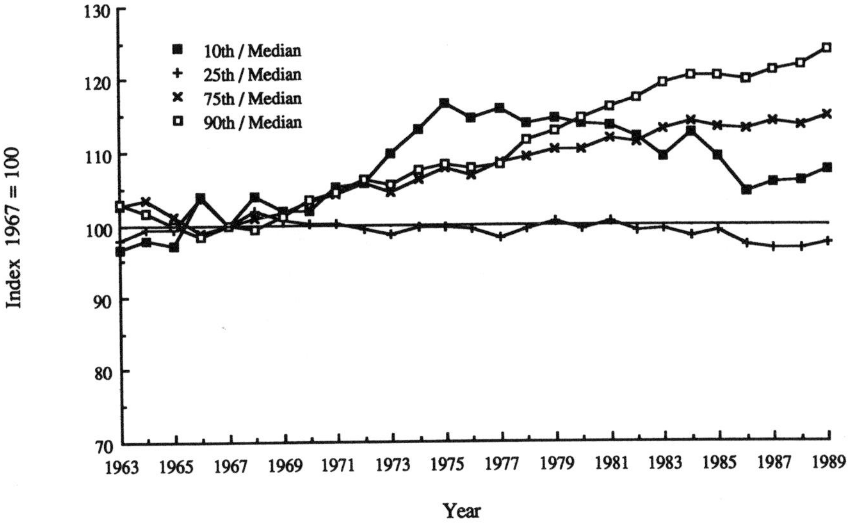

B. Adjusted Family Income (AFI)

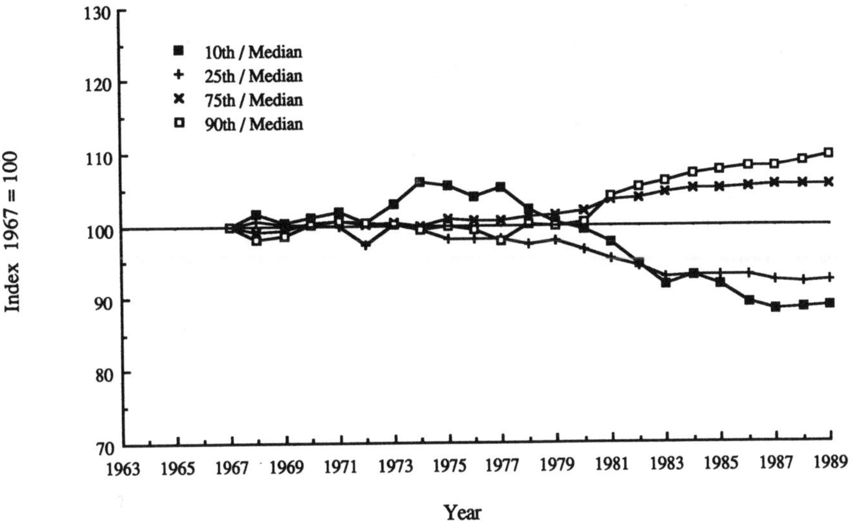

Source: Tabulations using CPS microdata from 1964 to 1990.

Figure 2.5 Inequality Among All Individuals
Percentiles Relative to Median Income

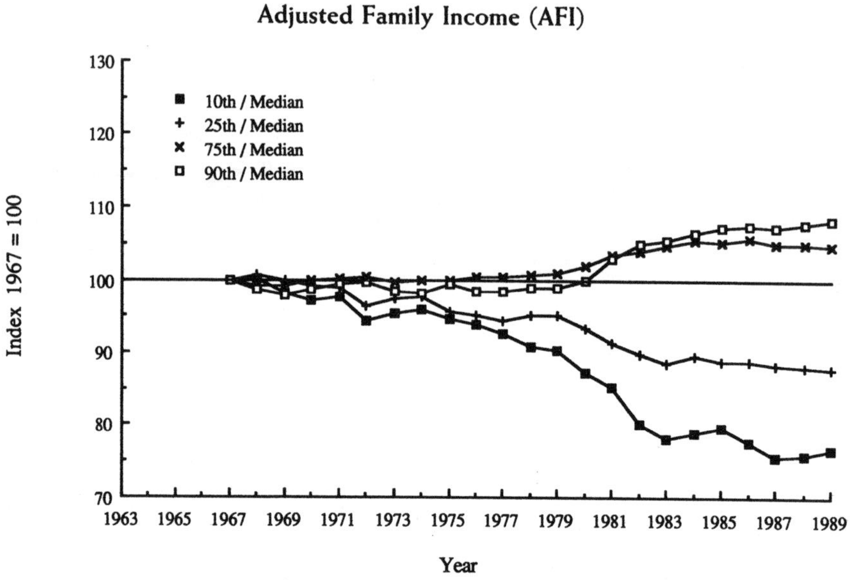

Source: Tabulations using CPS microdata from 1964 to 1990.

some differences in the timing of the changes and where in the distribution the changes are taking place.

For families (excluding unrelated individuals), there is evidence of increasing dispersion in both measures of income. Using family income as the metric (Figure 2.3A), the 10th percentile declined relative to the median from 1974 onwards, while the 25th percentile showed a relative decline over the entire period. In contrast, the 75th and 90th percentiles grew relative to the median starting about 1967, with an increasing rate of growth after 1977. Thus, dispersion is increasing in both tails of the distribution, with an acceleration in the trend after 1977. This pattern is consistent with the Census Bureau data reported in Figure 2.1, which use the same unit of analysis and measure of income.

The adjustment for differences in family size reinforces these conclusions (Figure 2.3B). Using AFI as the metric sharpens the contrast between the relative losses at the bottom of the distribution and the relative gains at the top. The 10th and 25th percentiles have lost ground relative to the median since the mid-1970s, and the more modest gains in the 75th and 90th percentiles began in 1980. Compared to FI, there is a larger increase in the gap between the 10th and 90th percentiles when changes in family size are accounted for. Thus, while the rich have been getting richer, the poor have become even poorer.

Expanding the sample to include unrelated individuals does little to alter the pattern of increasing dispersion (Figure 2.4). Using AFI as the more appropriate metric, the relative gains of families at the top of the distribution did not begin until 1980. In contrast, there is evidence of a U-turn in the relative status of those at the very bottom of the distribution: the 10th percentile, after growing faster than the median until 1974, declined in relative terms thereafter. Likewise, since 1974, the 25th percentile has declined relative to the median. By 1989, AFI at the 90th percentile was almost nine times that of the 10th percentile, whereas the ratio had been about 7:1 in 1967.

Finally, when the unit of analysis is the individual, rather than the family, the same pattern emerges (Figure 2.5). Since the distribution of AFI among individuals comes the closest to measuring the distribution of economic well-being, there is strong evidence that inequality, as reflected in the changing shape of the distribution, has increased. For instance, the lower tail of the distribution measured by the 10th and 25th percentiles failed to grow as fast as median income over the entire period. At the same time, the upper tail grew at approximately the same rate as the median until 1980, and increased thereafter. As a result, AFI among individuals in the 90th percentile grew from 5.6 to 7.8 times the level at the 10th percentile. These trends again point to growing inequality first in the lower tail of the distribution and later in the upper tail. Furthermore, the declining fortunes of individuals in the bottom of the distribution exceeded the gains of those at the top.

The changes in the shape of the distribution, especially since 1979, appear quite dramatic for all five time-series. One striking feature of the distributional changes is the failure of the economic recovery of the 1980s to significantly improve the relative well-being of families and individuals in the bottom segments of the income distribution. Thus, while the most recent increase in dispersion coincides with the economic downturns of the late 1970s and early 1980s, there is no indication that dispersion declined through the late 1980s as the economy expanded. There is some comfort to be found, however, as the growth in dispersion seems to have leveled off since about 1983, with some indication of a very modest relative growth at the 10th percentile. Even so, there is little to suggest that the recent growth in inequality is a temporary phenomenon, soon to be reversed.

A Comparison with Other Studies

The results indicated in Figures 2.3, 2.4, and 2.5 clearly point to increasing dispersion in income among both families (including unrelated individuals) and individuals, even after adjusting for differences in family size. How

Figure 2.6 Inequality Among Families in Total Family Income (FI) Absolute Income Class Shares Using CPI and CPI-X

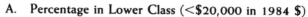

A. Percentage in Lower Class (<$20,000 in 1984 $)

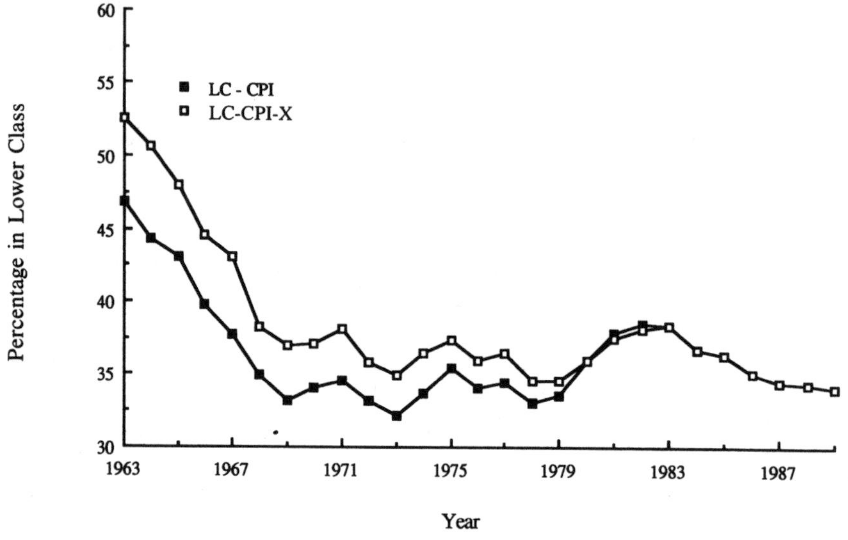

B. Percentage in Middle Class ($20,000–50,000 in 1984 $)

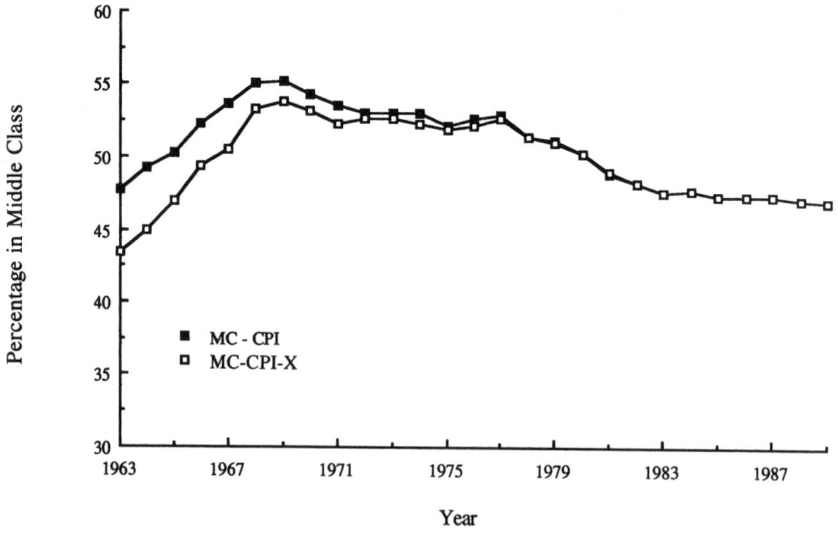

C. Percentage in Upper Class (>$50,000 in 1984 dollars)

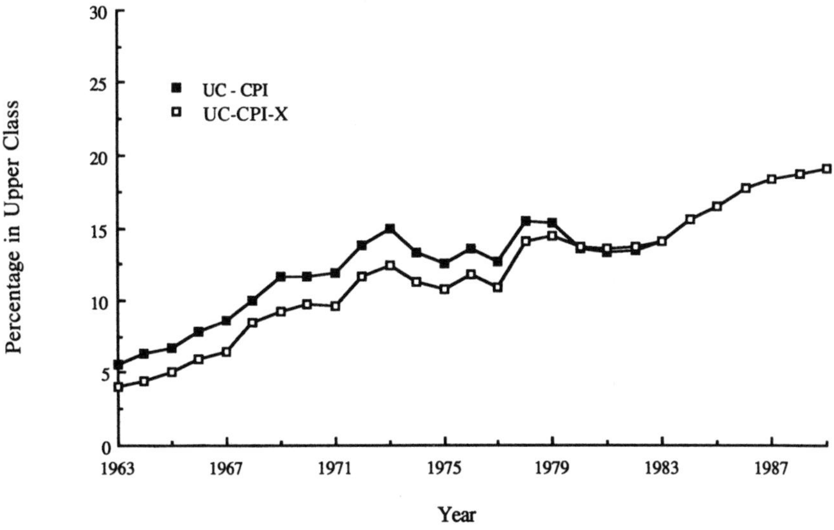

Source: Tabulations using CPS microdata from 1964 to 1990.

do these findings compare to those of previous researchers?[24] In terms of methodology, the CBO (1988) study is most comparable, focusing upon the changing shape of the distribution of adjusted family income for families and unrelated individuals. The trends in various income percentiles, reported in the CBO analysis, are similar to those shown in Figure 2.4B. Most of the other recent studies, however, have relied upon the class-based methodology, using either absolute or relative class cutoffs.

As noted earlier, the trend in class shares when absolute class cutoffs are used to define classes will be sensitive to the choice of deflator. A popular definition of the middle class is those families earning $20,000 to $50,000. For example, using only the 1974 and 1985 CPSs, Bradbury (1986) used these cutoffs in 1984 dollars (using the CPI) to define the LC, MC, and UC for a sample of families excluding unrelated individuals. Figures 2.6A, 2.6B,

[24]The focus of comparison will be those studies that also used the CPS microdata files to evaluate the trend in inequality among families and individuals. Other researchers have relied upon tabulated data published by the Census Bureau and are therefore not strictly comparable to these results (e.g., Winnick, 1989; Maxwell, 1990). The decennial Censuses have also been used to analyze trends in family inequality. For example, Smith (1988) uses microdata from the decennial Censuses for 1940 through 1980, focusing upon families excluding unrelated individuals.

and 2.6C report the results from replicating this methodology (and Bradbury's results) for the same sample over the period 1963 to 1989, using both the CPI and the CPI-X.[25]

As seen in the three panels in Figure 2.6, compared to the CPI-X, the decline in the LC and the rise in the UC is somewhat smaller when the CPI is the deflator. More importantly, for year-to-year comparisons, the two deflators can provide different results. For example, Bradbury concluded that from 1973 to 1984 the LC increased by 4.6 percentage points (from 32.1 to 36.7 percent). Using the CPI-X as the deflator, the increase in the LC is only 1.8 percentage points (from 34.9 percent in 1973 to 36.7 in 1984). In contrast, there is a larger increase in the percentage of families in the UC when the CPI-X is used (from 12.4 to 15.6 percent versus 14.9 to 15.6 percent using the CPI). Thus, Bradbury's conclusion that the growth in the LC was greater than the growth in the UC is reversed when the more appropriate deflator is used. Nevertheless, both deflators show about a 5-percentage point decline in the middle-class share since 1970.

These results differ from the pattern of increasing dispersion in both tails of the distribution shown in Figure 2.3. This difference is explained by the fact that the trend in class shares based on absolute cutoffs will reflect both changes in the level and shape of the distribution. To illustrate, Figures 2.7A and 2.7B show the trend in the percent of the population above the LC (100 − LC) and the percent in the UC (measured on the left axes of Figures 2.7A and 2.7B) versus the trend in real median income (measured on the right axes). The two panels of Figure 2.7 demonstrate that, in most cases, when real median income is growing, the percent in the LC is declining (100 − LC is rising) and the percent in the UC is rising. The bottom line is that absolute class shares may obscure important changes in the shape of the distribution. For example, the relatively flat trend in the LC in Figure 2.6A from 1969 to 1989 masks the increase in dispersion in the lower tail of the distribution evident in Figure 2.3A.[26]

Relative class shares are used by Blackburn and Bloom (1986, 1987) to examine the trend in the distribution for FI for families and unrelated individuals, and the trend in AFI for individuals. As noted earlier, measuring the trend in class shares using relative cutoffs is the complement to measur-

[25] Because the CPI uses the same methodology as the CPI-X starting in 1983, the two deflators will lead to the same results from 1983 to 1989.

[26] Horrigan and Haugen (1988) also find that trends in absolute class shares hide changes in the shape of the distribution among families. Using various absolute dollar cutoffs (inflated using the CPI-X), they report that, over the 1969–1986 period, the LC is flat or declining slightly, the UC is rising steadily over the period, and the MC is declining. Despite the flat trend in the LC share, the share of income held by the LC declined over the period, indicating a rise in dispersion in the lower tail.

Figure 2.7 Inequality Among Families in Total Family Income (FI)
Trend in Absolute Income Class Shares vs. Trend in Real Median Income[1]

A. (100 − Percentage in Lower Class) vs. Real Median Income

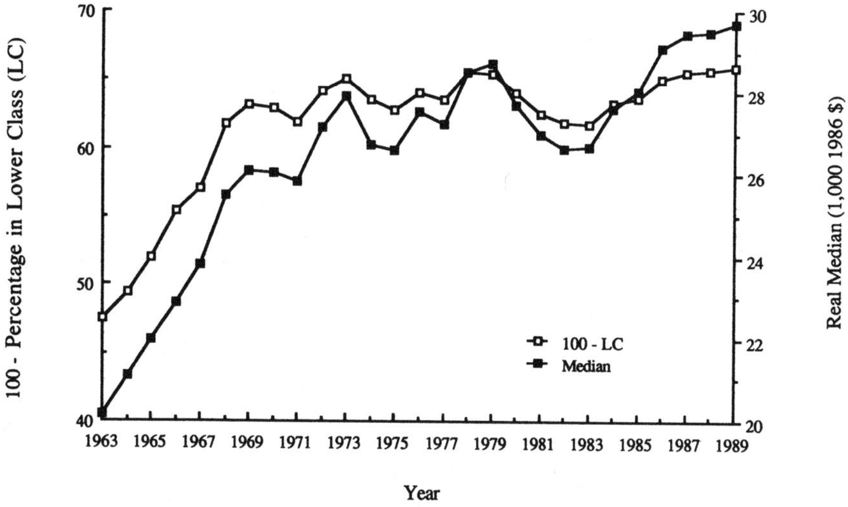

B. Percentage in Upper Class vs. Real Median Income

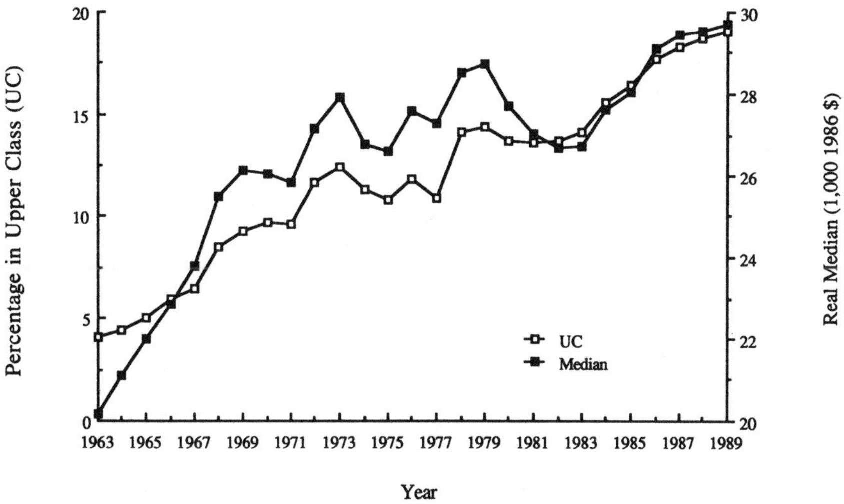

Source: Tabulations using CPS microdata from 1964 to 1990.

[1]The CPI-X is used to deflate family income (FI) and to calculate absolute class shares.

ing the trend in relative percentiles, and indeed their findings are similar to those reported here. For example, they find no trend in the percent of families and unrelated individuals in the LC and an increase in the UC. The LC, as defined, includes about 30 percent of the population, while the UC contains about 10 percent. The flat trend in the LC and upward trend in the UC is consistent with the results reported in Figure 2.4A showing no change in the 25th percentile relative to the median and an increase in the 90th percentile. However, their approach misses the increase in inequality below the 25th percentile, namely the U-turn in the 10th percentile (Figure 2.4A). Blackburn and Bloom also examine inequality in adjusted family income across individuals and conclude that most of the increase in inequality occurred from 1980 to 1985. Their measure of the UC (about 9 to 10 percent of the population) shows an increase starting in 1980 similar to the increase in the 90th percentile shown in Figure 2.5. Likewise, the trend in the 25th percentile and their definition of the LC is similar. Again, they do not detect the relative decline in the 10th percentile since 1967.

Other methods have also been used to summarize the trends in inequality among families and individuals. Danziger, Gottschalk, and Smolensky (1989) and the Committee on Ways and Means (1989) both use quintile or decile shares to examine the trend in inequality in adjusted family income among individuals (the former study restricts the analysis to individuals in families headed by a man under the age of 65). Based on a comparison of peak and trough years (1973, 1979, 1982, and 1987), they report that the income shares of the lowest three deciles declined while the top three deciles increased over the entire period. The CBO study reports similar results for the trend in quintile shares in AFI among individuals for 1973, 1979, and 1987. The findings of both of these studies, based on selected years, are consistent with the full time-series reported in Figure 2.5.

Disaggregating the General Trends

Although Figures 2.3 through 2.5 provide a picture of the overall trend in inequality, they obscure the experiences of different segments of the population. How have families with different characteristics fared?[27] This section focuses upon how the distribution of adjusted family income (AFI) has changed for families with children, and families and unrelated individuals

[27] A number of recent studies have conducted detailed analyses of the distribution of income for different types of families. For example, Danziger and Gottschalk (1986) examine inequality in real family income for families with children disaggregated by headship and race, while the studies by the CBO (1988) and the Committee on Ways and Means (1989) disaggregate the trend in inequality in adjusted family income for families of differing compositions (unrelated individuals and families, dual- and single-parent families, families with and without children).

characterized by the race of the head of the family, the age of the head, and the type of family head. While a detailed disaggregation of the trend in family inequality is beyond the scope of this analysis, this section provides some indication of the change in the distribution of economic well-being for different types of families.

In 1987, slightly more than half of all families included a child under the age of 18. For this group, the level and distribution of economic well-being, as measured by AFI, is shown in the top half of Table 2.2 for selected years. In absolute terms, families with children in the 10th percentile of the distribution experienced a 22 percent decline in real income from 1973 to 1987, while real income grew 23 percent at the 90th percentile. Relative to the median, the incomes of the 10th and 25th percentiles declined steadily from 1967, at the same time that the incomes of the 75th and 90th percentiles showed constant gains. As shown in the bottom half of Table 2.2, this same pattern of increasing dispersion in both the lower and upper tails of the distribution is evident when each person rather than each family is counted once. Compared to all families, families with children experienced slower growth in median income and a larger increase in inequality (compare Table 2.2 with Table 2.1).

Families and unrelated individuals, regardless of the race/ethnicity of the head of the family, experienced an increase in the dispersion of income, albeit to varying degrees.[28] Table 2.3 shows that, in absolute terms, white families fared best over the period, with a 24.8 percent growth in median AFI between 1970 and 1987. In contrast, over the same period, median AFI grew 20.1 percent among black families and only 8.6 percent for Hispanic families. Furthermore, unlike their black or Hispanic counterparts, white families experienced positive real income growth at each point in the distribution. Among whites, the gains in the 10th percentile are more modest compared to the 90th percentile, so the relative percentiles do show a slight increase in dispersion since 1979. Black and Hispanic families at the 10th and 25th percentiles experienced absolute declines in AFI since 1973. Coupled with the absolute income gains of the 75th and 90th percentiles, inequality increased to a greater degree for these families.

At the same time that inequality has been increasing, there have been important shifts in the composition of families based on the age of the head and the type of family head. The changing age distribution is shown in Table 2.4 by an increase in the share of families and unrelated individuals where the head is between 25 and 44 years old, and a decrease in the repre-

[28] Information regarding the ethnicity of the head of the family has been available only since the 1971 CPS. To maintain a consistent breakdown by race/ethnicity, the data in Table 2.3 are reported for selected years beginning with 1970.

Table 2.2 Absolute and Relative Percentiles of Adjusted Family Income[a]: Families with Children

	Absolute Percentile					Percentile Relative to the Median			
Year	10th	25th	50th	75th	90th	10th	25th	75th	90th
A. Families with Children[b]									
1967	0.91	1.54	2.33	3.31	4.51	0.389	0.662	1.422	1.935
1973	0.94	1.75	2.74	3.89	5.27	0.343	0.640	1.420	1.924
1979[d]	0.88	1.74	2.87	4.18	5.64	0.308	0.608	1.457	1.965
1987	0.71	1.60	2.95	4.54	6.48	0.239	0.540	1.538	2.194
B. All Individuals in Families with Children[c]									
1967	0.86	1.46	2.22	3.14	4.30	0.388	0.658	1.411	1.935
1973	0.93	1.71	2.67	3.79	5.13	0.347	0.638	1.418	1.921
1979[d]	0.89	1.72	2.81	4.10	5.55	0.316	0.612	1.456	1.972
1987	0.72	1.59	2.90	4.45	6.34	0.246	0.546	1.531	2.182

[a]Measured as total family income divided by the poverty line, where the 1967 poverty threshold is inflated using the CPI-X to calculate the poverty lines after 1967.
[b]Weighted by families.
[c]Weighted by persons in families.
[d]Using 1980-based population weights.

Table 2.3 Absolute and Relative Percentiles of Adjusted Family Income[a]: Families and Unrelated Individuals,[b] by Race/Ethnicity

	Absolute Percentile					Percentile Relative to the Median			
Year	10th	25th	50th	75th	90th	10th	25th	75th	90th
				A. White Non-Hispanic					
1970	0.89	1.66	2.78	4.23	5.98	0.320	0.599	1.521	2.154
1973	1.02	1.83	3.03	4.62	6.58	0.338	0.603	1.526	2.170
1979[c]	1.06	1.90	3.21	4.91	6.91	0.332	0.593	1.533	2.154
1987	1.07	1.96	3.47	5.51	7.95	0.307	0.565	1.586	2.290
				B. Black Non-Hispanic					
1970	0.46	0.82	1.54	2.64	4.10	0.301	0.533	1.712	2.655
1973	0.53	0.89	1.68	2.94	4.39	0.313	0.527	1.749	2.614
1979[c]	0.52	0.91	1.78	3.21	4.78	0.294	0.511	1.804	2.689
1987	0.41	0.86	1.85	3.43	5.22	0.222	0.465	1.855	2.825
				C. Hispanic					
1970	0.64	1.09	1.85	2.92	4.07	0.345	0.589	1.580	2.203
1973	0.71	1.14	1.97	3.13	4.33	0.362	0.578	1.592	2.200
1979[c]	0.67	1.15	2.07	3.31	4.93	0.323	0.553	1.596	2.378
1987	0.55	1.02	2.01	3.53	5.35	0.274	0.509	1.761	2.667

[a]Measured as total family income divided by the poverty line, where the 1967 poverty threshold is inflated using the CPI-X to calculate the poverty lines after 1967.

[b]Weighted by families.

[c]Using 1980-based population weights.

Table 2.4 Inequality in Adjusted Family Income[a]: Families and Unrelated Individuals,[b] by Group

	Group Share		Group Mean		Variance of Logarithm of Income			
	1967	1987	1967	1987	1967	1979	1987	1987[c]
Age of Head								
<24	7.0	7.3	2.25	2.26	0.592	0.614	0.892	
25–34	17.6	23.9	2.77	3.58	0.429	0.506	0.736	
35–44	19.5	20.8	2.84	4.12	0.422	0.499	0.669	
45–54	19.6	14.4	3.34	4.70	0.475	0.531	0.690	
55–64	16.9	13.4	3.24	4.26	0.643	0.624	0.766	
>65	19.4	20.2	2.04	3.12	0.622	0.496	0.556	
Inequality								
Between group					0.047	0.038	0.044	0.046
Within group					0.521	0.535	0.694	0.695
Total					0.569	0.573	0.738	0.740

Type of Head								
Husband-and-wife family								
0 or 1 spouse works	38.0	23.1	2.65	3.65	0.405	0.457	0.592	
Both spouses work	31.8	30.1	3.52	4.96	0.352	0.299	0.371	
Male-headed family	1.9	2.8	3.06	3.67	0.600	0.563	0.688	
Female-headed family	8.4	11.2	2.07	2.37	0.765	0.741	0.977	
Male unrelated indiv.	7.4	15.2	2.70	3.75	0.788	0.641	0.864	
Female unrelated indiv.	12.4	17.5	1.87	2.78	0.719	0.555	0.694	
Inequality								
Between group					0.078	0.091	0.106	0.092
Within group					0.490	0.482	0.632	0.589
Total					0.569	0.573	0.738	0.682

[a] Adjusted family income is total family income divided by the family's poverty line.
[b] Weighted by families.
[c] Inequality in 1987 holding group shares constant at the 1967 level.

sentation of families headed by a person aged 45 to 64. There are also important compositional shifts that occurred among families defined by headship (see Table 2.4). As noted earlier, unrelated individuals have increased their representation among all family units, at the same time that the percentage of traditional husband-and-wife families has declined. It is interesting to note that two-parent families with both spouses working actually declined as a fraction of family units when unrelated individuals are included, even though they became the majority of husband-and-wife families. Finally, female-headed families increased their representation among both families and families and unrelated individuals.

Table 2.4 also shows the trend in inequality in AFI as measured by the variance of the logarithm of income for families by age of the head or headship. Consistent with Figure 2.4B, from 1967 to 1987, the total variance of the logarithm increased from 0.569 to 0.738, although there was little change in the 1967 to 1979 time period. The disaggregation shows that all age and headship groups experienced an increase in inequality from 1979 to 1987. Four of the six age groups, and husband-and-wife families with only one spouse working, experienced an increase in inequality in the earlier period as well.

Given the changes in family composition, it is possible that inequality increased as a result of increases in the share of families with lower or higher incomes and higher inequality. This issue can be examined by calculating what inequality would have been if the 1967 composition of families based on age and headship had remained unchanged. As shown in the final column of Table 2.4, holding the age distribution constant results in roughly the same level of inequality that actually occurred (0.740 versus 0.738). In contrast, if there had been no change in the composition of families based on headship, the variance of the logarithm of income would have been 0.682, which is below the actual 1987 level (0.738), but still above the 1967 level (0.569). Thus, in the case of families defined by headship, the compositional changes shifted toward families with lower average income and higher inequality. However, this shift explains only about one-third of the increase in inequality from 1967 to 1987 [(0.738 − 0.682)/(0.738 − 0.569)]. The remaining increase is the result of an increase in inequality between and within each of the groups from 1979 to 1987.

Inequality Among Workers

The debate over the trend in inequality also focuses on labor income among workers. Since the largest source of income for most families and individuals derives from the labor market, the distribution of labor income is the primary component of the overall distribution of economic well-being. In addition, changes in the distribution of labor income provide signals about underlying changes in the labor market, from compositional changes in the workforce to more fundamental changes in the structure of wages.

One of the first studies to renew interest in this topic was an analysis by Harrison, Tilly, and Bluestone (1986a, 1986b) showing a U-turn in the variance of logarithm of annual wage and salary income beginning in 1978 (1975 for full-time year-round workers). Another study by Bluestone and Harrison (1986) evaluated the growth of "low wage" jobs using a class-based methodology, and again pointed to increased dispersion in labor income. While the U-turn thesis advanced by Bluestone and Harrison implies a reversal of a stable or declining trend in inequality, several earlier studies demonstrated increased inequality in labor income among workers during the 1970s, particularly among men (Henle, 1972; Henle and Ryscavage, 1980; Plotnick, 1982; Dooley and Gottschalk, 1984, 1985). Thus, it is uncertain whether the recent increase in inequality is a new phenomenon or simply the continuation of an earlier trend. Although recent analyses generally point to an increase in inequality, they do not always produce similar conclusions regarding either the timing of the changes or where in the distribution the changes are taking place.[29]

Conceptual Issues

Important conceptual issues again confront the researcher. While it may seem obvious that the unit of analysis is the worker and that labor income is the metric, there are more subtle choices about which workers to include and how to measure labor income. For instance, the recent debate over the inequality of earnings has been couched in terms of "good jobs versus bad jobs," yet the unit of analysis is always the individual worker.[30] Which workers are included in the sample for purposes of evaluating the distribution of earnings has differed in practice. In some analyses, individuals with nonzero labor income are included, whether they are wage and salary workers or self-employed (Blackburn and Bloom, 1987). A portion of the earnings

[29]Loveman and Tilly (1988) review most of the recent studies through 1988. Other more recent analyses include Blackburn and Bloom (1987); Bluestone and Harrison (1988); Hilley (1988); Kosters and Ross (1988a, 1988b); Bluestone (1989); Juhn, Murphy, and Pierce (1989); Burtless (1990); Moffitt (1990); and Karoly (1992).

[30]The distribution of earnings among workers differs from that among jobs in several ways. First, a worker may hold more than one job. In the CPS, earnings from multiple jobs are not differentiated. Secondly, the earnings associated with unfilled or vacant jobs are not included in CPS-based estimates of the distribution of earnings. Thus, any analysis of earnings inequality based on the CPS measures the distribution among individual workers, not among jobs.

of the self-employed, however, is a return to past capital investments and not a return to labor. Thus it is more appropriate to exclude the self-employed and focus exclusively on wage and salary workers.[31] This group has been defined as workers with nonzero wage and salary income (Harrison, Tilly, and Bluestone, 1986a, 1986b; Bluestone and Harrison, 1986; Moffitt, 1990) or as workers with wage and salary income exceeding their self-employment income (Burtless, 1990). However, applying either of these definitions to the CPS results in a sample that still contains self-employed workers.[32] In this analysis, as in Karoly (1992) and Kosters and Ross (1988a), the sample includes only wage and salary workers as defined by the Census Bureau (which excludes the self-employed in incorporated businesses). For purposes of comparison, some results will be presented for the sample of workers with nonzero wage and salary income.

The "good jobs, bad jobs" debate suggests researchers can assess how the "quality" of jobs has changed over time. The metric that is used in all of these analyses, however, is the labor income of the individual worker, which only proxies for job quality. The definition of labor income or earnings has also varied across studies. Ideally, labor income would be measured as total monetary and nonmonetary compensation, including the value of fringe benefits such as health insurance or pension contributions. However, a measure of total compensation is not easily computed from the CPS. Instead, monetary compensation is used to measure labor income.[33] In addition, for the same reasons that the self-employed should be excluded from the sample, self-employment income should also be omitted from the measure of labor income. Thus, labor income will be measured as annual wage and salary income in the year prior to the survey.

Due to differences in work effort, annual wage and salary income may

[31] Self-employed workers can have negative labor income as well as very large labor income. By excluding this group of workers from the sample (about 8 to 10 percent of all workers), earnings inequality is lower in each year than it would be if the self-employed were included.

[32] Some workers whose main source of income is self-employment may also have some wage and salary income and will therefore be included in the sample. In addition, the Census Bureau defines the earnings of workers who are self-employed in incorporated businesses as wage and salary income. Thus, if the sample is defined to include only individuals with positive wage and salary income, it will include individuals who are self-employed but whose earnings are counted as wage and salary income. The CPS does identify the self-employed in incorporated businesses so that they can be excluded from the sample of wage and salary workers (about 3 percent of the sample).

[33] Since the portion of total compensation that is paid in the form of nonmonetary benefits has grown over time, this measure of labor income will exclude a growing fraction of total compensation (Kosters and Ross, 1987). Depending upon the distribution of nonmonetary compensation across workers, the distribution of total compensation may be more or less equal than the distribution of money labor income.

not be the best metric for assessing changes in the distribution of labor income. The distribution of annual wage and salary income will contain many individuals with low earned income because they have worked, voluntarily or involuntarily, only part-year and/or part-time. Particularly because of the growth in part-time employment, trends in inequality in annual wage and salary income may be biased due to changes in the distribution of annual hours worked. To the extent that the concern is over the "quality of jobs," a correction needs to be made to account for differences across workers in annual hours worked.

One approach has been to restrict the analysis to full-time year-round (FTYR) workers, since this group has worked close to the same number of annual hours (Blackburn and Bloom, 1987; Kosters and Ross, 1987, 1988a, 1988b; Bluestone and Harrison, 1988; Bluestone, 1989; Juhn, Murphy, and Pierce, 1989; Karoly, 1992).[34] This approach, however, introduces another potential bias because FTYR workers are a selected sample of all workers.[35] For example, during a business cycle downturn, the increase in unemployment results in fewer full-year workers. Those workers who become part-year workers in a recession are not likely to be a random sample of all workers. Consequently, the approach of restricting the analysis to FTYR workers will not necessarily reflect the trends for all workers.

The alternative is to include all wage and salary workers in the sample and adjust for weeks worked by using a measure of the weekly wage, or adjust for annual hours by using a measure of the hourly wage. Using the March CPS, a measure of weeks worked in the previous year is available, although the information is recorded in intervals in the surveys prior to 1976. A measure of hours worked per week during the previous year is available only for the CPS surveys starting with 1976.[36] Using this information, I have computed three alternative earnings measures: (1) the weekly wage calculated as annual wage and salary income divided by annual weeks worked, where the midpoint of the interval is used as the estimate of weeks worked in the surveys prior to 1976; (2) the weekly wage calculated as in (1), except that annual weeks worked are calculated consistently over time using the midpoint of the weeks worked interval for all survey years; and (3) the hourly wage calculated as annual wage and salary income divided by annual hours (annual weeks worked times usual hours per week). The trend

[34] Full-time year-round (FTYR) workers are those who worked 35 or more hours per week and 50 or more weeks per year. In this group of workers, there is still variation in annual hours worked, primarily due to variation in hours worked per week.

[35] From 1967 to 1987, the percentage of all workers who work FTYR has ranged from 54 to 60 percent. This percentage has generally varied procyclically, reaching troughs in 1975 and 1982 during cyclical downturns, and peaking during the recent recovery.

[36] Prior to 1976, usual hours worked per week during the survey week were coded.

in inequality in wage and salary income is compared for these three wage measures as well as for annual wage and salary income.[37]

Finally, another complication arises from the potential selection bias in the sample of workers with earned income. Since individuals who do not work have no labor income, they are excluded from the sample of workers. In some cases, these individuals never participated in the labor market; in other cases, they have retired. Others may work in one year and not in the next as a consequence of an economic downturn. Thus, the composition of the workforce is constantly changing due to a variety of factors. This type of movement is problematic if workers who leave the labor market in any given year are not a random sample of all workers. For example, in an economic downturn, low-wage workers may disproportionately leave the labor force. Alternatively, the trend toward early retirement may result in a disproportionate loss of middle- or high-wage workers. Clearly, this type of selection behavior has implications for changes in the distribution of labor income. While it is easy to acknowledge this potential problem, an effort to correct for selection bias is beyond the scope of this chapter.

As was the case for inequality among families and individuals, there is no single way to assess the trend in inequality in labor income among workers. To examine the sensitivity of results to various methods and to allow comparisons with other studies, I present results for inequality among workers defined as all wage and salary workers (excluding all of the self-employed). Some comparisons are made for the sample defined as all workers with positive wage and salary income. Labor income is defined as wage and salary income measured (1) annually, (2) weekly, (3) weekly using a consistent methodology, and (4) hourly. Since the weekly and hourly wage series control for differences in labor supply, I focus the discussion on the results for these wage series. The annual wage series is provided for comparison. In addition, results will be presented for all workers and separately by sex. In all cases, the sample is restricted to individuals aged 16 and over who are not in the military and who worked at least one week in the year prior to the survey.

Changes in the Level of Income Distribution

The trend in real median wage and salary income for all wage and salary workers and separately for men and women is shown for the four wage

[37] Since the annual hours measure is based on "usual weekly hours" times weeks worked in the previous year, method (3) is only an approximation to the true hourly wage distribution. This method is comparable to that used by Blackburn and Bloom (1987) and Hilley (1988). Kosters and Ross (1988a) and Karoly and Klerman (1991) examine inequality based on reported hourly wages and usual weekly wages from the monthly CPS surveys.

Figure 2.8 Real Median Wage and Salary Income[1] for Wage and Salary Workers

A. All Wage and Salary Workers

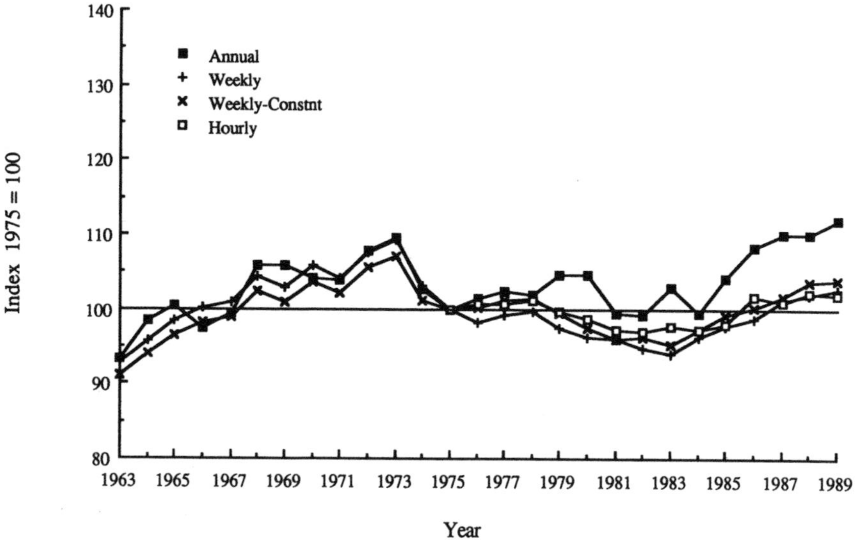

B. Wage and Salary Workers: Men

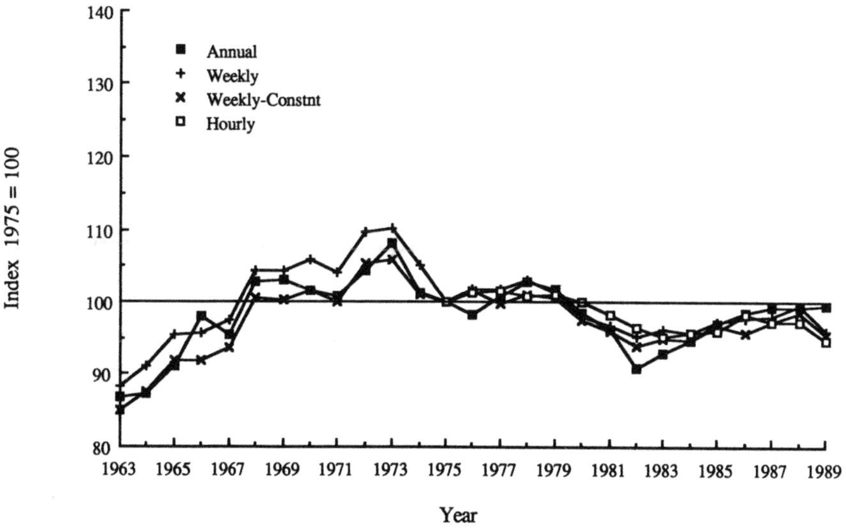

[1]The CPI-X is used to deflate all four measures of wage and salary income.

C. Wage and Salary Workers: Women

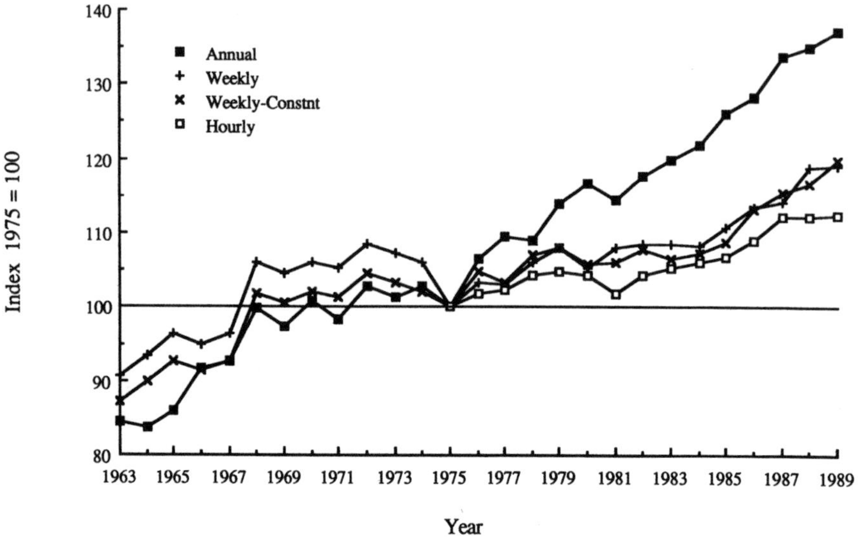

Source: Tabulations using CPS microdata from 1964 to 1990.

measures in Figures 2.8A, 2.8B, and 2.8C.[38] Since the hourly wage series is not available until 1975, all real median wage and salary income series are indexed to equal 100 in 1975 to facilitate comparisons between the four wage measures over the 1975 to 1989 period. This is also the period when the data are most comparable (see the discussion in Appendix 2A).

The trends evident in Figure 2.8 confirm the well-documented stagnation in the level of the wage distribution as measured by real median labor income. The general pattern for all four wage series is one of real wage growth through the 1960s and early 1970s, followed by declining real wages from 1973 to the early 1980s. There is a subsequent return to positive wage growth starting about 1983. Even with the recent wage growth, however, real median labor income for men in 1989 was more than 10 percent below the 1973 peak. In contrast, depending upon the wage series, real median labor income for women grew 10 to 30 percent between 1973 and 1989. Despite some stagnation in real wages during the 1970s, women workers have experienced substantial real wage gains in the past twenty-five years.

The trends in real wages differ for points above and below the median. Table 2.5 summarizes the pattern of real growth in weekly and hourly wage

[38]The absolute percentiles are tabulated in Table 2B.2 in Appendix 2B for all wage and salary workers and by sex for three of the wage series.

Table 2.5 Percentage Change in Real Absolute Percentiles of Wage and Salary Income: Various Years

	Weekly (Consistent) Percentile					Hourly Percentile				
Period	10th	25th	50th	75th	90th	10th	25th	50th	75th	90th
A. All Workers										
1967–1974	12.5	2.0	2.2	8.7	10.1					
1975–1979	6.8	6.1	−0.6	4.1	3.7	7.5	3.4	0.3	3.2	2.8
1979–1987	−6.4	−5.5	2.2	0.7	5.9	−8.8	−4.8	1.2	3.7	4.2
B. Men										
1967–1974	−1.1	1.7	7.8	10.5	13.8					
1975–1979	3.3	−0.5	1.5	6.0	6.4	1.8	0.1	1.5	4.8	1.6
1979–1987	−12.8	−10.0	−3.5	1.2	4.7	−13.5	−8.0	−3.7	−2.3	4.2
C. Women										
1967–1974	18.9	12.2	10.1	6.5	4.9					
1975–1979	12.0	10.9	8.4	4.5	4.4	10.4	7.6	4.9	3.2	4.5
1979–1987	−1.3	1.2	6.8	17.9	17.7	−3.7	−3.1	7.1	11.6	14.5

and salary income at the 10th, 25th, 50th, 75th, and 90th percentiles for various time periods.[39] Among men, real wage declines have almost exclusively fallen on those in the bottom half of the distribution. For these men, weekly and hourly wages have declined in real terms from the 1967 level. The sharpest declines have occurred since 1979, as the 10th percentile fell about 13 percent in real terms, while the 25th percentile declined around 10 percent. In contrast, the 75th and 90th percentiles grew faster in every period compared to the other percentiles of the distribution. Overall, the gap in weekly wages between men at the 10th and 90th percentiles has grown about 35 percent since 1967. In the recent period, this growing gap is the result of substantial declines in real wages at the bottom of the distribution and more modest gains at the top.

In real terms, women at each point in the distribution were better off in 1987 than they were in 1967. Between 1967 and 1979, real wages grew three to four times faster at the 10th percentile compared to the 90th percentile. However, the rapid wage growth at the lower tail of the distribution slowed after 1979, and actually turned negative. At the same time, wage growth accelerated at the top of the distribution. As a consequence, since 1979, the wage gap between the 10th and 90th percentile has risen nearly 20 percent. Unlike the rise in inequality among their male counterparts, this rise in inequality among women is due to small real wage declines at the bottom of the distribution and substantial real wage growth at the top.

The Changing Shape of Income Distribution

The differential changes in real incomes at the top and bottom of the distribution indicate that the overall shape of the distribution has not remained constant. Figures 2.9 through 2.11 further illustrate the changes in the shape of the distribution of labor income. These figures record the trends in the 10th, 25th, 75th, and 90th percentiles relative to the median separately for men and women workers and then for all wage and salary workers.[40]

All three wage series shown in Figure 2.9 demonstrate that inequality among men has been increasing since the early 1960s. Since 1963, there has been a steady growth in the upper tail of the distribution, with the 75th and 90th percentiles growing 10 percent faster than the median since 1975, and

[39] As discussed in Appendix 2A, changes in CPS survey procedures mean that the data prior to 1975 are not strictly comparable with the data from later years. Consequently, the time periods in Table 2.5 are calculated with a break in the time series between 1974 and 1975.

[40] Due to the similarity in the trends based on the two weekly wage-series, the results are reported only for the consistent weekly wage series. Again, the time-series for the percentiles relative to the median are indexed to equal 100 in 1975 to allow comparisons of the relative changes across the three wage-series.

Figure 2.9 Inequality Among Wage and Salary Workers: Men—Percentiles Relative to Median Income

A. Annual Wage and Salary Income

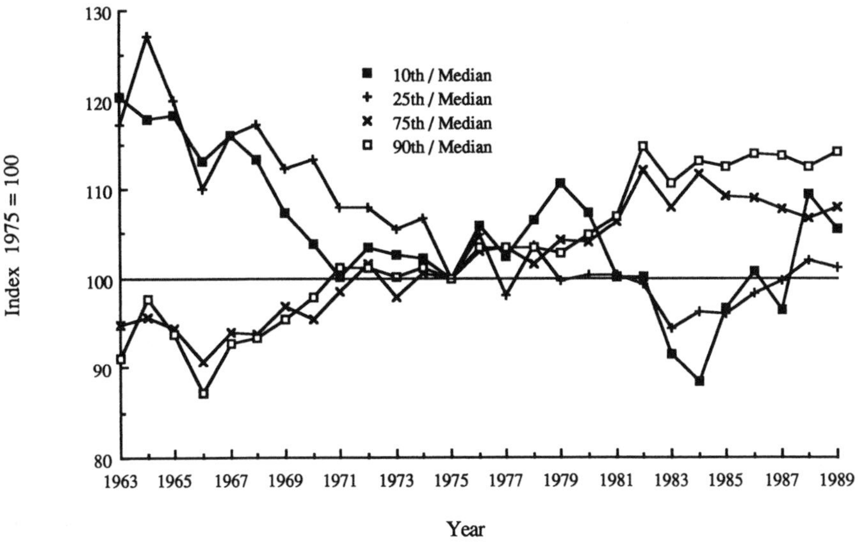

B. Weekly (Consistent) Wage and Salary Income

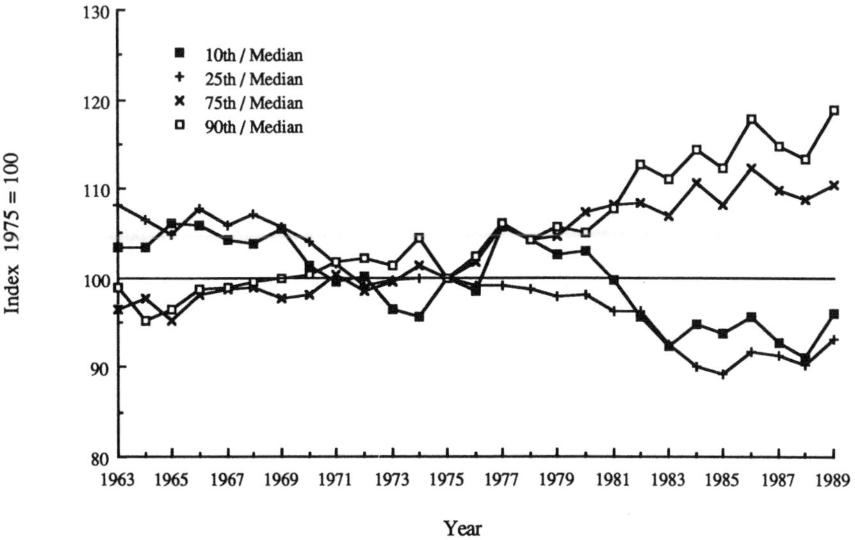

C. Hourly Wage and Salary Income

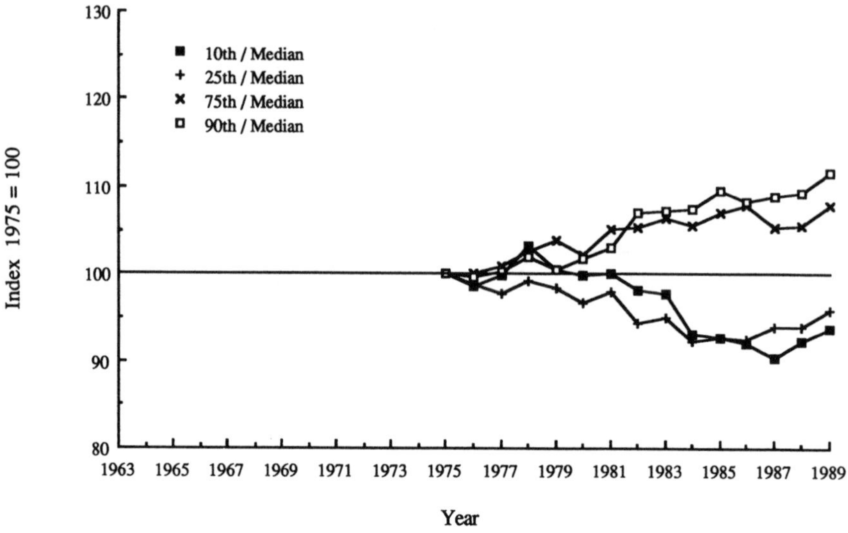

Source: Tabulations using CPS microdata from 1964 to 1990.

about 15 to 20 percent relative to the median since 1963. In contrast, the lower tail of the distribution declined over the entire period, with a sharper drop starting about 1978–1979.[41] The only period of relative stability in the distribution of labor income among men was between 1975 and 1979. In addition, the improvement in the lower tail of the annual wage distribution since 1984 (Figure 2.9A) is not evident once annual weeks or annual hours are controlled for (Figures 2.9B and 2.9C).[42]

[41] In Figures 2.9B, 2.10B, and 2.11B, the magnitude and direction of change for the 10th and 25th percentiles is similar from 1975 onward. Prior to that time, the movement in the two series is parallel but at different levels. The sharp jump in the 10th percentile from 1974 to 1975 can be attributed to the change in the income imputation procedures introduced with the 1976 CPS survey, as discussed in Appendix 2A. The effect of these changes is only evident for the 10th percentile using wage and salary measures that control for annual weeks or hours worked. In these cases, the 25th percentile provides a more consistent measure of the changing shape of the lower tail over time.

[42] Kosters and Ross (1988a) suggest that the relative decline in the lower tail of the hourly wage distribution may be affected by the decline in the real minimum wage from 1980 through 1988. This is not an issue for men, since the 10th percentile is always above the real minimum wage (Figure 2.9C). For all workers, the 10th (25th) percentile is always below (above) the real minimum wage (Figure 2.11C). The sharper decline in the 10th percentile as compared to the 25th percentile may reflect the declining real minimum wage. The same factor may explain the divergence of the 10th and 25th percentiles for women workers (Figure 2.10C).

At the same time that inequality among men was rising throughout the late 1960s and 1970s, the distribution of labor income among women was becoming more equal (Figure 2.10). Due to the variation in labor supply across women, the weekly and hourly wage measures (Figures 2.10B and 2.10C) are best. For these two measures, wage dispersion declined from 1963 to 1979, as wage income at the bottom of the distribution grew faster than the median. At the same time, incomes in the top of the distribution essentially kept pace with the growth in the median. Starting in 1979, however, inequality started to increase as the growth in incomes in the top of the distribution outpaced the growth in median income. Wages in the bottom of the distribution also fell in relative terms, leaving workers in the lower tail worse off in 1987 than they had been in 1975.

Figure 2.11 shows the trend in relative percentiles for the combined sample of male and female workers. Again, focusing on the weekly and hourly wage measures, there is evidence that inequality increased among all workers beginning around 1979. Prior to that year, wages at the 10th, 75th, and 90th percentiles increased almost steadily relative to the median. At the same time, the 25th percentile stayed unchanged in relative terms until 1975 when it grew faster than the median. Thus, despite the increasing inequality

Figure 2.10 Inequality Among Wage and Salary Workers: Women—Percentiles Relative to Median Income

A. Annual Wage and Salary Income

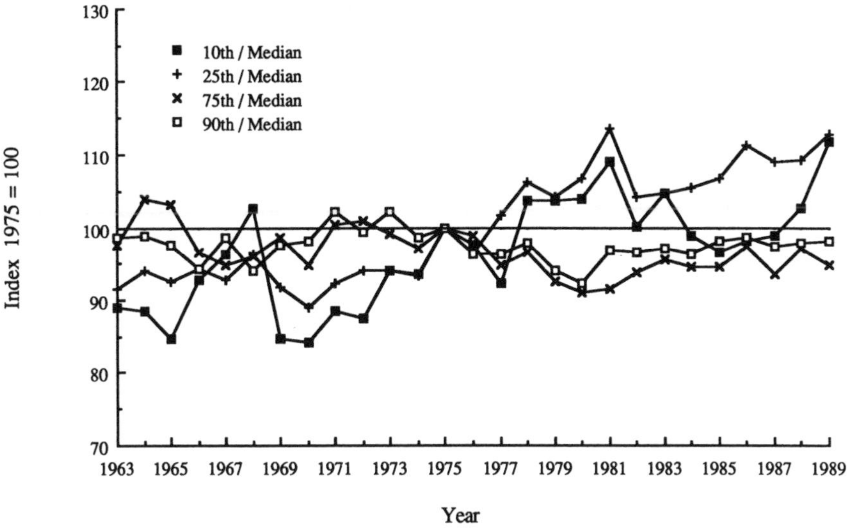

B. Weekly (Consistent) Wage and Salary Income

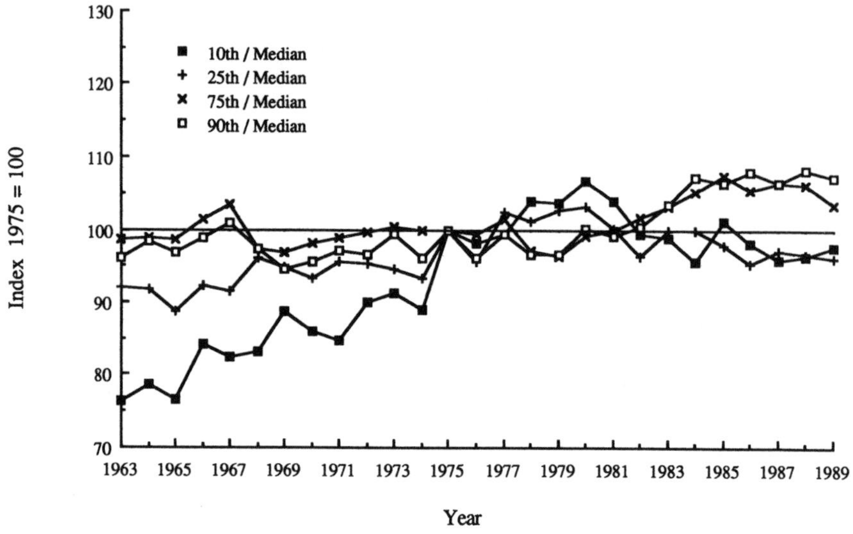

C. Hourly Wage and Salary Income

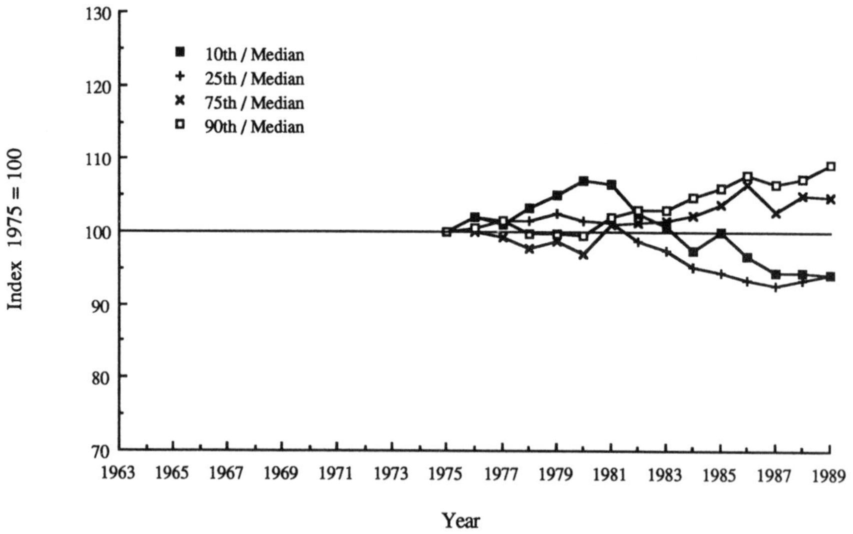

Source: Tabulations using CPS microdata from 1964 to 1990.

Figure 2.11 Inequality Among All Wage and Salary Workers
Percentiles Relative to Median Income

A. Annual Wage and Salary Income

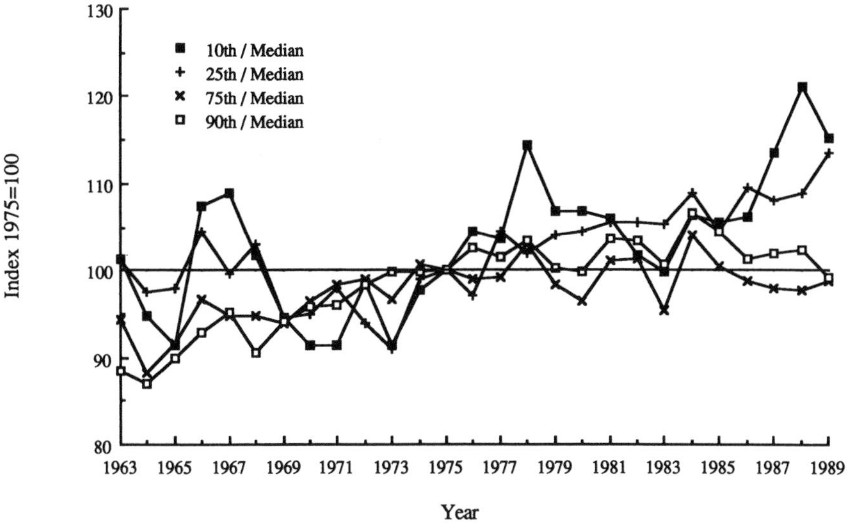

B. Weekly (Consistent) Wage and Salary Income

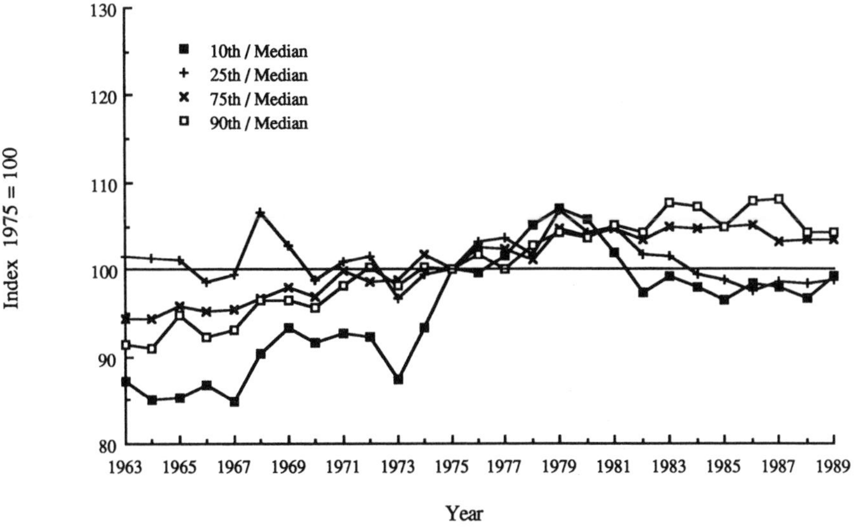

C. Hourly Wage and Salary Income

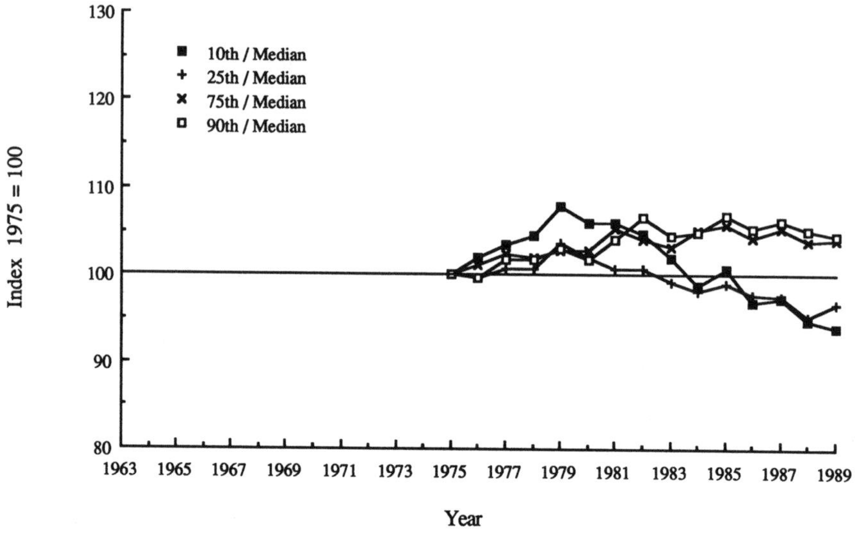

Source: Tabulations using CPS microdata from 1964 to 1990.

among men during this period, the overall distribution is dominated by the relative wage gains among women in the lower tail of the distribution. The combined effect is a decrease in inequality between 1963 and 1979.

The turning point comes in 1979 as both the 10th and 25th percentiles began to decline relative to the median, while the 75th and 90th percentiles continued to their relative growth. This is the period when inequality is increasing among both men and women due to relative wage gains at the top of the distribution and relative wage losses at the bottom. The similarity of the trends for the weekly and hourly wage series indicates that the growing wage dispersion in both the lower and upper tail of the distribution is not due solely to changes in annual hours worked.[43] In addition, the results for the annual wage and salary income, a measure that does not control for differences in labor supply, are somewhat different than the weekly or hourly measure (contrast Figure 2.11A with Figures 2.11B and 2.11C). In particular, there is more cyclical variation in the 10th percentile of annual income relative to the median. For instance, unlike the trends for the weekly

[43] An increase in inequality is also observed when the sample is restricted to FTYR workers. For FTYR workers, the increase in dispersion among men precedes the more recent increase in inequality among women. As with the sample of all workers, inequality has increased since 1979 due to growing dispersion in both the lower and upper tails of the distribution.

or hourly wage series, the 10th percentile in the annual wage distribution shows a relative decline between 1967 and 1971 and a relative improvement between 1983 and 1988.

Disaggregating the data further by sex and race/ethnicity reveals the same general patterns observed separately for men and women. Table 2.6 summarizes the trend in absolute and relative percentiles for weekly wage and salary income for men and women, separately by race/ethnicity.[44] In absolute terms, only Hispanic men experienced real declines in median income between 1970 and 1987. The gains in median weekly wages among black men and women were higher compared to those among white men and women, thereby increasing the black:white earnings ratio. Although dispersion increased in both the upper and lower tail for the three groups of men, black and Hispanic men at the 10th percentile appeared to have fared better than their white counterparts. The trend in the 10th percentile relative to the median is flat for black and Hispanic men, while it is declining for white men. Hispanic women are the only group of women who show a relative improvement in the 10th percentile in every period since 1970. Thus, there is some indication that the overall declines in the relative standing of low-wage workers did not hold for all groups.

Finally, it is worth noting that the increase in inequality observed among workers has not been reversed in the 1980s as the economy has expanded. Typically, inequality is expected to vary countercyclically, rising during economic downturns and falling during economic expansions. The trend in the hourly wage-series is the most convincing, since it adjusts for changes in the pattern of annual hours worked (Figures 2.9C, 2.10C, and 2.11C). For all workers, as well as for men and women separately, dispersion has at best leveled off, and in some cases continued to grow, since 1983. For example, while the 10th percentile of hourly wages for men shows modest gains relative to the median since 1987 (Figure 2.9C), the gap between the 90th and 10th percentile has changed little. Thus, it appears that the economic recovery has not improved the economic status of lower-wage workers.

Comparison with Other Studies

A variety of other approaches have been used to assess the trend in inequality in labor income among workers.[45] How do those results compare with the

[44] The time-series in Table 2.6 begins with 1970, since this is the first year that information on an individual's ethnicity is available on the CPS public-use files.

[45] The focus of the comparisons will be with other studies using the March CPS. Other data sources have also been used. For example, Grubb and Wilson (1989) rely upon the 1950, 1960, and 1970 Censuses. For workers with nonzero annual wage and salary income, they find an

Table 2.6 Absolute and Relative Percentiles of Weekly (Consistent) Wage and Salary Income: All Workers, by Sex and Race/Ethnicity

	Absolute Percentile[a]					Percentile Relative to the Median			
Year	10th	25th	50th	75th	90th	10th	25th	75th	90th
A. Men: White Non-Hispanic									
1970	124.82	280.85	432.72	596.13	800.96	0.288	0.649	1.378	1.851
1975	116.07	267.33	424.26	598.44	802.66	0.274	0.630	1.411	1.892
1979[b]	119.20	261.44	435.73	628.51	842.41	0.274	0.600	1.442	1.933
1987	109.89	240.74	433.04	662.43	906.75	0.254	0.556	1.530	2.094
B. Men: Black Non-Hispanic									
1970	76.66	171.63	274.61	405.68	525.30	0.279	0.625	1.477	1.913
1975	89.82	183.47	308.07	458.66	593.18	0.292	0.596	1.489	1.925
1979[b]	85.86	174.29	296.06	464.78	610.02	0.290	0.589	1.570	2.060
1987	77.66	157.95	283.90	454.24	624.57	0.274	0.556	1.600	2.200
C. Men: Hispanic									
1970	118.58	219.44	324.70	457.69	598.12	0.365	0.676	1.410	1.842
1975	112.78	201.81	305.78	457.13	590.70	0.369	0.660	1.495	1.932
1979[b]	112.35	203.34	305.01	464.78	628.51	0.368	0.667	1.524	2.061
1987	102.38	170.34	273.58	443.79	662.43	0.374	0.623	1.622	2.421

				D. Women: White Non-Hispanic					
1970	48.23	112.23	208.41	312.06	426.84	0.231	0.538	1.497	2.048
1975	53.16	112.38	203.56	310.35	438.60	0.261	0.552	1.525	2.155
1979[b]	58.78	122.56	221.37	326.16	450.25	0.266	0.554	1.473	2.034
1987	57.92	125.90	236.58	378.53	545.08	0.245	0.532	1.600	2.304
				E. Women: Black Non-Hispanic					
1970	37.89	85.26	168.80	265.38	390.08	0.224	0.505	1.572	2.311
1975	49.69	106.93	194.93	305.78	416.92	0.255	0.549	1.569	2.139
1979[b]	58.10	125.93	214.50	319.54	455.14	0.271	0.587	1.490	2.122
1987	57.92	124.26	227.61	359.60	501.93	0.254	0.546	1.580	2.205
				F. Women: Hispanic					
1970	47.75	104.11	192.67	260.05	358.87	0.248	0.540	1.350	1.863
1975	54.87	122.31	192.98	275.20	382.22	0.284	0.634	1.426	1.981
1979[b]	67.72	137.14	203.64	290.49	406.68	0.333	0.673	1.426	1.997
1987	68.89	123.20	199.71	321.75	461.01	0.345	0.617	1.611	2.308

[a]Measured in 1986 dollars using the CPI-X.
[b]Using 1980-based population weights.

Figure 2.12 Inequality in Annual Wage and Salary Income Among Workers: Variance of Logarithm Using Two Sample Definitions

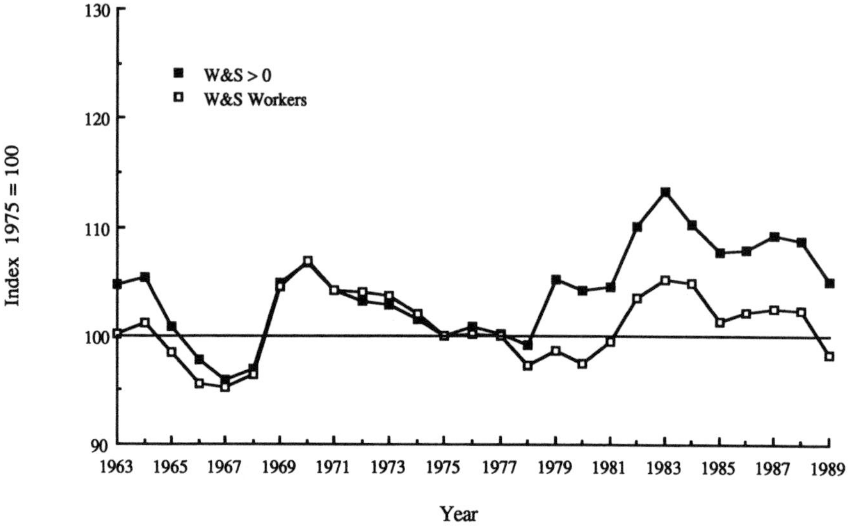

Source: Tabulations using CPS microdata from 1964 to 1990.

findings just presented? One theme in the recent literature is the U-turn hypothesis of Bluestone and Harrison. The U-turn story is based upon the trend in the variance of the logarithm of income and in class shares using absolute class cutoffs, both showing a period of decreasing inequality from the 1960s through the mid-1970s, and an increase in inequality thereafter. The finding of a U-turn is sensitive, however, to the inequality measure, the sample of workers, and the definition of labor income.

First, consider the evidence based upon summary measures of inequality. Updating previous analyses, Bluestone (1989) shows a U-turn in 1978 in the variance of the logarithm for workers with nonzero annual wage and salary income. Although the variance declines from 1983 to 1985, it increases again from 1985 to 1987. Figure 2.12 shows the trend in the variance of logarithm (VLOG) of annual wage and salary income for the sample used by Bluestone (all workers with nonzero annual wage and salary income) and the sample

---

increase in Theil's entropy measure between 1959 and 1969 as well as between 1969 and 1979. This is consistent with the trend in the variance of logarithm reported below for the same sample. However, when the sample is restricted to wage and salary workers only, inequality declines from 1969 to 1979.

used in this analysis (wage and salary workers only).[46] The trend in the two series is quite similar until 1978, when they begin to diverge. Although both series exhibit a U-turn (in 1978 for the Bluestone sample and in 1980 for the sample used in this analysis), excluding the self-employed results in a smaller increase in the variance of the logarithm of income during the recessions in the late 1970s and early 1980s.

However, based on the complete time-series observations in Figure 2.12, the 1978 U-turn is not the only change in the direction of the trend in inequality, as there are another trough in 1967 and relative peaks in 1970 and 1983. Changes introduced with the March 1970 CPS may be responsible for the sharp increase in inequality between 1968 and 1969.[47] If the time frame is restricted to the 1970 to 1989 period when the data are most comparable, 1978 does mark a U-turn in the trend in inequality. The upward trend is reversed, however, in 1983. After leveling off between 1985 and 1988, inequality declines further from 1988 to 1989. This drop in VLOG in the last full year of the economic expansion reflects relative gains in the distribution of annual wage and salary income below the 10th percentile.

The variance of the logarithm of annual wage and salary income is only one of several summary measures of inequality. For the sample of wage and salary workers, Figure 2.13 reports the trend in VLOG and in three other summary measures: the coefficient of variation (CV), Theil's entropy measure (ENTROPY), and Theil's mean logarithmic deviation (MLD). All four measures show similar turning points, including an increase in inequality in 1978 or 1980 and a decrease around 1983.[48]

[46] Using the Bluestone (1989) sample definition, I am able to replicate the point estimates from 1969 onwards. However, my results reported in Figure 2.12 differ significantly for the earlier years. The Bluestone (1989) estimates decline from 1.98 to 1.79 from 1963 to 1968, while my estimates decline from 1.80 to 1.67. In my series, there is a sharp increase from 1968 to 1969, while the Bluestone series shows a smaller increase. My results do replicate those initially reported as evidence of a U-turn by Harrison, Tilly, and Bluestone (1986a).

[47] Beginning with the March 1970 CPS, information about income and work experience in the previous year were collected in the same survey. Prior to that year, work experience data were collected in the February and April surveys and matched to the March data. It is not clear a priori that this change, or other revisions introduced at the same time, would have increased measured inequality. Bluestone and Harrison (1986) argue that the CPS data prior to March 1970 are not comparable with the data from subsequent years, and they therefore focus on the 1969 to 1983 period.

[48] Since these summary measures capture changes in the shape of the distribution, they should provide a picture similar to the analysis based on relative percentiles. Indeed, the turning points evident in the summary measures mirror the pattern in the 10th percentile relative to the median (Figure 2.11A). For example, a comparison of Figure 2.11A with Figure 2.13 shows that the 10th percentile peaks relative to the median when VLOG reaches a trough, and vice versa (e.g., 1967, 1970, 1978, and 1983). This is consistent with the sensitivity of VLOG to changes in the lower tail of the distribution.

Figure 2.13 Inequality in Annual Wage and Salary Income Among Wage and Salary Workers

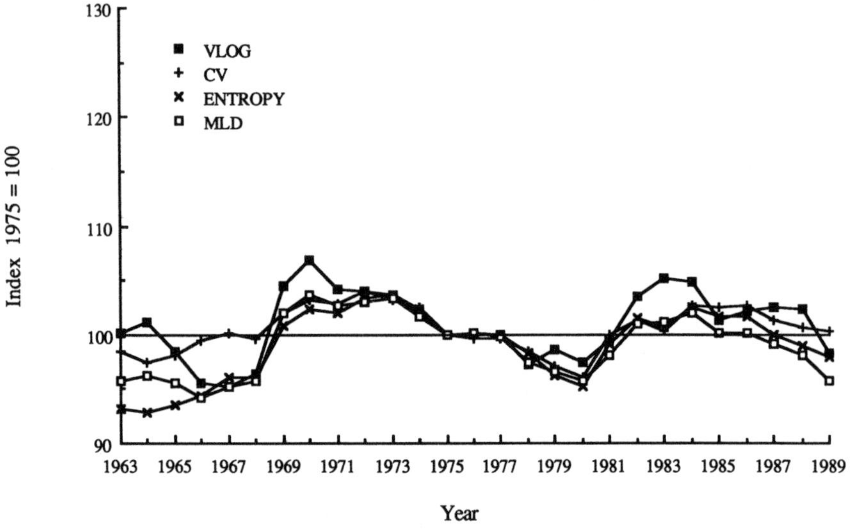

Source: Tabulations using CPS microdata from 1964 to 1990.

As shown in Figure 2.14A, when the weekly wage is the measure of labor income, there is no sign of a significant downturn in inequality in the last decade. After declining from 1975 to 1980, there is a steady increase in inequality between 1980 and 1986 as measured by CV, ENTROPY, and MLD. Only VLOG shows a break in a steady upward trend between 1983 and 1985. The other three measures begin to level off in the late 1980s, although two of the measures (VLOG and CV) increase between 1988 and 1989. In all cases, inequality in weekly wage and salary income for all workers is higher in 1989 than it was in 1980. This is also true for inequality in weekly wages among men (Figure 2.14B). Inequality continues to rise through 1989, although the rate of increase slows in the late 1980s. Thus, while the economic recovery may have slowed the increase in inequality, once annual weeks worked are controlled for, there is no indication that the expansion reversed the rise in wage dispersion.[49]

[49] In both Figures 2.14A and 2.14B, the weekly wage-series shows a sharp decrease between 1968 and 1969 and between 1974 and 1975. Again, these discontinuities can be attributed to revised survey procedures. Due to these CPS revisions, it is difficult to determine the long-run trend in inequality over the full 1963–1989 time period.

Figure 2.14 Inequality in Weekly Wage and Salary Income Among Wage and Salary Workers

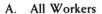

A. All Workers

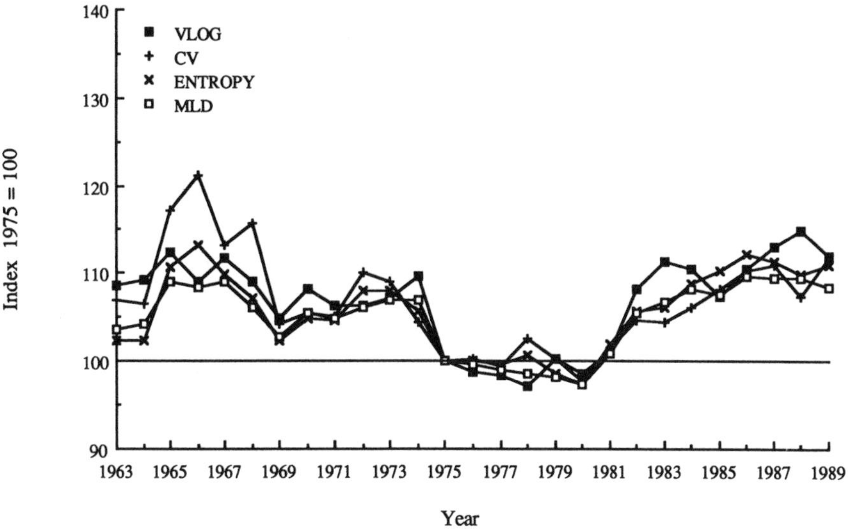

B. Men

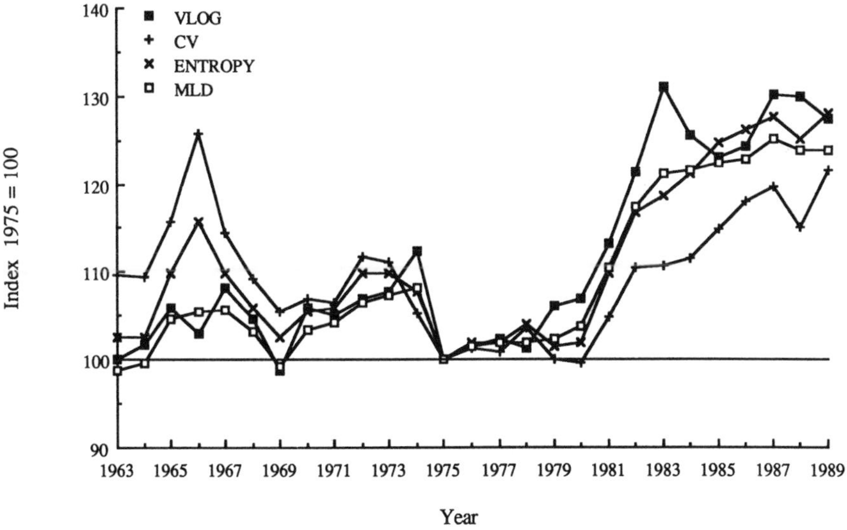

Source: Tabulations using CPS microdata from 1964 to 1990.

It is interesting to note that other studies using summary measures have not reached the same U-turn conclusion. For example, Blackburn and Bloom (1987) conclude that there is no upward trend in inequality in earnings among all workers based upon the CV, MLD, and Gini coefficient. However, they base their conclusion regarding the trend in inequality upon regressions of the summary measures on a linear time trend and a control for the business cycle. If there has been a U-turn in inequality in the late 1970s, rather than a continuous increase, their linear regression analysis is likely to show an absence of a trend. In fact, some of the summary measures they report do show a change in the direction of the trend around 1980.[50]

The evidence for a U-turn in inequality is also based on a class-shares analysis by Bluestone and Harrison (1986, 1988) and updated by Bluestone (1989). While the initial Bluestone and Harrison (1986) analysis used a sample of all workers, their subsequent studies focused upon FTYR workers only. For FTYR workers, the low-wage class (LC) is defined by an absolute income cutoff of $11,104 in 1986 dollars. Figure 2.15A replicates the Bluestone and Harrison methodology from 1963 to 1989 (using the CPI-X instead of the CPI to deflate annual wage and salary income) for the sample of FTYR workers. Figure 2.15A also plots the trend in real median annual wage and salary income. In contrast, Figure 2.15B plots two measures that isolate changes in the shape of the distribution: the percentage in the LC using the Kosters and Ross (1988a) definition (less than 50 percent of the median), and the 10th percentile relative to the median. The trend in the LC share based on relative income cutoffs is similar to the trend in the relative percentile.[51]

Contrasting the share in the LC from Figures 2.15A and 2.15B shows the difference obtained by using absolute versus relative class cutoffs. For example, from 1963 to 1972, the LC using absolute cutoffs declines while the LC using relative class cutoffs shows no clear trend. This is a period when the shape of the distribution is essentially unchanged but there is real growth in the level of the distribution. Both measures of the LC show a U-turn around 1978 to 1981, but the trend since that period also varies for the two measures. Once again, absolute income cutoffs obscure changes in

[50] The difference in their results may also be due to the inclusion of the self-employed in their sample and self-employment income in their measure of labor income.

[51] In general, for the same samples and the same relative point in the distribution, the results for the trends in class shares based on relative class cutoffs presented by Kosters and Ross (1987, 1988a) are comparable to those presented here based on relative percentiles. For example, for all workers, Kosters and Ross find that the share of workers in the LC (less than 50 percent of the current year median) declines slightly from 1967 to 1986. This is consistent with the modest increase in the 25th percentile relative to the median shown in Figure 2.11A. However, as Kosters and Ross define the LC, they miss any changes below the 30th percentile, and hence do not capture the changes in the 10th percentile shown in Figure 2.11.

Figure 2.15 Inequality Among FTYR Wage and Salary Workers Using Absolute and Relative Class Shares

A. Absolute Income Class Shares vs. Real Median Income[1]
(LC defined as <$11,104 in 1986 $, deflated using CPI-X)

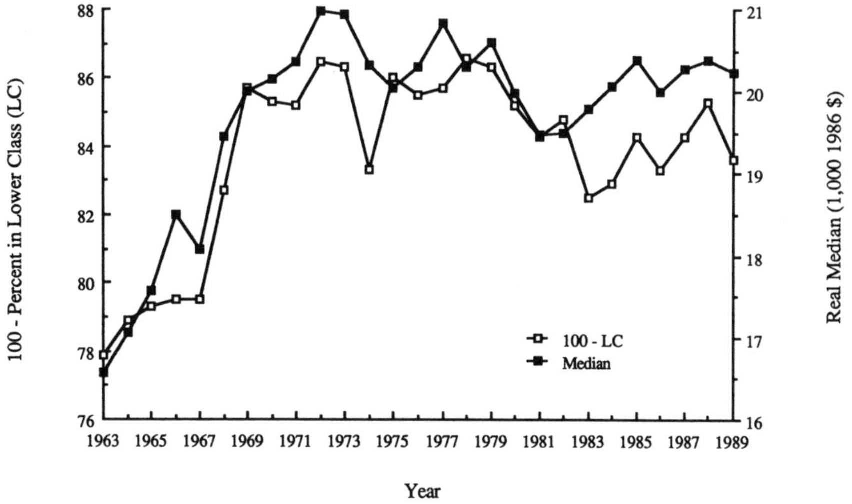

B. Relative Income Class Share vs. Relative Percentile
(LC is <50% of median income)

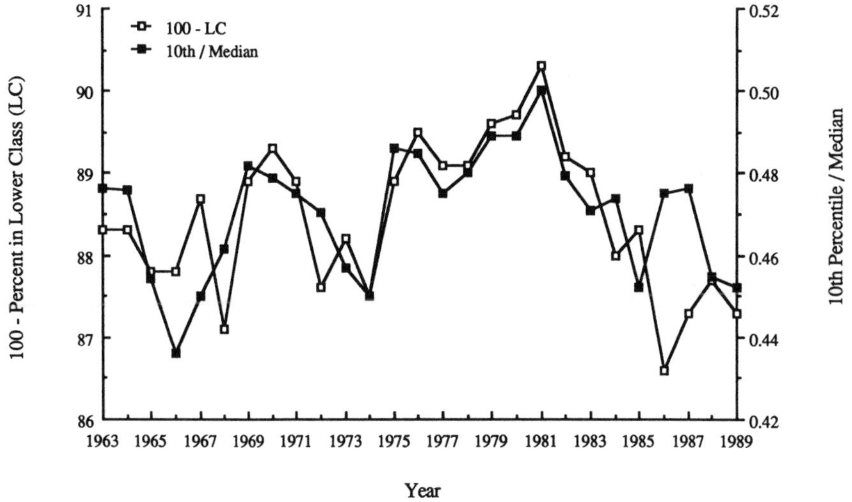

Source: Tabulations using CPS microdata from 1964 to 1990.

[1]The CPI-X is used to deflate annual wage and salary income and to calculate absolute class shares.

the shape of the distribution. Consequently, the findings of Bluestone and Harrison will differ from those of Kosters and Ross simply due to the methodological differences associated with measuring class shares based on absolute versus relative class cutoffs.

Some studies restrict the analysis to FTYR workers in an effort to control for annual hours worked. For example, the percentile method is employed by Juhn, Murphy, and Pierce (1989), who use the CPS surveys from 1963 to 1987, as well as the 1960 Census. They focus upon weekly wages for men who worked full time and find an increase in dispersion beginning in 1975. Other researchers have examined the distribution of hourly wages either directly or by using the decomposition property of the variance of the logarithm of income (Tilly, Bluestone, and Harrison, 1986; Blackburn and Bloom, 1987; Hilley, 1988; Burtless, 1990). In general, these studies have concluded that most of the increase in inequality in annual wage and salary income since the late 1970s is the result of an increase in inequality in hourly wages and not simply greater variance in weeks or hours worked. These findings are consistent with those reported here, which show similar increases in dispersion for wages measured annually, weekly, or hourly.

The one exception to this general finding is an analysis by Kosters and Ross (1988a) based upon the usual weekly and hourly wage data collected in the May CPS from 1973 to 1978 and the monthly Outgoing Rotations Group (ORG) CPS supplements from after 1979. In contrast to data based on the March CPS, Kosters and Ross report that the CV for hourly wages is flat or declining during the 1980s. Karoly and Klerman (1991), using the same data, demonstrate that once an adjustment is made for top-coding the wage data, the May/ORG CPS data produce the same trend in inequality as the March CPS data.[52]

While the U-turn hypothesis characterizes the trend in inequality for all workers since 1970, it does not apply when men and women workers are considered separately. This result, illustrated in Figures 2.9 and 2.10, is also supported by other research. For example, using summary measures of inequality, Blackburn and Bloom (1987), Karoly (1992), and Burtless (1990) find a positive trend for men since the 1960s with an acceleration in the trend since 1979, while the growth in inequality among women began around 1980. Similarly, using class shares defined by relative class cutoffs, Kosters and Ross (1987, 1988a, 1988b) show an increase in the LC and UC for men, but a decrease in the LC and stable UC for women. Again, these

[52] As Kosters and Ross (1988a) note, their results may be sensitive to the top-coding of the weekly wage data. Karoly and Klerman (1991) find that when there is no adjustment for the top-coding, the CV shows a spurious decline due to the increased truncation of the upper tail of the distribution over time.

findings are consistent with those reported earlier based on relative percentiles.

A number of other recent studies have further disaggregated the trend in inequality among workers by other characteristics such as education, experience, and industry (Dooley and Gottschalk, 1984; Blackburn and Bloom, 1987; Burtless, 1990; Juhn, Murphy, and Pierce, 1989; Karoly, 1992). Most importantly, these studies find that the overall trend in inequality is the result of increasing inequality both between groups and within groups. In the same way that inequality has increased for both men and women since 1979, inequality has also increased among more- and less-educated workers, among more- and less-experienced workers, and among workers in particular industries. The evidence of increasing inequality within groups is consistent with findings by other researchers that, even after controlling for individual characteristics using a standard log wage regression, there is an increase in inequality as measured by the variance in the regression residuals (Juhn, Murphy, and Pierce, 1989; Moffitt, 1990).

Table 2.7 presents a decomposition of the variance of the logarithm of income separately for men and women based on groups defined by education and experience.[53] Regardless of whether wage and salary income is measured annually, weekly, or hourly, inequality between and within education and experience groups increased from 1967 to 1987 for both men and women, with most of the increase occurring during the 1979 to 1987 period. The last two columns of Table 2.7 show what the variance of logarithm would have been in 1987 if the education-experience composition of the workforce were fixed at the 1975 or 1967 level. In all cases, total inequality and inequality within groups would have been higher under this hypothetical scenario, indicating that the compositional shifts served to dampen the increase in inequality. This is further evidence that the overall trend is the result of changing inequality within groups and not simply the result of the changing composition of the workforce.

These findings have important implications for any analysis that seeks to explain the trend in inequality among workers. For example, studies that examine the changing structure of wages by considering only changes in relative wages between groups of workers defined by their characteristics (e.g., sex, education, and experience) can only explain what is happening to the between-group component of overall inequality, leaving a large part of the overall trend unexplained.[54] Consequently, as part of any explanation of

[53] The sample of men and women wage and salary workers is disaggregated into four education groups by years of schooling (<12, 12, 13–15, 16+) and four experience groups defined as age minus years of schooling minus five (0–9, 10–19, 20–29, and 30+).

[54] Some recent examples include Bound and Johnson (1989), Katz and Revenga (1989), and Blackburn, Bloom, and Freeman (1990).

Table 2.7 Decomposition of Variance of Logarithm For Wage and Salary Workers by Education and Experience Groups,[a] by Sex

	Year					
				1987 using weights from year:		
	1967	1975	1979[b]	1987	1975	1967
			A. Men			
Annual						
Total inequality	1.205	1.340	1.361	1.564	1.674	1.672
Between group	0.447	0.478	0.443	0.531	0.546	0.513
Within group	0.758	0.863	0.918	1.033	1.128	1.159
Weekly (Consistent)						
Total inequality	0.756	0.699	0.741	0.910	0.965	0.973
Between group	0.199	0.217	0.200	0.271	0.271	0.252
Within group	0.557	0.482	0.541	0.639	0.695	0.721
Hourly						
Total inequality	. . .	0.459	0.490	0.614	0.638	. . .
Between group	. . .	0.118	0.113	0.159	0.153	. . .
Within group	. . .	0.341	0.377	0.455	0.485	. . .

B. Women

Annual						
Total inequality	1.617	1.691	1.660	1.712	1.782	1.801
Between group	0.296	0.295	0.261	0.337	0.360	0.348
Within group	1.321	1.395	1.399	1.375	1.422	1.454
Weekly (Consistent)						
Total inequality	0.980	0.832	0.825	0.944	0.967	0.979
Between group	0.130	0.121	0.104	0.164	0.167	0.159
Within group	0.850	0.711	0.722	0.780	0.800	0.820
Hourly						
Total inequality	. . .	0.435	0.432	0.544	0.543	. . .
Between group	. . .	0.060	0.051	0.087	0.081	. . .
Within group	. . .	0.376	0.381	0.457	0.462	. . .

[a]The decomposition uses four education groups (<12, 12, 13–15, 16+ years of schooling) and four experience groups (0–9, 10–19, 20–29, 30+ years of experience).

[b]Using 1980-based population weights.

the increase in inequality, researchers need to consider the causes of rising inequality between groups defined, for example, by education and experience, as well as the increase in inequality within these groups.

Conclusions

The changes in the distribution of income among families and workers in the United States in the last twenty-five years represent a serious challenge to the conventional wisdom. Rather than a stable income distribution, income inequality has been increasing in the last two decades on two fronts: among families and individuals, and among workers.

For families and individuals, the analysis of CPS microdata from 1963 to 1989 shows the following:

- Despite overall positive growth in real median income since 1963, family incomes have not grown equally throughout the distribution. For example, among families and unrelated individuals, even after adjusting for family size, real income at the 10th percentile declined 6 percent from 1979 to 1987, while real income grew 14 percent at the 90th percentile.
- These differential changes reflect underlying changes in the shape of the distribution. Even after adjusting for changes in family size, there is evidence of an increase in dispersion since the mid-1970s in both the lower and upper tails of the distribution for families (including unrelated individuals) and for individuals. Inequality first increased due to relative declines in the incomes of families and individuals in the bottom of the distribution. Since 1980, dispersion has also increased in the top of the distribution, as the income gains of wealthier families and individuals outpaced their counterparts at the median. By 1987, the income level of a family at the 90th percentile was almost nine times as great as a family's income at the 10th percentile.
- While a definition of the middle class is somewhat arbitrary, these trends in relative income percentiles indicate that lower and upper classes have been increasing in the 1980s, implying a corresponding decline in the middle class.
- As the economy expanded during the latter part of the 1980s, there is evidence that the distribution has stabilized at a higher level of dispersion compared to that of the 1960s and 1970s. However, there is no sign that inequality has started to decline.
- The pattern of increasing dispersion in both the lower and upper tails

of the distribution is even more pronounced when the sample is restricted to families with children, or when the data are disaggregated by the race/ethnicity of the head of the family. Inequality increased to a greater degree among black and Hispanic families than among whites.

- Inequality also increased among families differentiated by the age of the head and by the type of head. A decomposition analysis shows no effect of the changing age composition on the increase in inequality. The changing demographic composition of households based on headship explains about one-third of the increase in inequality since 1967.

The analysis of the changing distribution of labor income among workers produces the following findings:

- Real median wage growth varied for men and women. While male workers have experienced real wage declines, particularly since 1975, female workers have benefited from long-term positive wage growth. Again, the pattern of wage growth differed for workers above and below the median.
- Regardless of the wage measure, the shape of the distribution of labor income has become less equal for all workers since 1979. The increase in inequality for all workers reflects the combined effect of the experiences of male and female workers. Among men, inequality has been increasing since the 1960s, with growing dispersion in both the lower and upper tails. In contrast, inequality declined for women through about 1980, as the lower tail gained relative to the median while the shape of the upper tail showed little change. Since about 1980, female workers have also experienced growing dispersion in both the upper and lower tail of the distribution.
- These findings are not affected by the data measurement issues associated with the CPS such as top-coding. Furthermore, the timing of many of the changes occurs after 1975, which is the period when the CPS labor income data are most comparable.
- Again, there appears to have been some leveling off in the trend toward dispersion since about 1983 or 1984. When annual weeks worked are controlled for, there is no evidence that the trend in inequality has reversed as the economy expanded.
- The trends evident for all workers are replicated when the sample is restricted to full-time year-round workers. There are some differences in the experiences of workers of different racial/ethnic backgrounds, primarily among low-wage workers.

- A decomposition analysis shows that the increase in inequality among workers cannot simply be explained by shifts in the sex, education, or experience composition of the workforce. Instead, rising inequality within groups contributed to the increase in inequality.

This Chapter also demonstrates that choices regarding the inequality measure, the unit of analysis, and the measure of income are important. Recognizing these differences can help reconcile many of the contradictory findings of previous studies. For example:

- The trends in class shares using absolute income cutoffs tend to show different time-series patterns than those based on relative income cutoffs. Absolute class shares, by capturing both changes in the level and the shape of the distribution, often mask significant changes in the dispersion of the distribution.
- Depending upon how the class shares are defined, the time trend for relative class shares may still fail to record increases in dispersion within the lower or upper class. Typically, class shares place unequal percentages of the population in the upper and lower classes, making the measures more sensitive to changes in one tail of the distribution.
- Conclusions about turning points in the trend in inequality and about whether the changes are occurring in the top or the bottom of the distribution often vary for different definitions of the unit of analysis and the income measure.

Despite the methodological difficulties associated with evaluating the trend in inequality, there is no doubt that inequality has increased in the United States. Furthermore, this is not strictly a recent phenomenon. The economic status of families in the bottom of the distribution has been declining since the 1970s. The relative gains of the rich, however, are primarily a product of the 1980s. Inequality among men has been on the rise for more than 20 years, yet the trend has accelerated in recent times. Despite a long economic recovery, the data through 1989, the last full year of the expansion, give no indication that inequality has begun to decline significantly. At best, the trend has leveled off in the late 1980s. If there has been no lessening of inequality as a consequence of the latest economic expansion, it is unlikely that such lessening will occur during the current recession. Instead, the growth in inequality appears to be indicative of more fundamental changes in both the structure of the economy and the composition of families and workers.

APPENDIX 2A

The Current Population Survey

Microlevel data from the March Annual Demographic Survey are available from 1964 through 1990. These surveys provide a rich source of information about households, families, and individuals, including detailed demographic and income data. For this analysis, I have used the Uniform series data files prepared under the direction of Robert D. Mare and Christopher Winship from 1964 to 1967 and the Bureau of Census public-use files from 1968 to 1990. I have also used the CPS population weights for all results presented here.

Despite the advantages, it is important to recognize a number of data limitations associated with the CPS. These limitations include the imputation of missing income information, the top-coding of income amounts, and other changes in survey procedures. In general, the changes in survey procedures may reduce the comparability of surveys over time. For studies of inequality, it is important to identify the potential biases that these changes can introduce, particularly in light of findings that show U-turns or other sharp changes in the trends in inequality. If these U-turns coincide with changes in the survey procedures, they may be the result of the procedural changes and not true changes in the income distribution. In addition, it may be possible to correct for those biases introduced by the survey procedures so that the results are comparable over time.

Income Imputation

As with any survey, there will be some error in the income amounts that are reported by the CPS respondents. In addition to reporting error, the CPS suffers from substantial nonreporting error. The fraction of respondents who do not report at least one income item has grown from 9 percent in 1964 to a stable 27 percent in recent surveys. As noted by Lillard, Smith, and Welch (1986), the process used by the Census Bureau to impute income information when it is missing is biased, since it does not account for the relationship between the probability of not reporting and the individual's income level. Furthermore, the imputation procedure has changed over time, most significantly with the 1976 survey. At that time, the list of demographic variables used to define a match in the "hot deck" imputation procedure increased to include items such as the individual's education. In addition, earnings, weeks, and hours were imputed from the same "donor" whereas previously they had come from different donors. Juhn, Murphy, and Pierce (1989) demonstrate that this change, from the 1975 to the 1976 surveys, is particularly important for analyses of inequality in wage and salary income. The change in the weekly wage from 1974 to 1975 was much larger in the tails of the distribution (a large positive jump below the 10th percentile and a large negative jump above the 90th percentile) than the changes between other years. This compression of the distribution produces a discrete decline from 1974 to 1975 in many summary measures of inequality (e.g., the variance of logarithm) and sharp changes in percentiles in the tails of the distribution when the measure of labor income has been adjusted for weeks or hours worked.[1]

Income Top-coding

The public-use files of the CPS report the various income components up to a codeable maximum or top-code. The top-code has changed over time in nominal terms, from $50,000 for the 1968 to 1981 surveys, to $75,000 for 1982 to 1984, to $99,999 for 1985 to 1988.[2] Less than 1 percent of the sample of wage and salary workers have their wage and salary income top-coded, although the fraction does change over time. Similarly, up to 1.3 percent of total family income is ever top-coded. The problem of a constant nominal top-code (or changing real top-code) over time is not an issue when class-based measures are used to measure inequality, since the income cutoffs for the upper class are usually below the top-code. The same is true for percentiles that are below the 98th percentile. Trends in summary measures of inequality that are sensitive to the upper tail of the distribution may be sensitive to the top-coding.

Several researchers have adjusted for the top-coding problem by using constant dollar top-codes (Blackburn and Bloom, 1987) or by dropping a constant percentage of the upper tail from the sample (Burtless, 1990). In addition, other researchers have truncated the bottom tail of the distribution. For example, Juhn, Murphy, and Pierce (1989) drop individuals with wages below $67 per week in 1982 dollars. As with the use of the nominal top-codes, the use of constant-dollar top-codes or bottom-codes truncates a different percentage of the distribution over time. Trends in percentiles of the

[1] The discrete jump is due to the different allocation of annual weeks worked and usual weekly hours before and after the 1976 survey. Summary measures of inequality based on total wage and salary income are not affected by this change. However, adjusting annual wage and salary income for annual weeks or annual hours, or restricting the sample to FTYR workers, produces a large change in the time series from 1974 to 1975. For example, summary measures of inequality in wage and salary income for FTYR workers reported by Harrison, Tilly, and Bluestone (1986a), Blackburn and Bloom (1987), and Karoly (1988) exhibit a large downward "blip" from 1974 to 1975.

[2] The income amounts in the surveys from 1964 to 1967 do not appear to be top-coded, as incomes as high as $99,900 are reported. Likewise, the codeable maximum increased substantially with the 1989 survey, so that top-coding does not appear to be an issue for that year.

distribution, where the percentiles are beyond the truncation points in the sample, will be unaffected by the changes in the real value of the top-codes.

Other Changes in Survey Procedures

Several other changes have occurred that may prevent the data from different CPS surveys from being strictly comparable. One change has affected the sample weights in the CPS, which are based upon population estimates from the decennial Census. Beginning with the 1972 and 1981 surveys, the Census Bureau revised their weighting procedures to incorporate population estimates from the 1970 and 1980 Censuses, respectively. For purposes of comparison, the March 1980 public-use file was reissued using the new 1980-based population weights. In this analysis, I have used both of the March 1980 files and find that this change had little effect on the trend in inequality from 1978 to 1979. Thus, U-turns in the data that date to 1979 do not appear to be the result of changes in the weighting procedures.

More significant procedural changes were introduced with the March 1989 survey. For the first time since the 1976 survey, a new processing system was introduced to reflect changes in the CPS questionnaire, particularly the expanded detail regarding sources of income (46 income types versus 8 income types). Along with these changes, the imputation procedures were revised to impute each of the detailed income items separately and to impute entire sets of income and noncash benefits from the same interviewed person. The new imputation procedures resulted in an increase in aggregate income, particularly for nonearned sources, and a decrease in the poverty rate. To allow for comparisons over time, the March 1988 CPS was reissued using the 1989 processing system. Tabulations of the March 1988 data using both the old and new processing systems show that the distribution of total income among families and individuals is affected by the change (see the data reported in Table 2B.1). In particular, the sharp improvement in the lower tail of the distribution between 1987 and 1988 can be attributed to the new processing system. A comparison of the 1987 and 1988 data based on the same processing system shows that dispersion in the lower tail of the distribution remained relatively stable, while dispersion in the upper tail continued to increase.

The only available source of microdata from the 1964 to 1967 CPS surveys are the Mare-Winship Uniform Files. A number of procedural differences make the data from these earlier files less comparable with data from the later surveys. For example, a new processing system was introduced in 1967, which included revised procedures for imputing income. In addition, the sample sizes for these earlier years are about half those available for later years, and some information, such as the family's poverty line, is not available.

APPENDIX 2B

Table 2B.1 Absolute Percentiles for Families and Individuals

A. Families

	Total Family Income[a] Percentile					Adjusted Family Income[b] Percentile				
Year	10th	25th	50th	75th	90th	10th	25th	50th	75th	90th
1963	6309	12016	20168	29605	40789					
1964	6562	12630	21104	30844	41769					
1965	6965	13125	22006	31949	43291					
1966	7143	13975	22870	32919	45311					
1967	7554	14759	23795	33886	46386	0.96	1.64	2.61	3.91	5.55
1968	8763	15868	25506	36814	50219	1.01	1.71	2.69	3.99	5.63
1969	8635	16223	26117	37493	51435	1.03	1.78	2.82	4.19	5.93
1970	8475	15915	26040	37682	52146	1.02	1.78	2.81	4.22	5.97
1971	8501	15511	25827	38015	52163	1.03	1.78	2.82	4.25	6.09
1972	8889	16296	27160	39938	55486	1.08	1.88	3.02	4.53	6.47
1973	9209	16588	27907	40874	56512	1.11	1.94	3.08	4.64	6.59
1974	8899	16084	26755	39787	54852	1.08	1.89	3.02	4.51	6.35

1975	8752	15595	26612	39181	53901	1.06	1.86	2.99	4.51	6.39
1976	9041	16066	27557	40458	55535	1.08	1.89	3.09	4.63	6.51
1977	8847	15785	27257	40278	54082	1.08	1.90	3.10	4.64	6.38
1978	9075	16549	28519	42328	58744	1.12	2.00	3.27	4.93	6.94
1979[c]	9096	16619	28889	42919	60000	1.12	2.03	3.31	5.01	7.01
1979[d]	9062	16585	28741	42761	59852	1.11	2.02	3.30	5.00	7.01
1980	8573	15979	27699	41652	58407	1.05	1.95	3.22	4.90	6.84
1981	8321	15328	27007	41436	58394	1.00	1.86	3.15	4.85	6.91
1982	7913	14966	26670	41259	58658	0.93	1.82	3.12	4.85	6.99
1983	7701	14908	26711	41694	59196	0.92	1.83	3.19	4.99	7.15
1984	8010	15472	27624	43185	61639	0.96	1.91	3.29	5.18	7.52
1985	8053	15705	28053	43863	62765	0.98	1.93	3.34	5.26	7.72
1986	8304	16067	29110	45380	65278	1.01	2.00	3.46	5.46	7.95
1987[e]	8274	16357	29440	46071	65869	1.00	2.03	3.52	5.54	8.01
1987[f]	8405	16429	29585	46380	66393	1.02	2.05	3.54	5.57	8.07
1988	8550	16460	29657	46615	67127	1.04	2.04	3.56	5.61	8.22
1989	8637	16688	30012	47126	68966	1.05	2.06	3.59	5.70	8.41

Table 2B.1 (*continued*)

	B. Families and Unrelated Individuals									
	Total Family Income[a] Percentile					Adjusted Family Income[b] Percentile				
Year	10th	25th	50th	75th	90th	10th	25th	50th	75th	90th
1963	3750	8760	17780	27632	39053					
1964	3883	9091	18182	28435	39503					
1965	4064	9585	19169	29339	40942					
1966	4720	10851	20786	31134	43640					
1967	4482	10331	20515	31054	43825	0.74	1.40	2.43	3.76	5.41
1968	5030	11380	22156	33832	47066	0.78	1.46	2.52	3.86	5.50
1969	4958	11281	22284	34265	48189	0.80	1.51	2.62	4.03	5.75
1970	4907	11101	22016	34350	48594	0.80	1.50	2.60	4.04	5.80
1971	5010	10975	21781	34341	48601	0.81	1.50	2.61	4.06	5.85
1972	5247	11358	22711	36296	51496	0.85	1.56	2.78	4.31	6.21
1973	5581	11563	23256	36749	52326	0.89	1.64	2.84	4.41	6.33
1974	5439	11068	22046	35475	50633	0.89	1.58	2.76	4.27	6.10
1975	5474	10791	21501	35088	49710	0.88	1.55	2.74	4.28	6.10

1976	5535	11070	22114	35686	50941	0.89	1.59	2.81	4.37	6.22
1977	5451	10660	21557	35382	49826	0.90	1.59	2.81	4.38	6.12
1978	5591	11266	22487	37198	53593	0.92	1.66	2.96	4.63	6.60
1979[c]	5597	11317	22320	37258	53819	0.91	1.69	2.99	4.67	6.64
1979[d]	5566	11261	22259	37156	53680	0.91	1.68	2.98	4.67	6.63
1980	5360	10786	21571	35987	52746	0.88	1.62	2.91	4.59	6.51
1981	5255	10706	21179	35835	52555	0.85	1.57	2.86	4.58	6.61
1982	5161	10526	21106	35550	52939	0.82	1.55	2.85	4.57	6.68
1983	4990	10473	20904	35754	53289	0.81	1.55	2.90	4.69	6.84
1984	5265	10612	21437	37003	55170	0.85	1.61	3.00	4.87	7.15
1985	5190	10852	21747	37270	55879	0.85	1.63	3.04	4.94	7.28
1986	5130	11000	22500	38500	57660	0.85	1.68	3.13	5.10	7.52
1987[e]	5212	10965	22545	38909	58310	0.85	1.68	3.16	5.15	7.59
1987[f]	5301	11100	22627	39073	58749	0.87	1.70	3.18	5.17	7.63
1988	5334	11131	22719	39110	59361	0.88	1.71	3.21	5.23	7.76
1989	5414	11250	22735	39546	60389	0.89	1.73	3.24	5.27	7.89

Table 2B.1 (*continued*)

	C. All Individuals									
	Total Family Income[a] Percentile					Adjusted Family Income[b] Percentile				
Year	10th	25th	50th	75th	90th	10th	25th	50th	75th	90th
1963										
1964										
1965										
1966										
1967						0.87	1.49	2.34	3.48	4.88
1968						0.90	1.55	2.42	3.57	4.98
1969						0.93	1.62	2.55	3.76	5.21
1970						0.92	1.61	2.55	3.79	5.24
1971						0.93	1.61	2.56	3.81	5.31
1972						0.96	1.68	2.74	4.09	5.69
1973						1.00	1.75	2.82	4.18	5.79
1974						0.98	1.71	2.75	4.08	5.62

1975	0.96	1.66	2.73	4.06	5.66
1976	0.98	1.70	2.81	4.19	5.77
1977	0.99	1.73	2.88	4.30	5.91
1978	1.01	1.81	2.99	4.47	6.17
1979[c]	1.01	1.83	3.02	4.53	6.22
1979[d]	1.01	1.82	3.01	4.52	6.21
1980	0.95	1.74	2.93	4.44	6.10
1981	0.91	1.67	2.87	4.41	6.16
1982	0.85	1.63	2.85	4.40	6.23
1983	0.84	1.63	2.89	4.50	6.36
1984	0.88	1.71	3.00	4.70	6.66
1985	0.90	1.72	3.04	4.76	6.80
1986	0.91	1.78	3.15	4.95	7.06
1987[e]	0.90	1.80	3.20	4.99	7.15
1987[f]	0.92	1.81	3.21	5.03	7.19
1988	0.93	1.82	3.24	5.08	7.29
1989	0.95	1.83	3.27	5.12	7.40

[a] Measured in 1986 dollars using the CPI-X.

[b] Measured as total family income divided by the poverty line, where the 1967 poverty threshold is inflated using the CPI-X to calculate the poverty lines after 1967.

[c] Using 1970-based population weights.

[d] Using 1980-based population weights.

[e] Using old processing system.

[f] Using new processing system introduced in March 1989.

Table 2B.2 Absolute Percentiles for Wage and Salary Workers
(Measured in 1986 dollars using the CPI-X)

	A. All Wage and Salary Workers														
	Annual Wage and Salary Income Percentile					Weekly (Consistent) Wage and Salary Income Percentile					Hourly Wage and Salary Income Percentile				
Year	10th	25th	50th	75th	90th	10th	25th	50th	75th	90th	10th	25th	50th	75th	90th
1963	1316	4605	11891	19737	26316	60.37	148.35	271.32	406.95	559.21					
1964	1299	4675	12532	19481	27273	60.80	152.79	280.11	420.93	574.68					
1965	1278	4792	12780	20607	28754	62.64	156.61	287.54	438.51	613.92					
1966	1460	4969	12422	21118	28882	64.79	155.28	292.71	443.66	608.94					
1967	1506	4819	12651	21084	30120	63.89	158.13	295.30	448.85	620.13					
1968	1497	5308	13473	22455	30539	70.45	175.36	305.27	469.65	663.38					
1969	1393	4875	13465	22284	31755	71.63	166.49	301.05	469.71	655.42					
1970	1326	4820	13263	22546	31830	72.24	164.30	309.10	476.31	665.73					
1971	1323	4962	13232	22901	31807	71.85	165.39	304.17	483.46	673.55					
1972	1481	4938	13738	23953	33827	74.07	171.98	314.69	493.83	711.69					
1973	1395	4860	13953	23721	34884	71.14	166.11	319.20	501.60	706.79					
1974	1397	4958	13080	23207	32700	71.85	161.33	301.69	488.13	682.55					

1975	1392	4873	12733	22417	31875	76.08	160.53	298.13	474.49	672.18	3.18	4.78	7.50	11.35	15.93
1976	1476	4797	12915	22528	33137	75.97	166.05	298.73	488.14	684.75	3.26	4.79	7.54	11.53	15.97
1977	1476	5208	13021	22722	33073	78.13	168.35	301.72	491.59	680.83	3.31	4.84	7.55	11.69	16.32
1978	1623	5065	12987	23539	33591	81.17	165.52	302.39	487.01	700.28	3.36	4.87	7.59	11.71	16.39
1979[a]	1570	5333	13333	23259	33766	81.26	170.29	296.30	493.83	697.17	3.42	4.94	7.52	11.71	16.38
1979[b]	1556	5305	13333	23111	33450	80.85	170.29	296.30	493.83	697.17	3.42	4.94	7.48	11.64	16.38
1980	1555	5326	13316	22636	33289	78.33	162.92	290.28	480.14	678.83	3.33	4.81	7.41	11.52	16.00
1981	1466	5109	12652	22506	32847	74.39	161.80	286.25	477.08	678.67	3.28	4.68	7.30	11.63	16.13
1982	1404	5092	12615	22477	32683	71.28	157.40	287.17	472.21	674.58	3.23	4.67	7.28	11.47	16.47
1983	1430	5281	13091	22002	33003	71.84	155.31	284.03	474.56	689.12	3.17	4.63	7.33	11.44	16.25
1984	1473	5280	12672	23231	33791	72.47	155.04	289.87	482.73	701.35	3.06	4.57	7.30	11.62	16.25
1985	1529	5301	13252	23445	34659	72.81	157.27	295.82	494.24	699.57	3.14	4.64	7.35	11.76	16.66
1986	1600	5787	13800	24000	35000	75.00	156.86	298.85	500.00	727.27	3.13	4.75	7.62	12.02	17.04
1987[c]	1737	5792	13996	24131	35714	75.71	160.88	302.82	497.31	738.13	3.12	4.70	7.57	12.07	17.08
1987[d]	1737	5792	13900	24131	35714	76.05	160.88	302.82	497.25	738.13	3.13	4.70	7.57	12.07	17.09
1988	1854	5839	13902	24096	35855	76.53	163.55	308.93	508.82	726.89	3.09	4.65	7.66	12.03	17.11
1989	1796	6189	14147	24257	35367	78.69	164.70	309.46	509.07	728.14	3.06	4.72	7.65	12.05	17.00

Table 2B.2 (*continued*)

	B. Male Wage and Salary Workers														
	Annual Wage and Salary Income Percentile					Weekly (Consistent) Wage and Salary Income Percentile					Hourly Wage and Salary Income Percentile				
Year	10th	25th	50th	75th	90th	10th	25th	50th	75th	90th	10th	25th	50th	75th	90th
1963	2632	8931	16447	23026	29605	98.88	225.75	347.85	469.92	642.94					
1964	2597	9740	16558	23377	31932	101.86	229.18	358.26	490.20	636.62					
1965	2716	9585	17252	24048	31949	109.54	236.42	375.87	501.16	676.56					
1966	2795	9460	18571	24845	31988	109.61	243.58	376.44	517.60	694.19					
1967	2786	9711	18072	25084	33133	109.91	243.98	383.89	531.54	708.72					
1968	2934	10557	19461	26946	35928	117.41	264.18	410.94	569.45	763.18					
1969	2786	10139	19499	27855	36769	119.01	260.62	410.73	562.56	766.02					
1970	2653	10080	19218	27056	37135	115.86	260.05	416.08	572.11	780.15					
1971	2545	9542	19084	27735	38168	112.04	249.46	409.12	575.18	778.33					
1972	2716	9877	19753	29630	39506	118.71	256.60	431.47	595.50	823.05					
1973	2791	10007	20465	29535	40465	114.88	259.19	433.20	604.17	820.79					
1974	2608	9494	19198	28481	38397	108.68	248.20	413.67	587.41	806.65					

1975	2520	8772	18947	27953	37427	112.50	245.61	409.36	573.59	764.44	3.85	6.09	9.54	13.59	18.23
1976	2622	9041	18616	28303	38007	112.55	247.29	416.03	593.41	795.89	3.84	6.09	9.65	13.75	18.36
1977	2604	8681	19097	29167	39063	118.75	243.06	408.50	605.94	810.19	3.90	6.05	9.69	13.94	18.55
1978	2760	9351	19481	29221	39838	118.54	245.10	413.80	604.95	805.80	4.01	6.09	9.62	14.05	18.73
1979[a]	2896	9148	19259	29630	39259	116.19	244.37	415.40	607.83	813.36	3.92	6.10	9.69	14.25	18.52
1979[b]	2837	8889	19259	29630	39111	116.19	241.93	411.95	604.21	813.36	3.91	6.05	9.64	14.25	18.52
1980	2663	8655	18642	28628	38615	113.18	234.98	399.47	600.51	783.27	3.84	5.89	9.54	13.89	18.56
1981	2433	8477	18248	28630	38564	107.83	227.15	393.02	596.35	790.75	3.78	5.85	9.36	14.01	18.43
1982	2294	7913	17202	28440	38991	101.19	222.41	384.80	584.64	809.50	3.64	5.54	9.19	13.78	18.79
1983	2145	7701	17602	28031	38504	98.63	215.71	388.27	582.41	805.99	3.58	5.50	9.08	13.75	18.62
1984	2112	8000	17951	29567	40127	101.07	209.27	387.60	600.45	828.21	3.43	5.38	9.14	13.73	18.78
1985	2357	8155	18349	29562	40775	101.90	212.03	395.75	599.63	829.49	3.42	5.41	9.15	13.94	19.16
1986	2500	8500	18667	30000	42000	103.03	215.69	392.16	617.65	862.74	3.48	5.54	9.38	14.42	19.41
1987[c]	2413	8687	18822	29923	42278	101.35	217.65	397.46	611.31	851.69	3.38	5.57	9.28	13.92	19.31
1987[d]	2421	8687	18533	29923	42158	102.38	217.18	393.67	613.99	851.69	3.41	5.57	9.28	14.07	19.40
1988	2751	8897	18536	29657	41705	102.06	218.07	399.79	617.86	854.09	3.48	5.56	9.27	14.09	19.46
1989	2653	8842	18568	30062	42440	104.02	218.01	386.78	606.79	866.84	3.44	5.53	9.04	14.03	19.36

Table 2B.2 (*continued*)

	C. Female Wage and Salary Workers														
	Annual Wage and Salary Income Percentile					Weekly (Consistent) Wage and Salary Income Percentile					Hourly Wage and Salary Income Percentile				
Year	10th	25th	50th	75th	90th	10th	25th	50th	75th	90th	10th	25th	50th	75th	90th
1963	658	2168	6579	11546	16447	35.24	90.30	176.65	264.67	361.20					
1964	649	2208	6519	12201	16331	37.32	92.76	182.01	273.75	381.02					
1965	639	2236	6709	12460	16613	37.59	92.65	187.93	281.90	387.26					
1966	745	2422	7143	12422	17081	40.68	94.99	185.12	285.57	389.72					
1967	783	2410	7229	12349	18072	40.45	95.63	187.81	295.30	403.68					
1968	898	2695	7784	13473	18563	44.91	110.12	206.48	305.27	427.72					
1969	724	2507	7599	13496	18808	47.27	107.49	203.74	299.96	409.63					
1970	745	2523	7870	13414	19586	46.49	107.24	206.90	308.62	421.28					
1971	763	2545	7659	13837	19847	45.44	108.92	205.31	308.43	424.09					
1972	790	2716	8025	14568	20198	49.74	112.23	211.64	320.94	435.73					
1973	837	2674	7907	14098	20465	49.83	109.88	209.30	319.20	442.32					
1974	844	2690	8017	14019	20042	48.10	107.29	206.83	314.39	423.60					

1975	877	2805	7797	14035	19766	52.91	112.60	202.58	308.07	431.30	2.69	4.02	5.74	8.28	11.25
1976	911	2878	8303	14760	20295	54.27	112.73	212.07	320.65	434.12	2.80	4.18	5.85	8.43	11.53
1977	885	3125	8538	14583	20833	54.34	119.05	209.25	322.42	442.54	2.78	4.17	5.87	8.40	11.69
1978	992	3247	8506	14773	21104	58.91	121.75	216.80	319.93	445.63	2.90	4.26	5.99	8.45	11.71
1979[a]	1037	3345	8889	14815	21333	59.26	124.91	219.63	321.83	450.25	2.97	4.32	6.02	8.55	11.75
1979[b]	1037	3333	8889	14815	21209	59.26	124.91	219.03	320.96	450.25	2.96	4.31	6.01	8.55	11.75
1980	1065	3495	9108	14901	21305	59.65	122.71	214.09	322.80	456.53	3.00	4.25	5.98	8.36	11.65
1981	1095	3650	8929	14720	21898	58.28	119.44	214.68	326.28	453.22	2.92	4.15	5.85	8.52	11.70
1982	1032	3440	9174	15482	22485	56.68	116.93	218.46	337.29	466.74	2.87	4.14	5.98	8.73	12.08
1983	1100	3520	9351	16100	22992	55.64	119.72	215.71	338.66	474.56	2.86	4.13	6.05	8.85	12.22
1984	1056	3609	9504	16156	23231	54.31	120.68	217.40	347.85	495.98	2.78	4.06	6.09	8.98	12.50
1985	1067	3772	9829	16730	24465	58.25	119.93	220.34	359.78	499.69	2.87	4.05	6.13	9.17	12.74
1986	1104	4000	10000	17500	25000	58.82	121.40	229.41	367.82	527.73	2.83	4.09	6.25	9.61	13.22
1987[c]	1158	4083	10425	17568	25700	58.50	126.36	234.00	378.53	529.94	2.85	4.18	6.44	9.54	13.46
1987[d]	1216	4151	10328	17508	25579	59.71	126.81	234.00	378.53	530.32	2.84	4.18	6.44	9.58	13.51
1988	1275	4208	10426	18313	25950	60.66	127.21	236.24	381.62	545.17	2.84	4.21	6.44	9.80	13.58
1989	1415	4421	10610	18202	26525	63.16	130.03	242.71	381.41	554.78	2.83	4.25	6.45	9.78	13.87

[a]Using 1970-based population weights.
[b]Using 1980-based population weights.
[c]Using old processing system.
[d]Using new processing system introduced in March 1989.

This research was supported in part by the RAND Corporation, the Russell Sage Foundation, and Grant No. P-50-HD-12639 from the Center for Population Research, National Institute of Child Health and Human Development. I would like to thank Frank Levy for helpful comments on an earlier draft.

References

Atkinson, Anthony B. 1970. "On the Measurement of Inequality." *Journal of Economic Theory* 2:244–263.

———. 1983. *The Economics of Inequality*. Oxford: Clarendon Press.

Bamezai, Anil. 1989. "Rising Earnings Disparity and Technological Change." Unpublished Ph.D. dissertation, The RAND Graduate School.

Blackburn, McKinley, and David Bloom. 1985. "What Is Happening to the Middle Class?" *American Demographics* 7(1):19–25.

———. 1986. "Family Income Inequality in the United States: 1967–1984." *Proceedings of the Industrial Relations Research Association:* 349–357.

———. 1987. "Earnings and Income Inequality in the United States." *Population and Development Review* 13(4):575–609.

Blackburn, McKinley, David Bloom, and Richard B. Freeman. 1990. "The Declining Economic Position of Less Skilled American Men." In Burtless, Gary, ed. *A Future of Lousy Jobs?* Washington, D.C.: Brookings Institution.

Blinder, Alan S. 1980. "The Level and Distribution of Economic Well-being: Introduction and Preview." In Feldstein, Martin, ed. *The American Economy in Transition*. Chicago: University of Chicago Press.

Bluestone, Barry. 1989. "The Changing Nature of Employment and Earnings in the U.S. Economy: 1963–1987." Paper prepared for the Conference on "Job Creation in America" at the University of North Carolina at Chapel Hill, April 10.

Bluestone, Barry, and Bennett Harrison. 1986. "The Great American Job Machine: The Proliferation of Low Wage Employment in the U.S. Economy." Study prepared for the Joint Economic Committee.

———. 1988. "The Growth of Low-Wage Employment: 1963–1986." *American Economic Review* 78(2):124–128.

Bound, John, and George Johnson. 1989. "Changes in the Structure of Wages During the 1980s: An Evaluation of Alternative Explanations." NBER Working Paper No. 2983.

Bradbury, Katherine L. 1986. "The Shrinking Middle Class." *New England Economic Review* (September/October):41–55.

Burtless, Gary. 1990. "Earnings Inequality Over the Business and Demographic Cycles." In Burtless, Gary, ed. *A Future of Lousy Jobs?* Washington, D.C.: Brookings Institution.

Castro, Janice. 1986. "Is the Middle Class Shrinking?" *Time* (November 3):54–56.

Congressional Budget Office. 1988. *Trends in Family Income: 1970–1986*. Washington, D.C.: U.S. Government Printing Office, February.

Danziger, Sheldon. 1988. "The Economy, Public Policy and the Poor." In Rodgers,

Harrell R., Jr., ed. *Beyond Welfare: New Approaches to the Problem of Poverty in America*. New York: M. E. Sharpe, Inc.

Danziger, Sheldon, and Peter Gottschalk. 1986. "Families with Children Have Fared Worst." *Challenge* (March/April):40–47.

Danziger, Sheldon, Peter Gottschalk, and Eugene Smolensky. 1989. "How the Rich Have Fared, 1973–1987." *American Economic Review* 79(2):310–314.

Danziger, Sheldon, and Michael K. Taussig. 1979. "The Income Unit and the Anatomy of Income Distribution." *The Review of Income and Wealth* 25(4):365–375.

DasGupta, Partha, Amartya Sen, and David Starrett. 1973. "Notes on the Measurement of Inequality." *Journal of Economic Theory* 6:180–187.

Dooley, Martin D., and Peter Gottschalk. 1982. "Does a Younger Male Labor Force Mean Greater Earnings Inequality?" *Monthly Labor Review* 105:42–45.

———. 1984. "Earnings Inequality Among Males in the U.S.: Trends and the Effect of Labor Force Growth." *The Journal of Political Economy* 92(1):59–89.

———. 1985. "The Increasing Proportion of Men with Low Earnings in the U.S." *Demography* 22(1):25–34.

Grubb, W. Norton, and Robert H. Wilson. 1989. "Sources of Increasing Inequality in Wages and Salaries, 1960–1980." *Monthly Labor Review* (April):3–13.

Harrison, Bennett, and Barry Bluestone. 1988. *The Great U-Turn*. New York: Basic Books.

Harrison, Bennett, Chris Tilly, and Barry Bluestone. 1986a. *The Great U-Turn: Increasing Inequality in Age and Salary Income in the U.S.* Study prepared for the Joint Economic Committee.

———. 1986b. "Wage Inequality Takes a Great U-Turn." *Challenge* 29(1):26–32.

Henle, Peter. 1972. "Exploring the Distribution of Earned Income." *Monthly Labor Review* 95(12):16–27.

Henle, Peter, and Paul Ryscavage. 1980. "The Distribution of Earned Income Among Men and Women, 1958–1977." *Monthly Labor Review* 103(4):3–10.

Hilley, John. 1988. "Wages of American Workers in the 1980s." A study prepared by the staff of the Committee on the Budget, U.S. Senate, September.

Horrigan, Michael W., and Steven E. Haugen. 1988. "The Declining Middle-Class Thesis: A Sensitivity Analysis." *Monthly Labor Review* 111(5):3–13.

Juhn, Chinhui, Kevin M. Murphy, and Brooks Pierce. 1989. "Wage Inequality and the Rise in Returns to Skill." Paper presented at the Universities Research Conference Labor Markets in the 1990s, November 13.

Karoly, Lynn A. 1988. "A Study of the Distribution of Individual Earnings in the United States from 1967 to 1986." Unpublished Ph.D. dissertation, Yale University.

———. 1992. "Changes in the Distribution of Individual Earnings in the United States: 1967–1986." *The Review of Economics and Statistics* 74(1):107–115.

Karoly, Lynn A., and Jacob A. Klerman. 1991. "Regional Differences in Increasing Inequality." Paper presented at the 1991 annual meetings of the Population Association of America.

Katz, Lawrence F., and Ana L. Revenga. 1989. "Changes in the Structure of Wages: The U.S. Versus Japan." NBER Working Paper No. 3021.

Kosters, Marvin H., and Murray N. Ross. 1987. "The Distribution of Earnings and Employment Opportunities: A Re-Examination of the Evidence." *American Enterprise Institute Occasional Papers*, September.

———. 1988a. "The Quality of Jobs: Evidence from Distribution of Annual Earnings and Hourly Wages." AEI Occasional Papers, July.

———. 1988b. "A Shrinking Middle Class?" *The Public Interest* 90 (Winter):3–27.

Kuttner, Bob. 1983. "The Declining Middle." *The Atlantic Monthly* (July):60–69.

Lardner, James. 1989. "Rich, Richer; Poor, Poorer." *The New York Times* (April 19):27.

Lawrence, Robert Z. 1984. "Sectoral Shifts and the Size of the Middle Class." *The Brookings Review* (Fall):3–11.

Lazear, Edward P., and Robert T. Michael. 1988. *Allocation of Income Within the Household.* Chicago: University of Chicago Press.

Levitan, Star A., and Peter E. Carlson. 1984. "Middle-Class Shrinkage?" *Across the Board* 21(10):55–59.

Levy, Frank. 1987. *Dollars and Dreams: The Changing American Income Distribution.* New York: Russell Sage Foundation.

Lillard, Lee, James P. Smith, and Finis Welch. 1986. "What Do We Really Know about Wages? The Importance of Nonreporting and Census Imputation." *The Journal of Political Economy* 94(3):489–506.

Linden, Fabian. 1984. "Myth of the Disappearing Middle Class." *The Wall Street Journal* (January 23):20.

Loveman, Gary W., and Chris Tilly. 1988. "Good Jobs or Bad Jobs: What Does the Evidence Say?" *New England Economic Review* (January/February):46–65.

Maxwell, Nan. 1990. *Income Inequality in the United States, 1947–1985.* Westport, CT: Greenwood Press.

McMahon, Patrick J., and John H. Tschetter. 1986. "The Declining Middle Class: A Further Analysis." *Monthly Labor Review* 109:22–27.

Mishel, Lawrence. 1988. "Better Jobs or Working Longer for Less?" Economic Policy Institute Working Paper No. 101, July.

Moffitt, Robert. 1990. "The Distribution of Earnings and the Welfare State." In Burtless, Gary, ed. *A Future of Lousy Jobs?* Washington, D.C.: Brookings Institution.

Pechman, Joseph A. 1990. "The Future of the Income Tax." *The American Economic Review* 80(1):1–20.

Perkins, Joseph. 1988. "The Poor Are Trickling Upward." *The Wall Street Journal* (November 3):A2.

Plotnick, Robert D. 1982. "Trends in Male Earnings Inequality." *Southern Economic Journal* 48(3):724–732.

Rosenthal, Neal H. 1985. "The Shrinking Middle Class: Myth or Reality?" *Monthly Labor Review* 108:3–10.

Rothschild, Michael, and Joseph E. Stiglitz. 1973. "Some Further Results on the Measurement of Inequality." *Journal of Economic Theory* 6:188–204.

Samuelson, Robert J. 1983. "Middle-Class Media Myth." *National Journal* (December 31):2673–2678.

Smith, James P. 1988. "Poverty and the Family." In Sandefur, Gary D., and Marta Tienda, eds. *Divided Opportunities.* New York: Plenum Publishing Corporation.

Steinberg, Bruce. 1983. "The Mass Market Is Splitting Apart." *Fortune* (November 28):76–82.

Tilly, Chris, Barry Bluestone, and Bennett Harrison. 1986. "What Is Making American Wages More Unequal?" *Proceedings of the Thirty-Ninth Annual Meeting of the Industrial Relations Research Association*, 338–348.

Thurow, Lester C. 1984. "The Disappearance of the Middle Class." *The New York Times* (February 5):E2.

U.S. Bureau of the Census. 1988. *Measuring the Effect of Benefits and Taxes on Income and Poverty: 1986*. Current Population Reports, Series P-60, No. 164-RD-1. Washington, D.C.: U.S. Government Printing Office, December.

———. 1989a. *Money Income of Households, Families, and Persons in the United States: 1987*. Current Population Reports Series P-60, No. 162. Washington, D.C.: U.S. Government Printing Office, February.

———. 1989b. *Money Income and Poverty Status in the United States: 1988 (Advance Data From the March 1989 Current Population Survey)*. Current Population Reports Series P-60, No. 166. Washington, D.C.: U.S. Government Printing Office, October.

———. 1990. *Money Income and Poverty Status in the United States: 1989 (Advance Data From the March 1990 Current Population Survey)*. Current Population Reports Series P-60, No. 168. Washington, D.C.: U.S. Government Printing Office, September.

U.S. House of Representatives, Committee on Ways and Means. 1989. "Trends in Family Income and Income Inequality." In *Background Material and Data on Programs Within the Jurisdiction of the Committee on Ways and Means*. Washington, D.C.: U.S. Government Printing Office.

Wessel, David. 1986. "U.S. Rich and Poor Increase in Numbers; Middle Loses Ground." *The Wall Street Journal* (September 22):1, 19.

Winnick, Andrew J. 1989. *Toward Two Societies: The Changing Distributions of Income and Wealth in the United States Since 1960*. New York: Praeger.

Wohlstetter, Albert. 1988. "Own Data Misled Stagnation Prophets." *The Wall Street Journal* (November 3):A2.

PART TWO

Labor Market Changes and the Distribution of Earnings

3

Industrial Change and the Rising Importance of Skill

Kevin M. Murphy / Finis Welch

The extraordinary changes in wage structures of the 1980s have drawn more attention than any labor market phenomenon in recent memory. The popular press has applauded the increased wage premium for college over high school graduates and the narrowing female/male wage differential while denouncing the lack of progress in wages of blacks relative to whites and the declining wage and employment opportunities of young men who did not go to college. The employment-growth-through-creation-of-bad-jobs controversy was prominent during the 1988 presidential campaign. Economists and other social scientists have expounded hypothetical explanations much more rapidly than data analysts could sort through the numbers. We are left with the certainty that important changes have occurred and, perhaps, a plausible presumption that many of the changes have common origins. We are less certain about what those origins are.

In this chapter we attempt to do three things. The easiest is to summarize changes in wages from 1967 through 1989 by age, education, and gender. After doing so, we examine the similarity of these wage changes across industries. Then, using an assumption of constant differentials between industries, we calculate the impact of changing industrial employment distributions on average wages. Finally, we examine changes in average education across industries.

The summary of changes in average wages is provided to show the extreme nature of recent events. The analysis of wage changes within and between industries is a simple and direct attempt to learn about the process of change. First we ask whether change results from shifts in employment between industries where wages have traditionally differed, or whether wages change within industry. The good jobs–bad jobs discourse assumes that wages are fixed within firms; demand shocks (policy induced or otherwise) only affect numbers of jobs. In this view, wages are rents. Workers passively line up for jobs, and jobs do not compete for workers. Average wages rise if employment shifts to high-wage industries, and average wages fall if employment shifts to low-wage industries. According to this view, contraction in manufacturing and expansion in services would lower average wages.

The competitive view—preferred by the data—is that rents are arbitraged through competition, between workers for jobs and between jobs for workers, so that wage changes are broadly based. Moreover, average wages can rise even though employment is shifting toward low-wage industries. For example, schools and colleges typically pay lower wages to teachers than similarly aged and educated workers earn in other industries. Yet because the education industry employs proportionately more college graduates than other industries, the competitive view is that employment growth in education will either have no effect on relative wages or will increase the relative wage of college graduates.

We find that changes in the industrial composition of employment are only weakly related to changes in relative wages. If we predict changes in average wages by assuming that wages are constant within industry so that averages only reflect movement between high- and low-wage industries, we often find that the direction of the prediction is wrong. Even when the predictions go in the right direction, the movements in averages are dominated by changes within industries. Moreover, although there are idiosyncratic changes peculiar to each industry, the bulk of observed changes in average wages is common to many industries. These two points, that change occurs predominantly within industry and that patterns of change are broadly based, suggest that the competitive one-market paradigm is useful.

The final section of this chapter examines employment patterns by industry. We first ask whether relative growth in industries with high proportions of college graduates is sufficient to absorb the phenomenal rise in average education levels seen in the United States during the past two decades. And, as is true of wages, we find that most of the growth in national average education levels is reflected in increased education levels within industry, instead of in shifts to education-intensive industries.

This is hardly surprising for the first part of our sample period, when relative wages of college graduates fell and industries responded by hiring proportionally more of them. The second decade is more difficult: relative wages of college graduates increased greatly and, nevertheless, all but a few industries responded by hiring proportionally more of them. Obviously something has increased the relative values employers assign to college graduates, and most of the increase stems from changes within industry. Our major findings are that the within-industry growth in the demand for college labor is pervasive, and that growth in the demand for college graduates in the high-skilled areas of manufacturing and, most of all, in professional and financial services has been the most important source of recent demand changes. We also find evidence that changes in the industrial composition of employment have not represented an important component of the growth in the demand for college labor over the past decade.

In the next section of this chapter we describe the data. In the following section we summarize trends in relative wages; then we present the decomposition of changes in average wages into those occurring within industries versus industry composition effects, and the commonality of wage changes across industries versus wage changes that occur within them. The next section examines the impact of changes in industrial composition on the demand for college-educated workers. A brief conclusion follows.

Data

The data are from the March Current Population Surveys (CPS), 1968–1990. The March questionnaire contains the Annual Demographic Supplement with detailed questions about employment and earnings for the previous year. This, together with personal characteristics, provides employment and wage detail for the period 1967 to 1989. Two samples are created: a wage sample[1] that is used for measurement of earnings per week and an employment sample[2] that is used to compare distributions of employment by industry and personal characteristics.

The personal characteristics are gender, education, and potential work experience. Education is defined at four levels: (1) less than a high-school diploma (dropouts), (2) high school graduates, (3) one to three years of college, and (4) college graduates. Potential work experience is defined as approximate time since leaving school.[3] Observations are restricted to individu-

[1]The wage sample is restricted to full-time workers (usual hours exceed 34) who worked at least 14 weeks during the year. The sample excludes the self-employed, those with imputed wages, those who listed school or retirement as the reason for working only part of the year, and those who listed school as the major activity in the week preceding the interview.

[2]The employment sample includes everyone who worked during the year in question. Individuals with negative sample weights are excluded, however.

[3]For those who did not graduate from high school, potential experience is age minus 17 years. For others, potential experience is age minus *s* minus 6, where *s* is the number of years of school completed.

als with between one and forty years of potential experience. The summaries use eight five-year experience intervals: 1–5, 6–10, and so on.

With observations divided by gender (men and women), education (four levels), and experience (eight levels), there are a total of 64 (gender × education × experience) groups.

Calculations referring to industry use the two-digit taxonomy from the 1970 Census. This taxonomy involves 50 industry groups. To make the data comparable across years, we combine ordnance and aircraft manufacturing into one industry, so we work with 49 industries. In some of the presentations we aggregate to smaller numbers of industries.

Wages are annual wage and salary earnings divided by weeks worked. These are brought to 1982 levels using the GNP deflator for personal consumption expenditures. All calculations and presentations refer to the (natural) logarithms of average weekly earnings. Wage differentials between groups or industries are differences in average logarithms. When numbers are presented as percentage differences or changes, they are 100 times the corresponding logarithmic differentials. We refer to the 64 gender × education × experience groups as *skill groups*, and we use two measures of wages by skill groups. One, w_{ijt}, the average wage of skill group j in industry i in year t, is specific to industry, and the other, w_{jt}, is not. When wages are not specific to industry we use mean fitted values from a smoothing regression.[4] Residuals from the smoothing regression are averaged by industry within year and schooling groups to form an average industry-specific residual, ϵ_{ijt}, which is added to the fitted group mean, w_{jt}, to form the industry-specific wage $w_{ijt} = w_{it} + \epsilon_{ijt}$.

There are a number of cases when we aggregate. In these cases we used weights from the 1988 wage sample. For example, we use the industry residuals, ϵ_{ijt}, aggregated over skill group j and time t to estimate a fixed-industry effect, ϵ_i, that is used in ranking industries by wage-order. Time weights are uniform, and industry-by-skill weights are from the 1988 distributions. As another example, we aggregate over experience and sex for estimates of the time-series of college/high-school differentials using the 1988 wage sample frequencies within schooling levels.

Employment is counted as full-time weeks worked, with weeks discounted by one-half for those who work part-time. All employment aggregates are weighted using the Census's person weights.

[4]The wage-smoothing regression is computed separately by year, gender, and education group. Within each group the (logarithm of average weekly) wage is regressed on linear years of school completed, a quartic or fourth-order polynomial in potential experience, and interaction between the quartic and schooling. Since the high-school graduate class has only one level of schooling, the smoothing regression is a regression on the experience quartic only.

Wages in the 1970s and 1980s

Figure 3.1 summarizes the major changes in relative wages. Figure 3.1A traces the college/high-school differential (for men and women combined) for all experience levels and for those with one to five years of potential experience. The most obvious feature of both series is the increase in the relative wage of college graduates that occurred during the 1980s.

It may appear that the college premium was relatively stable until 1973, but from longer time-series we know that the college premium increased somewhat during the 1960s. Compared with the values of earlier periods, the 1973 values are high. The narrowing of the college/high-school wage gap during the 1973–1978 interval is one of the extraordinary changes that analysts noted during the 1970s. The changes during the 1970s, of course, pale in comparison to changes in the 1980s. On average, over all experience levels, college graduates earned 46 percent more than high-school graduates in 1973; the differential fell to 37 percent in 1978 and then increased. By the mid-1980s, the college premium matched earlier peaks, and the late 1980s' values are unprecedented. The 1989 measured logarithmic differential is 53 percent. The story is even more striking for recent job market entrants, where the 1973 differential of 42 percent shrank to a 1978 low of 33 percent and then matched its previous peak values (reached in 1971–1973) as early as 1982. The continual rise to a differential in the 57–59 percent range in the period since 1985 is remarkable.

The female/male wage differential is traced in Figure 3.1B. The increase for both high-school and college women during the 1980s parallels the growth in college wage premium. However, unlike in the case of the college wage premium, women's wages increased relative to men's wages during the 1970s as well as during the 1980s, though the growth during the 1980s was more rapid, particularly for high-school graduate women.

Since, as can be seen in Figure 3.1B, the gender differential is smaller for college than for high-school graduates, it must be that the college premium is greater for women than for men. This can be seen directly in Figure 3.1C, which traces the college premium separately for men and women (measured over all experience levels for each group). Although the decline during the late 1970s in the college premium is less pronounced for women than for men, the general patterns are remarkably similar, as are the changes between the early and late years of the series.

Figure 3.1D graphs log wage experience differentials between men with twenty-six to thirty-five years of experience and men with one to five years of experience. Differentials are shown separately for high-school and college graduates. The two measures follow an almost identical path of a widening differential between those at career wage peaks and new job market entrants

Figure 3.1 Trends in Relative Wages: 1967–1989

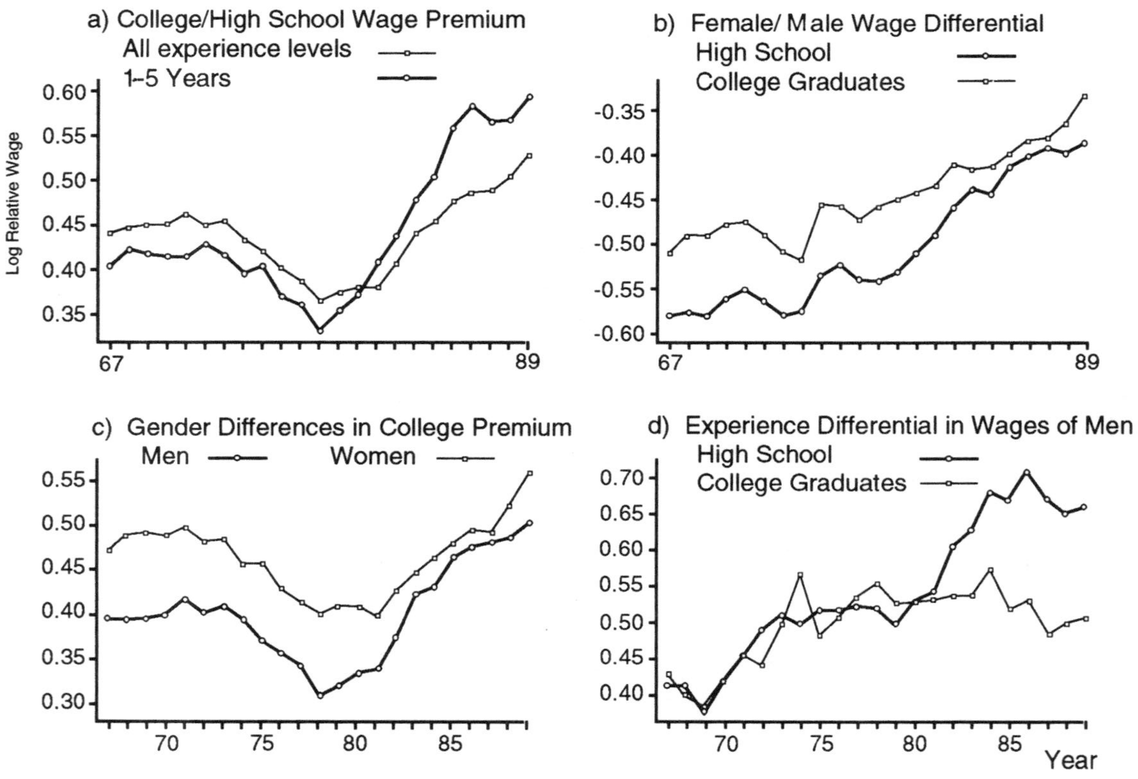

until 1980, but afterward the differential continues to widen for high-school graduates while it levels and then falls somewhat for college graduates.

In each of the series graphed in Figure 3.1, the trough-to-peak movement in relative wages is very large. For example, the college premium for new entrants was 1.8 times greater in 1989 than in 1978; when the premium is averaged over all experience levels, the 1989 value is 1.4 times the 1978 value. Between 1967 and 1974, women high-school graduates earned roughly 56 percent as much as men of the same age and schooling; by 1989 their relative wage had increased to 68 percent. In the same period, the relative wage of college graduate women increased from 60 to 72 percent of that of comparable males. In the late 1960s, men at the wage peak of their careers earned half again as much as new entrants, but by the late 1980s the advantage of peak earners over new entrants was almost 2 : 1 for high-school graduates. For college graduates, it was roughly 1.7 : 1.

Growth in the education and work experience premia represents the leading example of the rise in skill premia—what we term "the rising importance of skill." As we show below, the growth in the wage of women relative to men can probably best be regarded as a rise in the value of nonphysical skills.

It is, of course, possible that each of these trends—in education, experience, and gender wage differentials—results not from changes in the average wage workers of fixed quality but refers instead to changing quality. Where comparisons are possible, we think the evidence is to the contrary; namely, that the changes in relative wages we have seen result almost exclusively from changes in skill prices. Education is a clear example because comparisons can be made within cohorts, where issues of quality presumably do not arise.

This analysis is performed in Table 3.1, where we give the returns to college by cohort at five-year intervals from 1968 through 1988. The numbers at the bottom of the table summarize the changes in returns to schooling in two alternative ways. The first comparison, labeled "within experience," computes the average change in the returns to college between the indicated years, comparing individuals in the same experience categories in the two years averaged across our eight experience groups. For the second comparison, labeled "within cohort," we computed the change in the college/high-school differential across years following the same cohorts through time (hence we compare the returns to college for those in the first seven experience categories in the beginning year with the returns to college for the last seven experience categories in the subsequent year).

As can be seen by examining these summary measures of change or the detailed data in the top half of the table, the changes within cohort and experience are remarkably similar. In addition, the phenomenal rise in the returns for young workers occurs whether we use the increase from .350 to

Table 3.1 Education Returns by Cohort and Year: 1968–1988

Cohort	1968	1973	1978	1983	1988
1984–1988					.576
1979–1983				.476	.554
1974–1978			.350	.434	.542
1969–1973		.414	.356	.439	.535
1964–1968	.417	.423	.391	.475	.518
1959–1963	.416	.461	.434	.500	.515
1954–1958	.448	.515	.456	.504	.507
1949–1953	.500	.530	.468	.488	.500
1944–1948	.523	.524	.460	.454	
1939–1943	.537	.496	.425		
1934–1938	.521	.468			
1929–1933	.462				

Changes	1968/1973	1973/1978	1978/1983	1983/1988
Within Experience	+.001	−.061	+.053	+.060
Within Cohort	+.008	−.053	+.054	+.051

Notes: Data are average differences in log weekly wages between college and high-school graduates of the same sex, education, and experience level averaged across groups using the 1988 sample weights. Years refer to three-year simple averages centered on the indicated year (i.e., 1968 refers to 1967/1969). Cohort years refer to entry years for individuals in the center year of the three-year average.

.576 for the youngest experience groups in 1978 and 1988 or follow the 1974–1978 cohort through time from .350 to .542. These results should not be too surprising, however, since the relative wage movements between, say, 1973 and 1978, 1978 and 1983, or 1983 and 1988 span such short periods that the labor force at the end of each subperiod has most of the same people in it that it had at the beginning. It should be no surprise that the average change in the college premium within cohorts is similar to the overall average. Based on the results of Table 3.1, we conclude that the fluctuations through time in the college wage premium represent changes in the relative price of educated labor and are not artifacts of the changing composition of either college or high-school populations.

The quality issue is potentially more important for women because of growth in women's labor-force participation and the changing distinction between potential and actual work experience, which occurs both within and across cohorts. Figure 3.2 graphs the gender differential against potential

Figure 3.2 Changing Gender Differentials

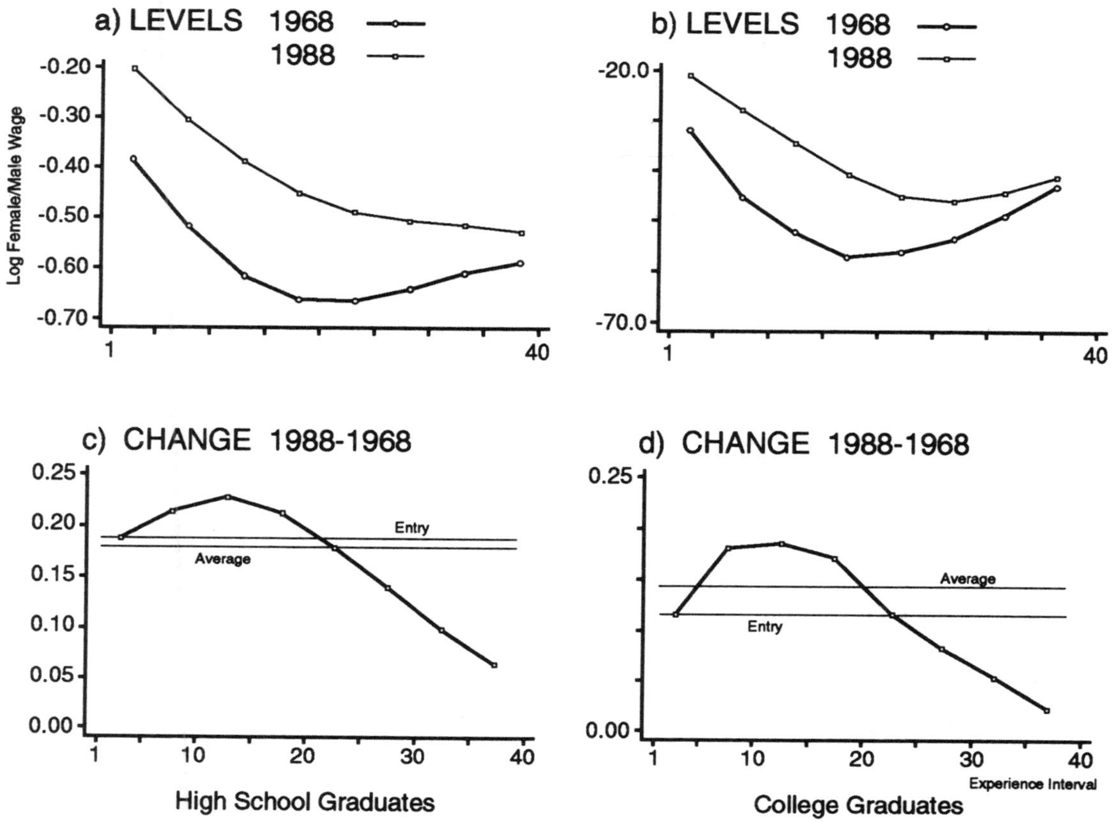

experience for 1968 and 1988.[5] Figures 3.2A and 3.2C refer to high-school graduates, and Figures 3.2B and 3.2D refer to college graduates. The top panels show the level of the general differential-experience profiles in 1968 and 1988, and the bottom panels show the changes from 1968 to 1988 over the eight levels of potential experience. For high-school and for college graduates, the relative wage of women in 1968 fell until the 16–20 years-of-potential-experience interval; it then increased slightly at higher levels of potential experience. The observed cross-sectional decline in women's relative wage as potential experience increases is usually attributed to a rising discrepancy between actual and potential experience.

Between 1968 and 1988, labor-force participation rates of women continued the increase begun in the early 1950s. As Smith and Ward (1985), O'Neill (1985), and others have noted, although increased participation will necessarily increase the accumulated work experience of women, it does not necessarily increase the experience of individual women who are working, that is, those for whom the wage comparisons apply. Increased participation that lengthens periods of employment for those already employed will obviously increase the experience of the employed. On the other hand, increased participation that is achieved when those who previously were not employed join the workforce will lower average experience of the employed unless, for some peculiar reason, the recent entrants have greater experience than those already working.

We rely on two observations to distinguish the part of the female/male wage convergence that results from convergence in skill levels (e.g., experience) from the part that results from convergence in the skill price. The first is that among new entrants, the gender difference in actual experience is unimportant, so that the entire increase in the relative wage of women reflects price increases for whatever skills distinguish them from men. The increase in the relative wage of women at one to five years of potential experience is 19 percent for high-school graduates and 11 percent for college graduates. We interpret this as indicating that the market price of women's skills relative to men's increased 19 percent among high-school graduates and 11 percent among college graduates.

Provided that these changes reflect skill price changes at all experience levels, the shape of the relative wage change profile results solely from different skill quantity changes at different levels of potential experience. Moreover, since the skill price is estimated by the relative wage change for new entrants, the skill quantity change at each level of experience is the observed change less the change at one to five years of experience. The horizontal

[5] Actually, the profiles reported in Figure 3.2 are three-year averages. The one for 1968 is the 1967–1969 average, and the one for 1988 is the 1987–1989 average.

lines (in Figures 3.2C and 3.2D) labeled "Entry" are drawn for contrast with changes at other experience levels.

We estimate that between 1968 and 1988 the actual work experience of women with twenty or fewer years of potential experience increased relative to men with equal potential experience. The opposite is true for older women. Evidently, for them increased participation has continued to widen the male/female skill gap. Although wage differentials have declined across the board, the analysis presented here suggests that, on average, the narrowing of skill quantity differentials among men and women of equal education has been restricted to cohorts who finished school after 1968.

The second horizontal line in Figures 3.2C and 3.2D gives the average height of the relative wage profile over all levels of experience.[6] The difference between the entry and average value lines identifies that part of the growth in women's relative wage that results from skill quantity convergence.

Note that the agreement between the entry and average increases for high-school graduates. Evidently for them, the gain in relative experience of the young is almost exactly offset by reductions in relative experience for older women. This would imply that the relative gain for high-school graduate women, graphed in Figure 3.1B, is almost exclusively a skill-price gain. Although the relative wage gain for college graduates is not as large as for high-school graduates, it appears nonetheless that part of it (about 20 percent of the average increase) is due to skill quantity convergence. However, even for college graduates the bulk of the relative wage gain (about 80 percent) is due to skill price changes.[7]

Thus we have a general pattern of relative wage growth for women, for more educated men and women, and for men who have greater work experience. This, we believe, is a pattern suggesting growth in the value of nonphysical activities. We call it growth in the value of skill. In the next section we examine the wage adjustment process, within and between industries, that has brought these changes about.

Industry Components of Wage Change

Earlier we defined w_{jt} as the quartic-regression-smoothed estimate of the (logarithm of the) wage of people in skill (gender × education × experience) group j in year t. We defined ϵ_{ijt} as the average residual from the regression

[6] As described earlier, the weights used in averaging are 1988 wage sample weights.

[7] The 1968–1988 decrease in the gender differential for new entrant college graduates is 11.4 percent, while the average gain over all experience levels is 14.3 percent.

for persons in industry i. We construct the industry average wage by group for year t, w_{ijt} as $w_{jt} + \epsilon_{ijt}$. In this section we decompose this wage as

$$w_{ijt} = w_j + \epsilon_{ij} + u_{ijt} = w_{ij} + u_{ijt},$$

where w_j is the time average of w_{jt} (defined above), ϵ_{ij} is the average difference between w_{ijt} and w_{jt} over time and industry, and u_{ijt} is the difference between the year by industry by group wage, w_{ijt} and $w_{jt} + \epsilon_{ij}$. The group wages, w_j, capture fixed differences in wages across groups over time. The industry by group effects, e_{ij}, capture average (over time) differences across industries in wages paid to particular groups, and the residual, u_{ijt}, captures differences in wages within industries by year.

We then decompose changes in average wages through time as

$$\begin{aligned} w_{jt} - w_{j\tau} &= \sum_{i=1}^{I} n_{ijt}w_{ijt} - \sum_{i=1}^{I} n_{ij\tau}w_{ij\tau} \\ &= \sum_{i=1}^{I} (n_{ijt} - n_{ij\tau})w_{ij} + \left(\sum_{i=1}^{I} n_{ijt}u_{ijt} - \sum_{i=1}^{I} n_{ij\tau}u_{ij\tau} \right), \end{aligned}$$

where n_{ijt} is the (normalized) number of workers in industry i in year t of type j. The first term in this decomposition captures the effect of changes in industrial composition (holding industrial wages fixed). The second term captures time-series changes in wages within industries.[8] We use the first components of the decomposition to measure the importance of changes in composition and the second to measure the within-industry components of wage change. It should also be noted that, to the extent that industrial differences in wages include differences in individual skills as well as market rents, the composition effect in this decomposition will tend to overstate the true effect of changes in industrial employment patterns. For example, if half of the differentials in industry wages represent industry rents (a number that seems high, given the results of Murphy and Topel, 1990), then the composition effect should be reduced by about 50 percent and the within-industry effect increased accordingly.

The composition effect measures changes in group j's average wage that would result if wages were constant within industries and employment shifted between industries, say, from low- to high-wage industries or vice versa. The within component is everything in the aggregate change (for group j) that is not composition. If the industrial distribution of employment

[8] Note that the second term also includes the employment × wage interactions.

Table 3.2 Total and Within-Industry Components of Changes in Real Wages for Specified Groups: 1967–1989

	Percentage Change					
	Total			Within Industries		
Group	1967–1989	1967–1978	1978–1989	1967–1989	1967–1978	1978–1989
All	3.7	7.3	−3.6	4.8	7.8	−3.0
Gender						
Men	−5.2	4.7	−9.9	−3.1	5.6	−8.7
Women	15.6	10.8	4.7	15.5	10.7	4.8
Education						
<12	−2.2	12.1	−14.3	0.6	12.0	−11.4
12	1.1	9.4	−8.3	3.2	9.7	−6.4
13–15	5.3	7.1	−1.8	6.3	7.6	−1.2
16+	9.7	1.8	7.9	8.3	2.7	5.6
Experience (men)						
1–5	−12.4	−0.4	−12.0	−8.7	1.1	−9.8
6–10	−10.7	0.7	−11.4	−8.1	2.0	−10.1
11–15	−8.0	3.2	−11.2	−6.4	3.6	−10.0
16–20	−4.4	5.4	−9.9	−2.8	7.2	−9.9
21–25	−1.7	7.6	−9.2	0.2	8.7	−8.4
26–30	1.6	8.7	−7.1	3.0	8.9	−5.9
31–35	3.3	9.8	−6.4	4.5	9.5	−5.0
36–40	6.4	13.1	−6.7	7.6	12.3	−4.7
Education (1–10 years' experience)						
<12	−7.9	6.7	−14.6	−3.3	6.7	−9.9
12	−12.2	3.1	−15.3	−6.2	5.4	−11.6
13–15	−0.7	6.6	−7.3	3.3	8.7	−5.4
16+	6.6	−4.4	11.0	4.6	−3.8	8.4

were constant, the within component would measure the time-series changes in wages within industry.[9]

Table 3.2 gives computed values for the total change and the within-industry component. The effect of composition changes can be deduced by subtracting the within-industry component from the total change. In these calculations, there are 49 industries corresponding to the two-digit designation for the 1970 Census. The three time intervals in the columns of Table

[9]When wages change within industry and industrial distributions also change, the within-industry component we measure will include the interaction effect, measuring whether employment has shifted toward industries where wages have risen or toward industries where wages have fallen relative to their time-series average.

3.2 refer to the full period, 1967–1989, and two subperiods of equal length, 1967–1978 and 1978–1989.

Notice that for the national average (top line), the within-industry change exceeds the total, so the direction of the change due to industry composition is perverse to the direction of change in the average. For men and women, changes in the gender-specific wages and the convergence of women's wages toward men's are essentially a within-industry phenomenon. This can be seen in Table 3.2, where the changes in wages within industry are essentially the same as the aggregate changes for these comparisons. Changes in industrial composition are simply not an important source of female/male wage convergence.

For education differences, the college/high-school differential within industry over the full period increases by 8.6 overall (9.7 − 1.1) and 5.1 of this increase is within industry (8.3 − 3.2). Between 1967 and 1978, the college/high-school differential falls 7.6 percent overall and 7.0 percent within industries. From 1978 to 1989, the college/high-school differential rises 16.2 percent overall and 12.0 percent within industries. For young workers, the 1967 to 1978 change is −7.5 overall and −9.2 within industries, implying that the composition effect goes against the direction of wage change. Comparing the changes from 1978 to 1989 with those from 1967 to 1978 for young workers, we find that the difference in the two changes is 33.8 (26.3 − (−7.5)) overall and 29.2 (20.0 − (−9.2)) within industries. This implies that the striking change in college returns during the 1980s relative to the 1970s is, once again, almost entirely a within-industry phenomenon. Similar conclusions can be drawn for experience differentials and other differences addressed in Table 3.2.

The conclusion from Table 3.2 is that, for a variety of skill-group partitions, the changes in average wages are changes that occur within industries; they are not simply artifacts of shifts in the industrial distribution of employment.

The next question is whether the changes are isolated in a few industries, or whether what occurs within industries is part of a general pattern. To address the uniformity question, we have combined industries in two ways, using four industry composites for each combination. In the first we aggregate industries by function. The manufacturing aggregate includes all manufacturing (23 two-digit industries). There is a service aggregate that includes all services (professional, business and repairs, personal, education and religious) together with finance, insurance, and real estate. Governments (federal, state, and local) are combined with transportation and public utilities, and there is a residential group that includes agriculture, forestry and fishing, and mining and construction. Figure 3.3 graphs the time-series for four relative wage ratios by industry. Panel (a) gives the college/high-school dif-

Figure 3.3 Industrial Patterns of Relative Wage Change

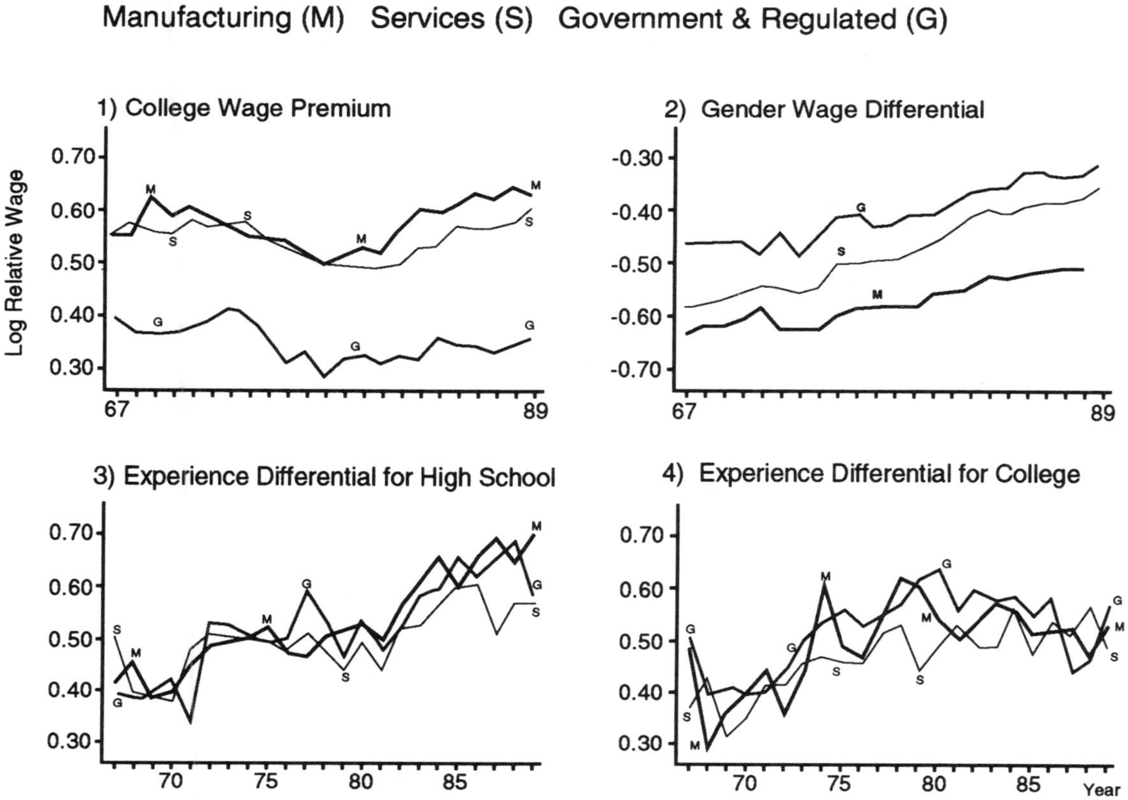

ferential, panel (b) traces the relative wage of women, and panel (c) for high-school and panel (d) for college graduates trace the experience differential (the wage of men with twenty-six to thirty-five years of experience relative to men with one to five years of experience). The series for the composite industries are fixed-weight aggregates of the two-digit industry component series. Thus they only include detailed within-industry changes and are not sensitive to changing industrial distribution of employment.

Our alternative method of combining industries uses the fixed industry wage effects, ϵ_{ij}, averaged over j to form a composite wage score, ϵ_i, for each industry. We order industries on the basis of their skill-mix-adjusted average wages and divide them into four groups that we call *wage quartiles.* Figure 3.3 parallels Figure 3.4 but uses wage order instead of industry function as the basis of aggregation.

Table 3.3 is the tabular equivalent of Figures 3.3 and 3.4. Table 3.3 isolates short periods and gives growth in relative wages during the subperiods. For comparison, it provides the aggregate relative wage series. Unlike the industry composites, the aggregate series includes all composition changes as well as the within-industry components. There are several interesting patterns of industrial differences in relative wages. For example, relative to high-school graduates, college graduates earn far less in government and regulated industries than in other sectors of the economy; the industries with the lowest average wages have the highest relative wages of college graduates. Relative wages of women have increased faster in the services than elsewhere, but as of 1989 they were still lower in services than in government and regulated industries. Women earn relatively more in low-wage industries. Finally, there is no clear pattern of difference using either aggregation base for wages of men at mid-career relative to the wages of new entrants.

The purpose of Table 3.3 and its companions, Figures 3.3 and 3.4, is first to show that the patterns of change within industries are similar across broad industrial groups. Moreover—see the last column of Table 3.3—the within-industry components generally closely follow the aggregate changes.

Much has been written about wage differences between firms and industries, and anyone who has examined data describing earnings of individuals must be aware of the incredible differences in wages observed for nominally similar individuals, i.e., people of the same sex, age, race, and schooling. Even though the possibility of reaching consensus about the sources of wage differences among individuals or firms may be remote, it should be clear from the summaries in Figures 3.3 and 3.4 and Table 3.3 that there are important elements of change in the education-experience-gender structure of wages that are common across seemingly diverse industries. We take the commonality of change as evidence that the market view with arbitrage of

Figure 3.4 Relative Wages by Industry Quartile

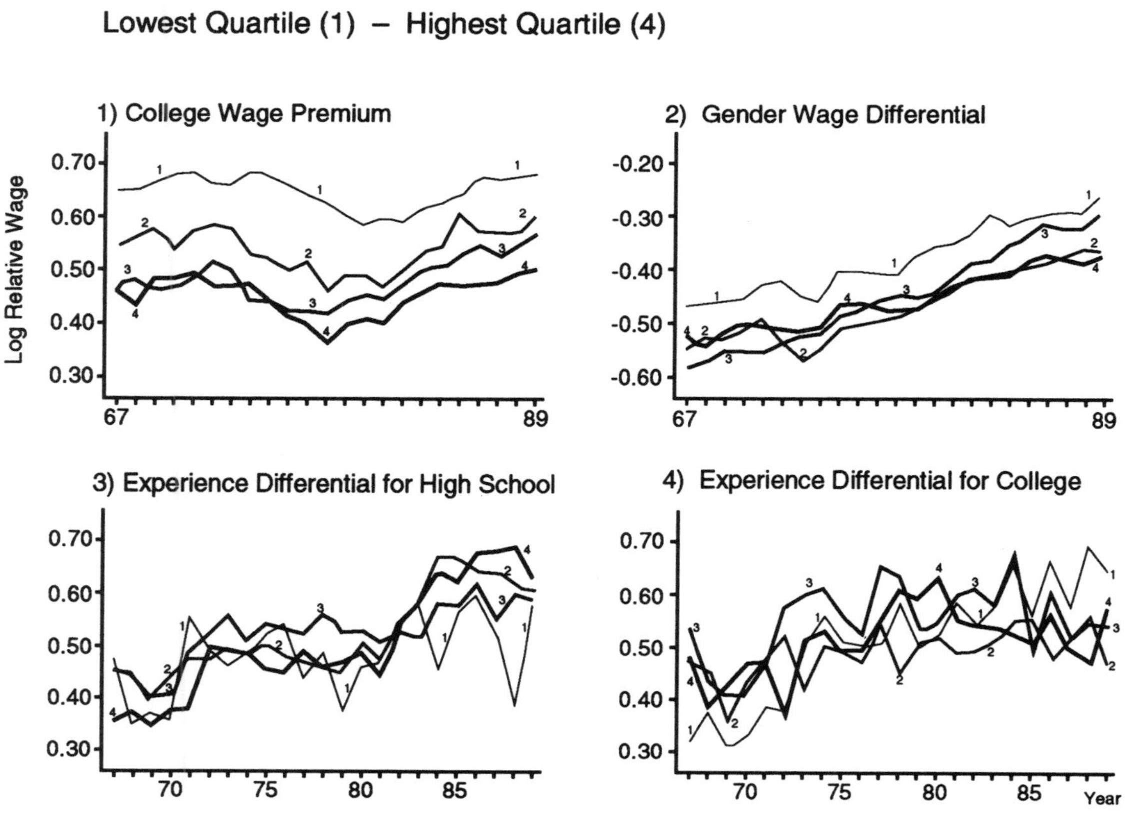

Table 3.3 Patterns of Relative Wage Change Between 1967 and 1989 and for Three Subperiods by Industry Group

	Percentage Change				
	Interval				Correlation with National Average
	1967–1989	1967–1973	1973–1978	1978–1979	(23 years)
Industries By Function					
	College Wage Premium				
Manufacturing	7.7	2.2	−7.9	13.4	.92
Services	4.8	1.7	−7.5	10.7	.90
Government & Regulated	−4.4	1.7	−13.7	7.6	.45
Other	1.1	−9.2	−2.9	13.1	.57
All Industries	8.6	1.3	−8.9	16.2	1.00
	College Wage Premium (Experience 1–5)				
Manufacturing	22.6	3.4	−10.5	29.6	.95
Services	8.0	0.5	−10.0	17.5	.78
Government & Regulated	−3.0	1.1	−15.0	10.9	.62
Other	1.1	−11.6	9.2	3.5	.61
All Industries	18.8	1.1	−8.6	26.3	1.00
	Relative Wage of Women				
Manufacturing	12.5	0.9	4.5	7.1	.98
Services	22.5	2.6	6.4	13.5	.99
Government & Regulated	15.1	−3.1	6.2	12.0	.97
Other	36.1	4.2	9.3	22.6	.98
All Industries	20.7	0.9	5.2	14.6	1.00
	Experience Differential (High-School Men)				
Manufacturing	11.5	−0.9	3.0	9.4	.95
Services	25.6	4.8	5.7	15.1	.82
Government & Regulated	10.8	−5.2	4.7	11.2	.87
Other	25.7	2.2	6.5	17.0	.90
All Industries	19.5	0.0	3.8	15.7	1.00
	Experience Differential (College Men)				
Manufacturing	19.9	−5.4	12.2	13.1	.80
Services	17.4	−0.7	4.6	13.4	.80
Government & Regulated	9.6	−10.2	5.0	14.8	.85
Other	53.7	6.4	20.3	27.0	.34
All Industries	17.7	0.0	5.1	12.6	1.00

Table 3.3 (*continued*)

	Percentage Change				
	Interval				Correlation with National Average (23 years)
	1967–1989	1967–1973	1973–1978	1978–1979	
Industries By Wage Quartile					
	College Wage Premium				
1	3.2	1.4	−3.5	5.4	.68
2	5.3	3.2	−11.7	13.7	.90
3	8.8	2.1	−7.8	14.5	.91
4	4.3	1.1	−10.0	13.2	.90
All Industries	8.6	1.3	−8.9	16.2	1.00
	College Wage Premium (Experience 1–5)				
1	−0.4	2.0	−11.8	9.4	.22
2	13.4	2.6	−9.6	20.5	.79
3	21.9	8.3	−7.1	20.7	.95
4	13.4	−1.6	−12.0	27.0	.94
All Industries	18.8	1.1	−8.6	26.3	1.00
	Relative Wage of Women				
1	20.2	1.4	4.0	14.9	.99
2	20.8	0.9	7.9	12.0	.98
3	24.6	2.2	7.5	14.8	.99
4	14.9	1.2	3.8	9.9	.99
All Industries	20.7	0.9	5.2	14.6	1.00
	Experience Differential (High-School Men)				
1	21.1	0.7	5.9	14.5	.56
2	23.2	4.1	7.2	11.9	.92
3	23.0	1.6	5.5	15.9	.94
4	10.6	−1.6	2.4	9.8	.97
All Industries	19.5	0.0	3.8	15.7	1.00
	Experience Differential (College Men)				
1	20.7	0.9	3.3	16.5	.81
2	17.4	−9.2,	6.1	20.5	.53
3	22.2	4.1	7.1	10.9	.80
4	20.9	−3.8	10.4	14.3	.77
All Industries	17.7	0.0	5.1	12.6	1.00

rents is useful. It is not that there is nothing in relative wages that is unique to some of the industries; indeed there is, and studies of industrial differences, say, in the college or in the experience premium, might yield important insight into wage determination. Our point, instead, is that the major changes in relative wages that we find for the aggregate are also observed in many industries; the pattern is so general that it is hard to believe its causes are independent.

Industrial Change and the Demand for Education

As our analysis in the previous sections has made clear, the past two decades have been witness to large fluctuations in the price of college labor. Between 1968 and 1978 the price of college labor relative to high-school labor, as measured by the overall college wage premium, decreased by 8 percent. In contrast, the price of college labor increased by 14 percent from 1968 to 1988, leaving the relative price of college labor 6 percent higher in the late 1980s than it was in the late 1960s. Over this same period, the fraction of labor input accounted for by college graduate labor increased from 26.7 percent in 1968 to 43.6 percent in 1988.[10] This change represents a phenomenal 14 percent increase in the ratio of college to high-school labor. The fact that the relative price of college labor increased during a period when its relative supply effectively doubled implies that there has been enormous growth in the demand for college graduates that has somehow outpaced the rapid growth in supply.

What accounts for this phenomenal growth in demand for college labor? Simple accounting says that such growth can only be accommodated in two ways, either by relative employment growth in industries that have greater relative demands for college labor than the average industry, or by individual industries increasing the fraction of college labor in the face of a rising relative price of college graduates. The first of these effects would have necessitated significant growth in college-intensive industries over our sample period. The second would have required that labor demand shift in favor of college graduates within individual industries. These shifts would have to have been more than enough to offset the incentive to substitute away from college labor that would naturally accompany the observed rise in the price of college labor.

Table 3.4 presents the data necessary to address the significance of each of these components. The first three columns of the table document the

[10] See notes to Table 3.4 for a description of how we aggregate to measure employment and the fraction of college labor.

Table 3.4 Employment Shares and Percentage College Labor by Industry: 1968–1988

	Employment Shares			Percentage College Labor		
Industry	(1) 1968	(2) 1988	(3) Percent Change 1968–1988	(4) 1968	(5) 1988	(6) Percent Change 1968–1988
Agriculture and Mining	4.8	3.3	−32.5	12.7	29.4	16.7
Construction	6.8	7.1	5.1	12.5	22.2	9.8
Low-Skill Mfg.	4.4	2.7	−39.5	9.4	17.1	7.7
Medium-Skill Mfg.	13.0	8.0	−38.1	14.8	25.9	11.1
High-Skill Mfg.	13.1	10.3	−21.6	27.7	44.8	17.0
Transportation and Utilities	7.6	7.3	−3.9	15.4	34.9	19.5
Wholesale	3.9	4.6	15.4	26.7	41.8	15.0
Retail	11.8	12.2	3.5	15.7	29.9	14.2
Professional and Financial	13.5	22.3	65.2	42.8	58.8	15.9
Education and Welfare	9.0	10.3	13.9	73.1	75.8	2.7
Government	7.1	6.8	−4.4	30.8	50.7	19.9
Other Services	5.0	5.3	5.3	12.8	27.7	14.9
All Industries	100.0	100.0	0.0	26.7	43.6	16.9

Notes: All quantities refer to fixed-wage weighted aggregates of annual hours across experience, sex, and education. For aggregation across education levels, those with less than a high-school degree are assigned a weight of .82 for aggregation with high-school graduates, those with 13–15 years of schooling are assigned a weight of .696 for aggregation with high-school graduates and a weight of .296 for aggregation with college graduates. Industry shares refer to the percentage of aggregate fixed-wage weighted labor hours employed in the industry. The percentage college labor refers to the percent of the fixed wage weighted labor accounted for by the college wage aggregate. 1968 refers to a simple average for the years 1967–1969, and 1988 refers to a simple average for the years 1987–1989.

change in the industrial composition of employment by listing the share of aggregate labor (measured using our fixed-wage aggregates) employed in each of 11 industry aggregates in 1968 and 1988, as well as the percentage change in each share between these two years. As these numbers make clear, low-skilled and medium-skilled manufacturing's shares of overall employment have both declined by about 40 percent, while agriculture and mining, and high-skilled manufacturing have declined by about 30 percent and 20 percent respectively. On the opposite end of the spectrum, both trade and education and welfare have increased by about 15 percent, while professional services and finance have grown a phenomenal 65 percent.

The within-industry changes in educated labor documented in the final three columns of the table have been equally dramatic. As can be seen in the final column, the fraction of college labor increased in all 11 industry aggregates. Clearly, the dramatic shift toward hiring more college labor has been at least as pervasive over this period as was the rise in the relative wage of college graduates.

What have been the relative contributions of the industrial composition changes documented in the first three columns of Table 3.4 and the within-industry changes in the shares of college graduates documented in the final three columns?

As we saw with employment changes, some simple algebra can help us understand the importance of the within- and between-industry changes. If we denote the fraction of overall labor employed in industry i in year t by K_{it}, and the share of college labor in the industry by R_{it}, then the aggregate fraction college, R_t, can be written as

$$R_t = \sum_{i=1}^{I} K_{it} R_{it}.$$

The change in this fraction from year τ to year t can be written as

$$R_t - R_\tau = \sum_i (K_{it}R_{it} - K_{i\tau}R_{i\tau}) = \sum_i (K_{it} - K_{i\tau})(R_{i\tau} - R_\tau) + \sum_i K_{it}(R_{it} - R_{i\tau}).$$

The first term in this expression captures the effect of the change in industrial composition, measured as the change in industry shares times the difference between the fraction college in the industry and the fraction college in the economy as a whole. As this expression makes clear, shifts in employment toward industries that employ a greater fraction of college graduates than the average, or away from industries that employ a smaller fraction of college labor than the average, both account for rising employment of college graduates relative to high-school graduates. The second term captures the fact that the college share also increases as each industry increases the share of its workforce accounted for by college labor.

Table 3.5 presents the results of this decomposition. The first three columns of the table replicate the levels and changes in the industry shares from Table 3.4 along with the changes in the fraction college in each industry. The fourth column, labeled the "Employment Effect," shows the absolute change in the industry's employment share times the difference between

Table 3.5 Decomposition of Growth in College Employment: 1968–1988

Industry	(1) 1968 Share	(2) Percent Change 1968–1988	(3) Change in Fraction College	(4) Employment Effect	(5) Within Effect	(6) Total Effect
Agriculture and Mining	4.8	−32.5	16.7	0.26	0.51	0.76
Construction	6.8	5.1	9.8	−0.05	0.70	0.65
Low-Skill Mfg.	4.4	−39.5	7.7	0.30	0.20	0.50
Medium-Skill Mfg.	13.0	−38.1	11.1	0.59	0.89	1.48
High-Skill Mfg.	13.1	−21.6	17.0	−0.04	1.76	1.72
Transportation and Utilities	7.6	−3.9	19.5	0.09	1.36	1.45
Wholesale	3.9	15.4	15.0	0.00	0.68	0.68
Retail	11.8	3.5	14.2	−0.10	1.78	1.68
Professional and Financial	13.5	65.2	15.9	1.52	3.45	4.97
Education and Welfare	9.0	13.9	2.7	0.52	0.35	0.86
Government	7.1	−4.4	19.9	0.06	1.29	1.34
Other Services	5.0	5.3	14.9	0.03	0.72	0.74
All Industries	100.0	0.0	16.9	3.16	13.70	16.86

Notes: Quantities are computed as noted in Table 3.4. Columns (4), (5), and (6) are aggregates of the corresponding statistics from the 49-industry taxonomy. (1) is the industry's share of aggregate labor in 1967/1969. (2) is the percentage change in the industry's share from 1976/1969 to 1987/1989. (3) is the absolute change in the fraction of total industry wage weighted hours accounted for by college graduates between 1967/1969 and 1987/1989. (4) is the change in the college graduate share of aggregate employment accounted for by the change in each industry's share of aggregate fixed wage weighted hours. This is computed as the change in industry share from 1967/1969 to 1987/1989 times the percent college labor in the industry in 1967/1969. (5) is the change in college labor's share of aggregate employment computed as the industry's employment share (fixed wage weighted) in 1987/1989 times the change in the fraction of college labor in that industry from 1967/1969 to 1987/1989. (6) is the sum of columns (4) and (5).

the fraction college labor in an industry and the fraction college labor in the economy as a whole, and captures the effect of changes in industrial composition (the first term in the above decomposition). The final entry in this column implies that, aggregated over all industries, this between-industry component accounts for 3.16 percentage points of the 16.86 (listed in the last column) percentage point increase in the college share of aggregate employment.

Inspection of the individual industry contributions to this change indicates several important points. First, except for three very small negative effects, all entries in this column are positive. This implies that employment has contracted in most of the industries that tend to employ high-school labor disproportionately and has expanded in sectors that hire more college graduates than the average. The largest contractions are found in agriculture and mining and in low- and medium-skilled manufacturing. The contractions in these three sectors contribute a total of 1.15 percentage points of the 3.16 percentage point increase in the share of college labor. The most significant expansions in the employment of college labor have come from the growth in professional services and finance and the expansion of education and welfare. The enormous growth in professional and finance accounts for 1.52 percentage points of the increase, and the growth in education and welfare accounts for another 0.52 percentage points.

While the changes in industry composition described above go toward increasing the relative demand for college graduates, they come far short of accommodating the overall growth in college labor, accounting for only about .19 (3.16/16.86) of the increase. The remainder of the growth in college labor from 1968 to 1988 was accommodated by an increase in the fraction of college graduates within each industry. Since the fraction of college labor expanded in every industry over this period, all of the within-industry effects listed in Column 5 are positive. Among these, the growth in the fraction of college labor in high-skilled manufacturing, transportation and utilities, retail trade, professional and finance, and the government sector are the most important. Hence, in spite of the general rise in the cost of college labor, the percentage of college labor increased in all 12 of the industrial classifications shown in the table (as well as in all 49 of the two-digit industries we used for the underlying analysis). Clearly, the demand growth for college labor in each of these industries has been more than enough to offset the incentive to substitute away from college labor, caused by its rising relative cost.

Examining the total effects listed in Column 6 of the table illustrates the importance of the financial and professional services sector in accounting for the growth in college labor. As these results illustrate, growth in the size of this sector (accounting for 1.52 percentage points) and its increased college-labor intensity (accounting for 3.45 percentage points) accounts for about .30 (4.97/16.86) of the growth in college labor. In spite of the general decline in employment, both medium- and high-skilled manufacturing together account for about .20 (3.20/16.86) of the growth in overall college employment, primarily because of rapid increases in the fraction of college labor within both of these sectors.

Although the results in Table 3.5 allow us to account for the change in the aggregate employment of college labor, they do not directly address the question of how the demand for college labor changed over time. The true-demand changes occurring over this period are mixed with the substitution response to the increasing price of college labor to produce the results in Table 3.5. This problem does not arise, however, when we compare two time periods where the price of college labor is the same. The longest time span available for such a comparison is between 1970 and 1984, when the college wage premium was .452 and .451 percent respectively. Since the college wage premium was essentially the same in 1970 and 1984, the results of the decomposition presented in Table 3.6 provide direct estimates of both the within- and between-industry components of demand change without the bias from factor substitution responses to price changes. Since the time period covered is only fourteen years (rather than the twenty-

Table 3.6 Components of Growth in the Demand for College Labor: 1970–1984

Industry	1970 Share	Percent Change 1970–1984	Change in Fraction College	Employment Effect	Within Effect	Total Effect
Agriculture and Mining	4.4	−12.1	15.9	0.13	0.56	0.69
Construction	7.0	−1.3	9.7	0.01	0.67	0.69
Low-Skill Mfg.	4.1	−29.0	8.3	0.22	0.24	0.47
Medium-Skill Mfg.	12.2	−31.6	9.0	0.49	0.76	1.25
High-Skill Mfg.	12.6	−13.5	14.3	−0.02	1.57	1.56
Transportation and Utilities	7.8	−2.9	15.3	0.07	1.11	1.18
Wholesale	4.3	12.6	12.1	0.01	0.58	0.59
Retail	11.8	0.1	11.9	−0.05	1.46	1.41
Professional and Financial	14.6	40.8	13.0	0.92	2.70	3.61
Education and Welfare	9.7	9.8	2.5	0.41	0.29	0.70
Government	6.9	−2.9	18.4	0.05	1.16	1.22
Other Services	4.6	8.1	11.4	0.00	0.51	0.51
All Industries	100.0	0.0	13.9	2.25	11.62	13.87

Notes: Statistics are as defined in the notes to Table 3.5. Here 1970 refers to a simple average of the data for the years 1969/1971, and 1984 refers to a simple average for the years 1983/1985.

year period covered in Table 3.5), the measured within- and between-industry changes in the fraction of college labor are absolutely smaller than those of Table 3.5.

In general, the results in Table 3.6 are quite similar to those in Table 3.5. Again, the between-industry effect accounts for only about 16 percent (2.25/13.87) of the overall change in demand for college graduates, and within-industry changes in the demand for college graduates accounts for the remaining 84 percent. Once again, for this period all industries in the sample show a significant growth in the relative demand for college graduate labor. Virtually all industrial output shifts go in this same direction. As in the results in Table 3.5, the most important demand shifts favoring college graduates have come in medium- and high-skilled manufacturing, transportation and utilities, retail trade, governments, and most importantly in professional and finance, which accounts for .26 (3.61/13.87) of the increase in the demand for college labor over this period.

The overall results in Table 3.6 imply that the demand for college labor increased by about .99 (13.87/14) percentage points per year over the 1970 to 1984 period, with about .16 percentage points accounted for by the shift in industrial employment toward college-intensive industries, and .83 percentage points per year coming from within-industry growth in the demand for college labor. These compare with a growth of .84 overall, .16 between industries, and .68 within industries in the percentage of college labor for the 1968–1988 period as a whole.

Although the slower growth of college labor over the 1968–1988 period as a whole (shown in Table 3.5) compared to the 1970–1984 subperiod (Table 3.6) may reflect differing rates of demand growth over these two intervals, one simple interpretation is that the differential growth in college proportions represents the substitution effect of the rise in the price of college labor observed over this longer period. The calculations in Table 3.7 adopt this interpretation of the data and compute the implied demand growth for the entire period by industry as well as the implied substitution effect, computed as the difference between the actual growth in the percentage of college labor between 1968 and 1988 and the growth in this percentage, predicted using the annual growth rate from 1970 to 1984. The results in the table are consistent with this interpretation, and imply that all industry aggregates substituted away from college labor over the 1968–1988 period due to the rise in its relative cost. Overall, these results imply that the demand for college labor grew by 16.6 percent from within-industry components over this twenty-year period, and that substitution away from college labor caused the actual change in college labor to be 2.9 percentage points less, or 13.7 percent.

Table 3.7 Estimated Demand and Substitution Effects: 1968–1988 Within-Industry Changes in Percentage of College Labor

Industry	(1) Predicted from 1970/1984 Change	(2) Actual Change	(3) Implied Substitution Effect
Agriculture and Mining	20.2	15.6	−4.6
Construction	13.9	9.8	−4.2
Low-Skill Mfg.	12.0	7.7	−4.2
Medium-Skill Mfg.	12.8	11.1	−1.6
High-Skill Mfg.	20.6	17.2	−3.4
Transportation and Utilities	20.9	18.7	−2.2
Wholesale	17.3	15.0	−2.3
Retail	17.6	14.6	−3.0
Professional and Financial	18.5	15.5	−3.0
Education and Welfare	3.9	3.4	−0.5
Government	25.0	18.9	−6.1
Other Services	14.9	13.6	−1.3
All Industries	16.6	13.7	−2.9

Notes: All statistics are share-weighted averages of the corresponding two-digit industry statistics using the employment shares from 1987/1989. (1) Is the predicted change in the percent college labor in the industry for 1967/1969 to 1987/1989 computed as 20/14 times the corresponding change from 1969/1971 to 1983/1985. (2) Is the change in the percent of college labor in the industry from 1967/1969 to 1987/1989. (3) Is the difference between Columns (1) and (2).

The results in Table 3.8 examine this substitution interpretation still further by comparing the change in the percentage of college labor within industry for the two subperiods, 1968–1978 and 1978–1988. As we showed in Figure 3.1, the wage premium paid to college graduates fell substantially between 1968 and 1978, from 45 percent to 37 percent. From 1978 to 1988, the college premium increased sharply from 37 percent to 51 percent. These patterns of price changes should cause industries to substitute toward college labor during the 1968 to 1978 period and away from college labor from 1978 to 1988. If patterns of demand growth are similar over these two periods, we would expect this to show up as greater growth in the fraction of college

Table 3.8 Within- and Between-Industry Components of the Growth in College Labor: 1968–1978 and 1978–1988

	Employment Effects			Within Effects			Total Effects		
Industry	1968–1978 (1)	1978–1988 (2)	Diff (3)	1968–1978 (4)	1978–1988 (5)	Diff (6)	1968–1978 (7)	1978–1988 (8)	Diff (9)
Agriculture and Mining	0.17	0.09	−0.08	0.38	0.20	−0.18	0.55	0.29	−0.26
Construction	−0.02	−0.04	−0.02	0.46	0.22	−0.24	0.44	0.18	−0.26
Low-Skill Mfg.	0.18	0.15	−0.03	0.15	0.08	−0.07	0.33	0.24	−0.09
Medium-Skill Mfg.	0.30	0.40	0.10	0.56	0.45	−0.11	0.86	0.85	−0.01
High-Skill Mfg.	−0.05	0.05	0.10	0.89	0.97	0.08	0.84	1.02	0.18
Transportation and Utilities	0.03	0.06	0.03	0.64	0.75	0.12	0.66	0.81	0.15
Wholesale	0.00	0.00	−0.00	0.48	0.20	−0.27	0.48	0.20	−0.27
Retail	−0.04	−0.06	−0.01	1.12	0.64	−0.48	1.07	0.59	−0.49
Professional and Financial	0.85	0.56	−0.29	1.45	1.68	0.23	2.29	2.23	−0.06
Education and Welfare	0.72	−0.18	−0.90	0.44	−0.08	−0.52	1.16	−0.26	−1.42
Government	0.03	0.01	−0.02	0.77	0.53	−0.24	0.81	0.54	−0.27
Other Services	0.13	−0.12	−0.24	0.35	0.30	−0.05	0.47	0.18	−0.29
All Industries	2.30	0.93	−1.36	7.68	5.95	−1.72	9.97	6.88	−3.09

Notes: All statistics are sums of the corresponding two-digit industry statistics. (1) and (2) are the employment effects computed as the change in industry share from the base years (1967/1969 in (1) and 1977/1979 in (2)) to the ending years (1977/1979 in (1) and 1987/1989 in (2)) times the difference between the percentage of college labor in the industry in the base year and the aggregate fraction of college labor in the base year. (3) is (2) minus (1). (4) and (5) are the effects on the aggregate share of college labor from the within-industry change in the percentage of college labor computed as the industry share in the ending years times the change in the percentage of college labor for the industry over the period. (6) is (5) minus (4). (7), (8), and (9) are the sums of (1) and (4), (2) and (5), and (3) and (6), respectively.

labor within each industry between 1968 and 1978 than between 1978 and 1988. If we observe that the share of college graduates grows faster from 1978 to 1988 than during the earlier period, this would be evidence that the demand shift favoring college graduates accelerated over the sample period. The within-industry changes in the percentage of college labor presented in Columns 4, 5, and 6 of Table 3.8 are largely consistent with the substitution explanation, since both overall and in 9 of the 12 industries, the percentage of college labor grew more slowly from 1978 to 1988 than from 1968 to 1978.

For high-skilled manufacturing, transportation and utilities, and professional and financial services, the percentage of college labor increases somewhat faster from 1978 to 1988 than from 1968 to 1978. Growth in the demand for college-trained employees must have been greater in the later periods for these three industries. Thus, there may be at least some role for accelerating within-industry demand growth in explaining the rapid growth in college wages during the 1980s.

For education, we find substantial evidence that industries have substituted away from college graduate labor as its price increased, but the substitution is incomplete; average education levels have increased within industry despite the rising price. Thus it must be that demand has increased *within* industry. In the aggregate, it is clear that the demand for college-trained employees has increased: both relative wages and relative employment levels increased. This could be caused by shifts toward education-intensive industries (growth in finance and professional services, for example) or it could be caused by shifts within industries.

The between-industry phenomena are easily understood. They include general trends toward services and the more recent changes associated with (or induced by) expansions in international trade and the United States trade deficit (see, e.g., the discussion in Murphy and Welch, 1990). But the results provided here (and supported in earlier calculations by Bound and Johnson, 1989) indicate that, although industry shifts are apparently pro-education, the between-industry component of the growth in demand for college-trained employees is not the whole story, nor even most of the story. During the 1980s, demand growth within industry dominates. This, of course, is not an explanation for the phenomenal wage changes of the 1980s. It does, however, narrow the range of acceptable explanations.

The changes documented here and elsewhere for the 1980s are more extensive than any that we can recall in a similar time span, and their causes remain elusive. We are sure that, as industries are defined, the shifts between them have not provided the primary impetus. We are less sure about the causes within industry.

Summary and Conclusions

During the past two decades, relative wages of workers classified by gender, education, or potential work experience have changed more than in any other period of similar length with which we are familiar. After describing wage changes through time, we ask whether these changes reflect change in what we call the pure price of skill, or whether they simply reflect changing quality of workers. With experience comparisons restricted to new entrants versus workers at earnings profile peaks, the quality issue cannot be addressed. We cannot say whether falling wages of young workers implies increasing wage premiums for added experience or declining quality of younger cohorts. We can probably be more precise for education, and perhaps for gender as well. The swings through time in the college/high-school wage differential that we see within cohorts closely parallels the full population changes. Since the quality issues do not arise within cohort once schooling is completed, we interpret the congruence as evidence of changes in skill price rather than skill quality. We reach essentially the same conclusion for the gender differential. The recent gains in women's relative wages are almost the same for new entrants (where questions of the differential effects of work experience are presumably less important) as they are on average over all levels of potential experience.

We next ask whether the changes in relative wages that we see for national aggregates are pervasive within industries, or whether they are averages over a spectrum of different patterns. To those who presume that wages are linked across markets via competition—between workers who search for higher wages and between firms who search for better workers at a given wage—it is perhaps not surprising that, as a general rule, patterns of wage changes are highly correlated among industries. The clearest agreement between changes within industries and the aggregate measures is for the narrowing gender differential and the widening experience differential among high-school graduates. Although the large majority of the changes that we measure are within industry, there is significant heterogeneity between industries in changes both in the college premium per se and in the experience premium among college graduates.

In sum, relative wages have changed hugely, the changes appear to be real phenomena that cannot be dismissed as reflections of changing quality differentials, and they are pervasive among industries. Narrowing our focus to the college-wage premium, which has increased over the full period, we add that average education levels have also increased so the demand for education must have increased. The final sections of the chapter examine the industry components of the aggregate increase in worker education.

The first and perhaps most significant finding is that growth in industries that are intensive in college-trained labor (finance and professional services) and the corresponding shrinkage in employment in industries using relatively unschooled labor (agriculture, mining, and low- and medium-skilled manufacturing) have contributed relatively little to the absorption of college labor. Fully 80 percent of the 1968–1988 growth is within-industry, despite the increased relative wage of college labor. From this it follows that the composition theories of growth in demand for skilled labor—see, for example, the "service economy" studies of the early 1970s and more recently our (1990) study where we describe the role of expanding international trade and especially the trade deficit—cannot explain the bulk of what has happened. Our result here reinforces the earlier conclusions of Bound and Johnson (1989), who observe that changes in industrial composition are insufficient to account for rapidly expanding education levels.

The final two sets of calculations ask whether, in contradiction to the full-period pattern of industry employment shifting toward college labor despite rising costs, there is evidence of substitution and, in reference to the overall trend of increasing demand for skill, whether there is evidence relevant to the timing of the increase. For each of the 12 industrial composites that we examine, we find that the average rate of growth in the college to high-school employment ratio is not as rapid over the full period, 1968–1988, when the relative price of college labor increased, as in the 1970–1984 subperiod, for which the price ratio was the same at the end as at the beginning. This, we believe, is evidence of substitution—the rising price of college labor during the 1980s is perhaps a result of slowing in the rate of growth in average education levels. As a counterpoint, we ask whether there is accompanying evidence that the growth in demand for college labor was more rapid during the 1980s than in the 1970s.

During the 1970s, the relative wage of college labor fell, but the subsequent increase in the 1980s swamped the earlier decline. We find that in transportation and public utilities, high-skilled manufacturing, and the finance/professional services composite, the college/high-school employment ratio actually increased more rapidly during the 1980s than the 1970s, so for these industries there is evidence of accelerating demand for skilled labor.

We are certain that demand for college labor has increased and that most of the increase is within-industry. Thus, explanations for whatever has generated the increase should be sought at the industry level. (The term "technological change" comes to mind, but it only underscores our ignorance.) We also believe, but are less certain, that industries substitute away from college labor as its cost rises. Finally, as we see the evidence, one cannot say whether—in the sense of growth in skill demand—the 1980s differ from the 1970s. The relative wage of college labor increased more rapidly during the 1980s, but average college/high-school employment ratios grew less rapidly.

There is strong evidence in favor of acceleration in some industries, but it is impossible to say whether there are equally important contradictions.

References

Bound, John, and George Johnson. 1989. "Changes in the Structure of Wages During the 1980s: An Evaluation of Alternative Explanations." NBER Working Paper No. 2983.

Murphy, Kevin M., and Robert H. Topel. 1990. "Efficiency Wages Reconsidered: Theory and Evidence." In Weiss, Yoram, and Gideon Fishelson, eds. *Advances in the Theory and Measurement of Unemployment*.

Murphy, Kevin M., and Finis Welch. 1990. "The Role of International Trade in Wage Differentials." In Kosters, Marvin, ed. *Workers and Their Wages: Changing Patterns in the United States*. Washington, D.C.: American Enterprise Institute.

O'Neill, June. 1985. "The Trend in the Male-Female Wage Gap in the United States." *Journal of Labor Economics* 3(2) (January): S91–S116.

Smith, James P., and Michael P. Ward. 1985. "Time-Series Growth in the Female Labor Force." *Journal of Labor Economics* 3(2) (January): S59–S90.

4

How Much Has De-Unionization Contributed to the Rise in Male Earnings Inequality?

Richard B. Freeman

In the 1980s, earnings inequality increased greatly among male workers in the United States. The differential between college graduates and the less educated, which had narrowed in the 1970s (Freeman, 1976), shot upwards, particularly among young men (Murphy and Welch, 1992; Katz and Revenga, 1989; Blackburn, Bloom, and Freeman, 1990). Professionals and managers had gains in real earnings while blue-collar men suffered declines. Dispersion of earnings within demographic groups also rose (Juhn, Murphy, and Pierce, 1989). This increase in within- and between-group inequality was not solely the result of change in cyclical conditions. Total earnings inequality grew in the 1983–1988 boom as well as in the 1981–1982 recession.

In the 1980s, the proportion of workers in unions declined precipitously. Between 1978 and 1988, union density fell by 10 percentage points. Among traditionally highly unionized 25- to 34-year-old blue-collar men the fall was even larger—18 percentage points over the decade.[1] As unionism compresses the distribution of earnings among organized workers and reduces the differential between white-collar and blue-collar workers (Freeman, 1980; 1982) it is natural to suspect that the decline in union density contributed to the rise in inequality.

In this chapter I follow this natural lead and examine the relationship of changing union density to earnings differentials and inequality among male

[1]These figures are based on tabulations of the 1978 and 1988 Current Population Survey files.

workers. I begin by documenting the facts that motivate the analysis: the rise in inequality in the 1980s, the concordant decline in union density, and the inverse association between unionism and earnings dispersion that suggests a causal link between them. I contrast the earnings of union and nonunion workers with the earnings of similar workers who change union status over time. I estimate the contribution of falling unionism to the increased white-collar/blue-collar and college/high-school earnings differentials, and to the rise in the overall variance in the logarithm (ln) of earnings. Finally, to allow for the possibility that unionism affects the wage distribution through mechanisms beyond collective bargaining for members (say, by influencing the pay policies of nonunion employers or national economic policies), I examine differences and changes in industrial earnings inequality between more and less highly unionized, developed OECD countries.

The empirical analysis yields three findings for the United States:

(1) The fall in union density did contribute to the 1980s increase in U.S. earnings inequality. Cross-section–based estimates of union wage effects suggest that the white-collar/blue-collar pay differential would have been 4 to 5 percentage points lower, and the college/high-school differential 1 to 4 percentage points lower in 1988 than they were, had union density remained at its 1978 level throughout the 1980s. These figures imply that 40 to 50 percent of the rise in the white-collar premium and 15 to 40 percent of the rise in the college premium are attributable to the fall in union density. Longitudinal-based estimates suggest that deunionization may have had a somewhat smaller effect.

(2) Unions are a major determinant of changes in within-group earnings inequality. Standard deviations of ln earnings are markedly lower among union workers than nonunion workers within skill groups. In addition, standard deviations of ln earnings decline sharply when nonunion workers become union members. This implies that the fall in union density contributed to the 1980s rise in within-group earnings inequality, accounting for about 20 percent of the overall increase in inequality in ln earnings among men.

(3) The dispersion of earnings grew as much among organized workers as among otherwise comparable nonunion workers, so that overall dispersion would have risen substantially even if the entire workforce has been organized. The market forces for greater inequality were too strong to allow unions to maintain the levels of dispersion among members that characterized earlier time periods. Thus deunionization was a factor in the rise in inequality, but was not the only factor behind this trend.

Cross-country comparisons yield two additional supportive findings:

(1) Earnings distributions are more compact among union workers than among nonunion workers in OECD countries despite differences in union densities, types of union movements, and union/nonunion wage differentials. This implies that the relation between unionism and dispersion is a general outcome of unionism, not something specific to institutions in the United States.
(2) Differentials in earnings between high-wage and low-wage industries for all workers are smaller and increased less in the 1980s in highly unionized countries than in less unionized countries, suggesting that strong national union movements can partially offset market pressures for rising inequality in the overall market.

Increasing Inequality and Declining Unionism in the 1980s

Although no one disputes that earnings inequality grew and union density fell in the 1980s, it is useful to review at the outset the dimensions of the phenomena to be explained.

Rising Inequality

Table 4.1 uses household and establishment survey data to document the ubiquitous rise in ln earnings differentials by skill.[2] Lines 1–2 give college/high-school differentials for men aged 25 to 64 and 25 to 34, and the managers and professionals/operatives differentials for these same groups of men from the widely used March Current Population Survey (CPS) annual earnings files. Although the increase in both measures of inequality is sizable for 25- to 64-year-olds, it is even larger among 25- to 34-year-olds, who are more likely to be in the "active job market" than older male workers. Since these men represent the future of the labor market, I distinguish them in ensuing analyses.

Line 3 records median usual weekly earnings differentials by occupation for all (female as well as male) full-time workers from a different CPS data file: the May outgoing rotation group. It shows rises in the differential of managers/laborers and of professionals/service workers that reflect an overall widening in white-collar/blue-collar pay gaps.

Lines 4–6 report differentials from non-CPS-based surveys. Line 4 records the increase in the differential of pay between specified groups of

[2] It is important to contrast CPS-based changes in differentials and inequality with changes in other data sets, because the CPS does not always give the same picture as these other data sets. In particular, CPS-based trends in union wage differentials in the 1980s do not agree with establishment-based trends given in the Employment Cost Index.

Table 4.1 Earnings Differentials and Changes in Differentials Between Higher- and Lower-Paid Groups of Workers in the 1980s[a]

Source and Groups	1979	1988	Change
(1) March CPS, Annual Earnings (males)			
College/high school, age 25–64	.40	.49	.09
College/high school, age 25–34	.15	.33	.18
(2) March CPS, Annual Earnings (males)			
Managers and professionals/operatives, age 25–64	.35	.48	.13
Managers and professionals/operatives, age 25–34	.23	.39	.16
(3) May/Annual CPS, Usual Weekly Earnings			
Managers/laborers	.52	.65	.13
Professionals/service workers	.67	.79	.12
(4) Employment Cost Index (1981 = 100)			
White-collar/blue-collar	. . .	.10	.10
Professionals/operatives	. . .	.12	.12
Managers/laborers	. . .	.16	.16
(5) BLS Establishment Survey			
Mfg./retail trade	.39	.48	.09
Petroleum/apparel	.79	.90	.11
(6) American Association of University Professors			
Professors in public universities/full-time year-round male workers	.43	.53	.10

Sources: Lines 1 and 2, Blackburn, Bloom, and Freeman (1990); Line 3, U.S. Bureau of the Census, *Statistical Abstract* (1982–1983, p. 404) and *Employment and Earnings* (January 1988); Line 4, *Monthly Labor Review* (January 1988); Line 5, *Monthly Labor Review* (January 1980 and 1989); Line 6, Bureau of the Census, *Statistical Abstract* (1989, Tables 263 and 727) and *Statistical Abstract* (1981, Table 741).

[a]Differentials are measured in ln points. For small numbers, they are approximately the same as percentage changes.

workers from the Bureau of Labor Statistics' (BLS) Employment Cost Index, which reports indices of earnings over time with a 1981 base period. The magnitude of increase in inequality is comparable to that found in the CPS. Line 5 gives earnings differentials and changes in differentials between high-wage and low-wage industries from the BLS's regular establishment survey. It shows a rise in inequality by industry—a pattern also found in the National Income and Products Account industry earnings figures (Bell and Freeman, 1991). Line 6 shows that the earnings of one narrowly defined group of highly educated and skilled workers (professors in public universities) rose by 0.10 points relative to the income of all year-round full-time male workers. Earnings figures for lawyers, doctors, or almost any other professional group would show a similar pattern.

The overall rise in earnings inequality among male workers in the 1980s was not only due to increased differentials between more- and less-highly skilled or educated workers, but also to increases in inequality within specified skill groups (see Karoly, Chapter 1 of this book). The upper deciles of the distributions for college graduates and high-school graduates had, for instance, greater increases in earnings than the lower deciles. A complete explanation of the rise in inequality should, therefore, account for changes in within-group income inequality as well as in across-group means.

As a result of the rise of differentials by group and of within-group inequality, the standard deviation of ln earnings rose from 0.49 to 0.52 from 1978 to 1988 for men aged 25 to 64, while the standard deviation of ln earnings rose from 0.44 to 0.50 for men aged 25 to 34.[3]

The Suspect: Declining Union Density

So much for the phenomenon. What about falling union density? As can be seen in Figure 4.1, the union share of nonagricultural workers, which had been falling modestly since the mid-1950s, plummeted in the 1980s by about one percentage point a year—a magnitude without precedent in American economic history. In 1969, 29 percent of the nonagricultural workforce was organized in unions; in 1978, 25 percent was organized; but in 1989, just 16 percent of the workforce were union members. The decline was endemic to the entire private sector: density fell in nearly all two-digit and three-digit industries, and in all major blue-collar occupational groups, reducing union membership to a bare 12 percent of private sector workers in 1989—a level comparable to that in the 1920s![4]

As the college/high-school differential rose in the 1980s, and as overall inequality increased rapidly in the 1980s as well (see Figure 4.1), the time-series evidence puts the fall in density at the "scene of crime" of rising inequality, and thus suggests the value of a more detailed look at the link between unionism and inequality.

[3]These figures are my tabulations from the CPS files. See Table 4.6.

[4]The ubiquity of the decline belies simple stories of deunionization due to changes in the composition of employment by industry or occupation, and directs attention to the failure of unions to organize workers in National Labor Relations Board representation elections as a result of adamant employer opposition (Freeman, 1985; Goldfield, 1987; and Farber, 1990), and to the slow growth of employment in existing union workplaces (Bronars and Deere, 1989).

Figure 4.1 Union Density, Log College/High-School Earnings Differential, and the Variances of Ln Weekly Earnings Among Men: 1968–1987

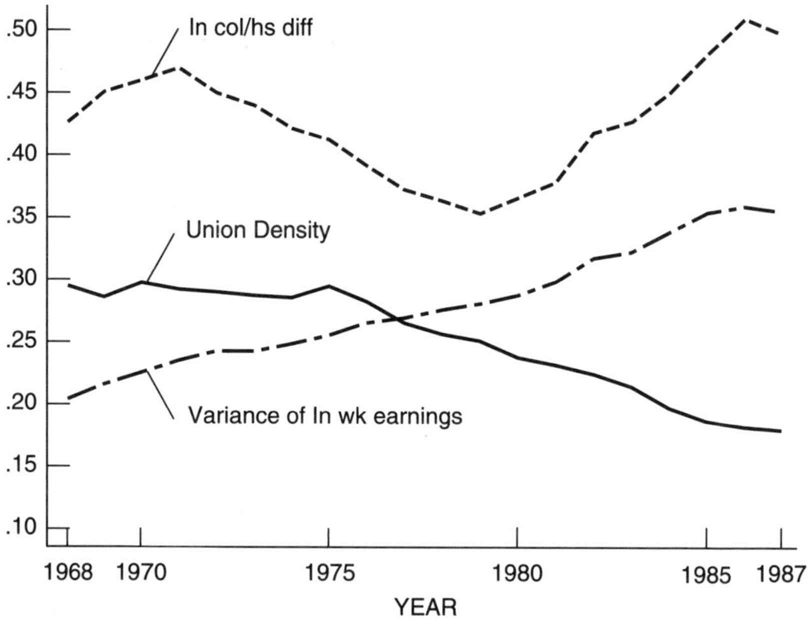

Sources: Unionization data, Troy and Sheffrin (1985) and Bureau of Labor Statistics *Employment and Earnings*, January edition; variance of earnings, Juhn, Murphy, and Pierce (1989); earnings differentials, Katz and Murphy (1990).

Unionism, Earnings Differentials, and Earnings Dispersion

What unions do to earnings inequality has long been controversial. Some analysts, such as Milton Friedman (1962), have criticized unions for producing horizontal inequality by increasing the wages of organized workers relative to those of otherwise comparable nonunion workers. Other analysts have stressed that union standard wage policies reduce inequality within the organized sector (Webb and Webb, 1902). As unions create differentials among observably identical workers, reduce inequality among organized workers, and raise the earnings of blue-collar workers relative to higher-paid white-collar workers, determining what unions do to inequality overall is an empirical question, dependent on the relative magnitude of the inequality-increasing and inequality-decreasing routes of impact.

In *Unionism and Relative Wages*, H. Gregg Lewis (1963) expressed the belief that the inequality-increasing effects of unionism dominated the inequality-reducing effects. Using microdata unavailable to Lewis at the time he wrote, Freeman (1980; 1982) found the opposite: the union-induced reductions in dispersion among organized workers and in the white-collar/blue-collar differential had a greater effect on overall inequality than the increase in dispersion due to the wage differential between organized and unorganized workers. Other studies of dispersion in the United States have yielded comparable results (see the summary in Freeman, 1984), producing a general consensus that unionism is associated with lower rather than greater wage inequality. (In his 1986 book, Lewis reversed his earlier assessment as a result of the newer evidence.) The question for this study, then, relates not to the net direction of the union effects but to whether they are sufficiently sizable, in conjunction with declining density, to contribute to the massive increase in earnings differentials.

To estimate the magnitude of union effects on skill differentials and dispersion of earnings in the United States, I analyze data on usual hourly earnings (hourly pay for those who report hourly pay and usual weekly earnings divided by usual hours worked, for those who do not)[5] of men in the 1988 Annual Merged CPS file and in the 1978 May CPS file (the last May survey to contain earnings information on all respondents). I limit my sample to 25- to 64-year-old male wage and salary earners who report earnings and who are employed outside agriculture and private household services, though analyses for female workers and for men and women together yield similar results.

The 1988 Merged Annual CPS file yields samples of 67,967 25- to 64-year-old male workers and 25,466 25- to 34-year-old male workers—sufficiently large numbers to infer the shape of earnings distributions as well as to estimate union effects on skill differentials. The May 1978 file contains data on 18,304 men aged 25 to 64 and 7,249 aged 25 to 34.

To test whether cross-section differences in earnings and earnings distributions between union and nonunion workers are potentially causal rather than spuriously resulting from the selectivity of workers into unionized jobs, I further analyze longitudinal data from the outgoing rotation groups of a matched file of the 1987 and 1988 Merged Annual CPS tapes. Because respondents in the CPS are in the sample for four months, then out of the sample for eight months, before returning for an additional four months (each respondent is in an outgoing rotation group twice) the data provide information on earnings and union status at two points in time. By matching

[5]The results are similar when I use usual weekly earnings/usual weekly hours for all workers from the same source.

the 1987 and 1988 files, I have information on 26,757 male workers aged 25 to 64, of whom 2,456 or 9.2 percent changed union status, and on 9,006 male workers aged 25 to 34, of whom 872 or 9.7 percent changed union status. I compare the earnings of the same workers before and after a change in union status to control for possible differing fixed characteristics of union and nonunion workers. As this longitudinal analysis of unionism is subject to serious problems of measurement error due to miscoding (Freeman, 1984), I view the longitudinal estimates not as better than the cross-section estimates, but as an alternative to help interpret the data and determine the bounds of the union causal effect.

Skill Differentials: Cross-Section Evidence

To see how much of the fall in union density may have contributed to the rise in the "collar" and education differentials, I use two related statistical techniques. My first technique is a shift-share analysis, in which I combine estimates of a base period union earnings premia and of changes in density to calculate the effect of the changes on earnings differentials:

$$d\text{SKILL} = (\text{DIFF})_h\,\text{dUN}_h - (\text{DIFF})_l\,\text{dUN}_l, \qquad (4.1)$$

where d is the difference operator, SKILL is the skill differential, DIFF is the base period union premium, and UN is the proportion of workers unionized. Subscripts relate to lower-paid (l) and higher-paid (h) workers.

I estimate the union differential for the base period May 1978 CPS by regressing ln earnings on a union dummy variable and a set of "control" variables: dummies for age, race, one-digit industry, and dummy variables either for education (in the occupation group regressions) or occupation (in education regressions). For consistency, I use the same controls in ensuing regressions as well. The estimated union differentials, shown in Column 1 of Table 4.2, are consistent with estimates of union wage differentials in previous work (see Lewis, 1986). Large premia are found for blue-collar workers and for high-school graduates compared to insignificant premia for white-collar workers and college graduates. Comparable estimates of union wage premia in the 1988 Merged File suggest that the CPS-based union differential was roughly constant over the period.

The next three columns of Table 4.2 record estimates of union density in 1978 and 1988 and changes in density between those years. Density fell sharply among less-educated and blue-collar men, with drops of 0.14 points for 25- to 64-year-old blue-collar workers compared to 0.05 points for 25- to 64-year-old white-collar workers; and by a massive 0.18 points among 25- to 34-year-old blue-collar workers compared to 0.06 points among 25- to

Table 4.2 Effect of De-Unionization on Earnings and Earnings Differentials by Education and Occupation, Male Workers: 1978–1988

	(1)	(2)	(3)	(4)	(5)	(6)	(7)	(8)	(9)
	Union Differential	Union Density			Effect on	Earnings Differential			Percent Change
Workers	1978	1978	1988	Change	Earnings	1978	1988	Change	Explained
Aged 25–64									
White-collar	.01	.18	.13	−.05	−.001	...	...	...	...
Blue-collar	.26	.47	.33	−.14	−.036	...	...	...	...
White-collar/blue-collar differential	...	...	...	...	.035	.29	.36	.07	50%
College	−.02	.17	.14	−.03	.001	...	...	...	...
High school	.16	.42	.30	−.12	−.014	...	...	...	...
College/high-school differential	...	...	...	...	.015	.32	.38	.06	25%
Aged 25–34									
White-collar	.03	.16	.10	−.06	−.002	...	...	...	...
Blue-collar	.28	.43	.25	−.18	−.050	...	...	...	...
White-collar/blue-collar differential	...	...	...	...	.048	.21	.32	.11	44%
College	.01	.18	.10	−.08	−.001	...	...	...	...
High school	.24	.40	.23	−.17	−.041	...	...	...	...
College/high-school differential	...	...	...	...	.040	.24	.35	.11	36%

Sources: Column 1, estimated by regression of ln earnings on age dummy variables, one-digit industry dummy variables, and a race dummy variable for the relevant groups in May 1978 CPS file. Columns 2 and 3, calculated as the proportion who are union members in the relevant surveys. Column 4, the difference between Columns 2 and 3. Column 5, the first two lines under each grouping are obtained by multiplying Line 1 by Line 4. The next line is the difference between the statistics for the more- and less-skilled group. Columns 6 and 7, estimated by regression of ln earnings on age dummy variables, one-digit industry dummy variables, a race dummy variable, and either education or collar dummy variables, with no union control. Column 8, the difference between Columns 6 and 7. Column 9, the ratio of Column 5 to Column 8.

34-year-old white-collar workers.[6] Multiplying the change in density by the estimated union earnings differentials gives the effect of deunionization on the earnings of each group, as shown in Column 5. Finally, the figures in the lines labeled white-collar/blue-collar give the estimated effects of the changes in density on the earnings differential between specified groups. For instance, the .035 for workers aged 25–64 indicates that the drop in density raised the earnings differential between white-collar and blue-collar workers by 3.5 percent. Altogether, these numbers show that deunionization widened differentials more for younger workers and those differentiated by occupation than it did for older workers and those differentiated by education.

The next set of columns in Table 4.2 presents estimates of the actual white-collar/blue-collar or college/high-school premia in 1978 and 1988, and of the change in these premia. These estimates are obtained from a multivariate regression of ln earnings on the relevant collar of occupation or education dummy variable with controls for race, industry, and age, as in Column 1, but not for union status. Consistent with the Table 4.1 calculations, they show rises in white-collar and college premia by 7 and 6 percentage points for all men from 1978 to 1988, and by 11 percentage points among younger men. Finally, to obtain the percentage of contribution of the fall in density to the rise in earnings differentials, I divide the estimated effect of deunionization on the differentials with the estimated changes in the differentials. These statistics, given in the final column, show that deunionization accounts for 44 to 50 percent of the increase in the collar differential, and from 25 to 36 percent of the increase in the college/high-school differential.

My second technique for assessing the effect of changes in unionization on skill differentials is based on adding a union dummy variable to the ln earnings equation that includes a collar or education dummy variable. If, as hypothesized, the decline in unionization contributed to the rise in skill differentials, inclusion of the union dummy should lower the estimated changes in skill differentials.

Formally, let X be a set of explanatory factors, D be a dummy variable for the relevant skill group, and UN be a dummy for unionism. Then, the equations I estimate are:

$$\ln W_t = a_t + b_t D_t + c_t X_t + v_t, \tag{4.2A}$$

[6]If within-group inequality increased more among blue-collar and less-educated workers than among white-collar and more-educated workers, this would lend additional support for the role of changes in unionization in the rise in inequality. However, the evidence supporting the trend in within-group inequality is mixed.

and

$$\ln Wt = a'_t + b'_t D_t + c'_t X_t + d'_t UN_t + v'_t. \qquad (4.2B)$$

The v's in the equations are error terms with the usual properties. Since unionism reduces skill differentials, the coefficient on the dummy skill variable in the equation controlling for union status (b'_t) should be larger than the coefficient in the equation without a union variable (b_t). Changes in the estimated skill differential in Equation (4.2A) between the 1988 and 1978 regressions give the estimated trend in skill differentials in Table 4.2. Moreover, insofar as the falling proportion of the workforce receiving the union premium contributed to the rise in differentials, the change in b' coefficients between 1988 and 1978 will be smaller than the change in b coefficients over the same period.

Table 4.3 summarizes the results of this analysis. The first column reports the estimated 1978–1988 change in differentials when unionism is excluded as an explanatory variable. The second column reports the change in differentials when the union dummy variable is included in the regressions. The third column gives the differences between the numbers in the first and second columns. This measures the effect of declining unionization on the trend in differentials. For workers differentiated by collar, these estimates are similar to those in the Table 4.2 decompositions, suggesting that 4 to 5 percentage points or roughly 40 percent of the growth in the collar-earnings gap is associated with the fall in union density. For workers differentiated by education, the estimated effect of deunionization in Table 4.3 is smaller than in the Table 4.2 decompositions: it accounts for 16 to 18 percent of the increase in differentials in this table.

Dispersion of Earnings: Cross-Section Evidence

If there are no differences in the distribution of jobs held or in the abilities of union and nonunion workers after controlling for measured characteristics, the differences in the shapes of cross-section earnings distributions between the two groups can be used to infer the effect of union wage policies on inequality (Freeman, 1980; 1982). Because the major difference between union and nonunion workers is that unionists are concentrated in blue-collar jobs, I limit my analysis of the effect of unionism on the shape of earnings distributions to blue-collar men.[7] Comparisons of distributions for white-

[7] It is possible to get a better fix on "otherwise similar" workers, say by comparing distributions for more narrowly defined groups (at the cost of fewer observations), or by comparing

Table 4.3 Effect of Including Union Dummy Variables on Earnings Differentials, Male Workers: 1978–1988

	Change in Differentials from Regressions		Change Due to Fall in Union Density	
Workers	Without Union Dummy	With Union Dummies	Absolute	Percentage
Ages 25–64				
White-collar/blue-collar	.07	.04	.03	48
College/high school	.06	.05	.01	16
Ages 25–34				
White-collar/blue-collar	.11	.06	.05	45
College/high school	.10	.08	.02	18

Sources: Column 1, calculated by regression of ln earnings on age dummy variables, dummies for the occupation or education group, race, and one-digit industry dummy variables for 1978 and 1988, and taking the difference in the estimated coefficients on the skill groups. Column 2, calculated by adding a union dummy to the regressions in Column 1 for 1978 and 1988 and taking the difference in the estimated coefficients on the skill groups. Column 3, the difference between Columns 1 and 2. Column 4, the ratio of Column 3 to Column 1.

collar workers and for female workers yield a similar picture to that given for blue-collar men.

Figure 4.2 shows earnings distributions in 1978 and 1988. It confirms previous research findings: that unionized workers have a less dispersed distribution of earnings than nonunion workers. In each panel of the figure, the distribution for union workers is more peaked and has a smaller range. Figure 4.3 shows two summary measures of the differing shapes of the distributions: the variance of ln earnings and the gap between ln earnings in the top and bottom deciles of the distributions. Both statistics show that the difference in distributions by union status are large. In 1988, for example, the variance of ln earnings is 0.09 points smaller among union than among nonunion 25- to 64-year-old workers, and 0.08 points smaller among union than among nonunion 25- to 34-year-old workers. The difference in ln earnings between the top and bottom deciles differs by 0.29 points (25- to 64-year-olds) and 0.24 points (25- to 34-year-olds).

The Figure 4.3 statistics show further that union/nonunion differences in

---

residuals from earnings equations (at the cost of specifying functional form). The gross comparisons in the figure suffice to demonstrate the effect of unionism on within-group dispersion in the 1980s.

Figure 4.2 Earnings Distributions of Blue-Collar Male Workers, by Union Status: 1978 and 1988

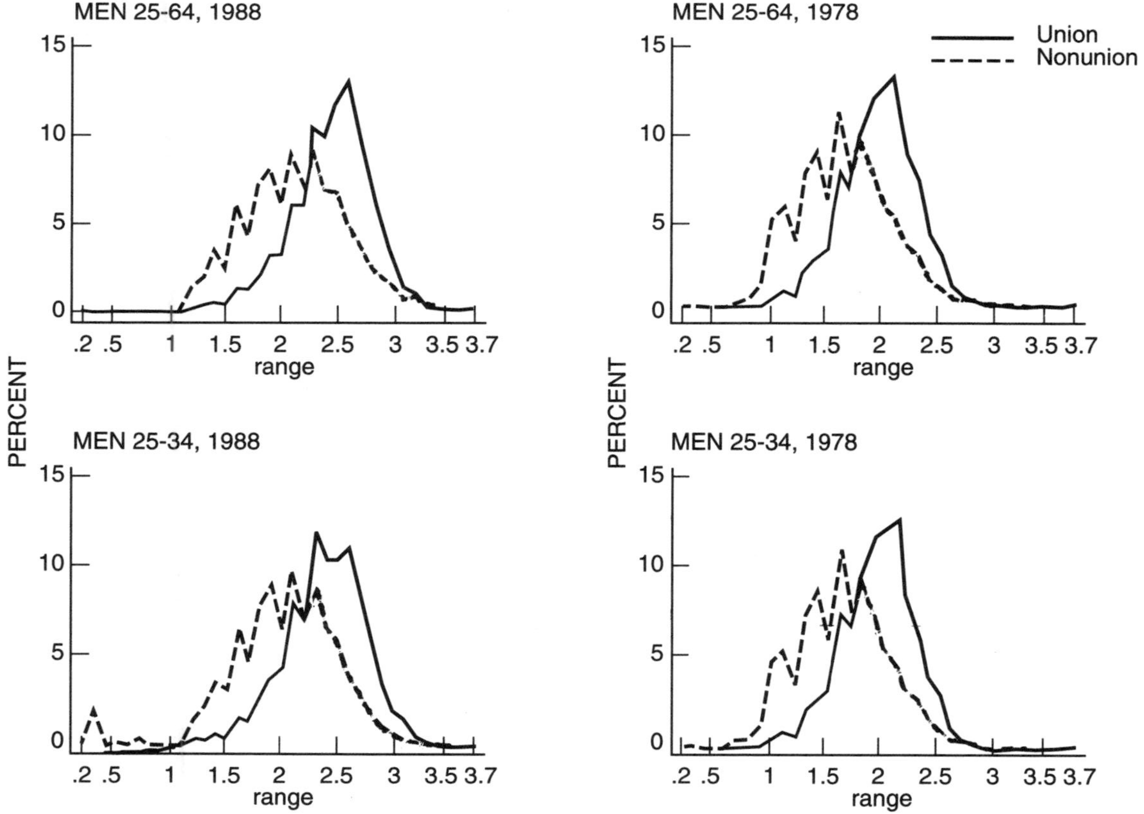

Sources: Tabulated by author from Current Populations Survey Tapes, May 1978; Annual Merged File, 1988.

Figure 4.3 Variances of Ln Earnings and Decile Differences in Ln Earnings, by Union Status, 1978 and 1988

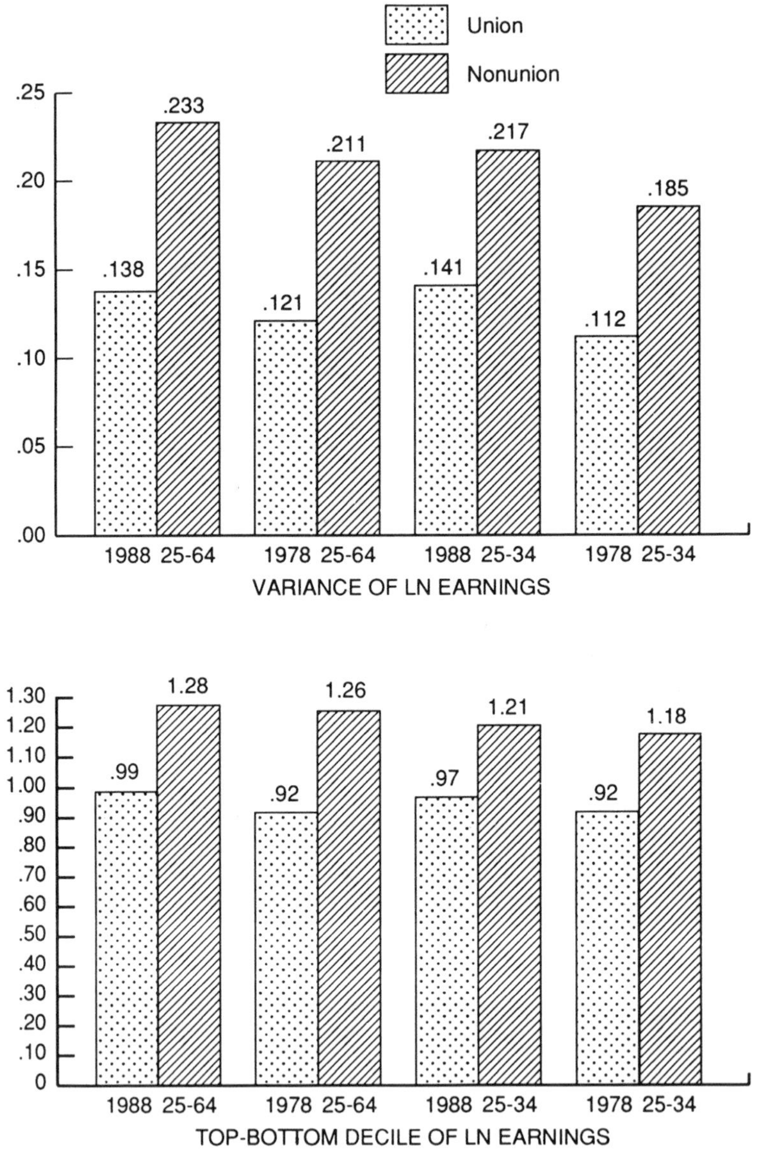

Sources: Tabulated by author from Current Population Survey Tapes, May 1978; Annual Merged File, 1988.

variances in 1978 are virtually identical to those in 1988, and that the union/nonunion differences in deciles are also remarkably similar in the two time periods. The similarity in the union/nonunion difference in variances and in deciles in a period of declining union density suggests that selectivity is unlikely to be a major cause of the observed differences.[8] This supports my use of base-period differences in variances to assess the effect of changing density.

The stability of the union/nonunion differences over time, however, implies that inequality of earnings rose roughly as rapidly among union as among nonunion workers. For instance, the variance of earnings went up by 0.02 points among 25- to 64-year-old blue-collar union workers and nonunion workers between 1978 and 1988, and by 0.03 points among both groups of 25- to 34-year-old workers. The implication is that unions were unable to slow the trend toward increased dispersion among members—a fact that should come as no surprise given the breakdown of pattern bargaining and the wage concessions that characterized the collective negotiations of the 1980s.

The increase in earnings inequality among unionists notwithstanding, the difference in dispersion between union and nonunion workers was sufficiently large for the decline in union density to have contributed significantly to the rise in overall dispersion. A 10 percent decline in the share of the workforce in a group having a variance in ln earnings 0.09 points smaller than that of other workers would, for instance, reduce overall variance by .009 points—or nearly half the within-group rise in variances for union and nonunion 25- to 64-year-old blue-collar workers shown in Figure 4.3.

Longitudinal Evidence

Matched CPS annual files that provide information on workers at two points in time can be used to test the frequently mentioned possibility that cross-section union/nonunion differentials are spurious because of the selectivity of workers into unions. Longitudinal analyses of union effects are, however, subject to considerable problems from measurement error in the union variable (Freeman, 1984).[9] On the basis of these considerations, I view longitudi-

[8] Selectivity would predict changes in the shapes of distributions that are highly likely to alter the difference in variances or in the ratio of deciles.

[9] An error in which 3 percent of workers in a sample had their union status misclassified in a way that would have essentially no effect on cross-section estimates of union earnings effects would substantially bias longitudinal estimates downward if, for example, only 5 percent of a sample truly changed status. This is because some 38 percent of observed changes in status [3/(5 + 3)] would be mismeasured. In addition, longitudinal analysis does not fully eliminate

nal estimates as providing a lower bound to true union causal effects, and cross-section estimates as providing an upper bound.

The results of longitudinal estimates of union effects on earnings using the matched CPS files are given in Table 4.4. The table distinguishes four groups of workers: those who were nonunion in both years (NN), those who were union in both periods (UU), those who became union (NU), and those who left unions (UN). There are two potential ways to measure the effect of unions on earnings in a longitudinal design. The first comparison shows what happens when workers become union, by contrasting the changes for NU and NN. The second comparison shows what happens when workers lose union status, by contrasting UN and UU. The table records statistics for both groups.

The upper two panels of the table present calculations for full-time workers who were either blue-collar or white-collar in both 1987 and 1988. The lower panels treat all men who were high-school or college graduates, based on their reported schooling in 1988.

The longitudinal analysis yields lower estimated effects of unionism on wages for blue-collar workers than does the comparable cross-section analysis, while confirming the seemingly insignificant effect of unionism on white-collar wages. On average, the effects in Table 4.4 for blue-collar workers are roughly one-third as large as those in Table 4.2.

Does this mean that the cross-section calculations in Tables 4.2 or 4.3 significantly overstate the percentage of the contribution of declining density to the trends in differentials? No, it does not. This is because it is erroneous to divide estimated union effects based on longitudinal analysis with estimated trends in differentials based on cross-section comparisons of earnings. The correct analysis is to compare union effects estimated from the longitudinal changes with trends in collar differentials estimated from longitudinal changes. The 1987–1988 matched file contains enough workers who change from blue-collar to white-collar jobs to permit such an analysis. Among men aged from 25 to 64, nonunion workers who shifted from blue-collar to white-collar jobs from 1987 to 1988 gained 10 percentage points in earnings relative to nonunion workers who remained in blue-collar jobs. This is roughly one-third as large as the cross-section–based collar differentials in Table 4.2. Thus, comparing likes to likes (longitudinally based estimates of union differentials to longitudinally based estimates of collar differentials) yields estimates of the effect of unionism on the collar differential that is of comparable percentage magnitude to that in cross-section data.

---

selectivity issues, as workers who join or leave unions are likely to differ from others, arguably in ways that would also bias estimated union effects downward (Freeman, 1984).

Table 4.4 Estimates of Ln Weekly Earnings and Changes in Ln Weekly Earnings, by Change in Union Status: 1987–1988

	Men Aged 25–64			Men Aged 25–34		
Group (# obs 25–64; 25–45)	1987	1988	Change	1987	1988	Change
Full-Time Blue-Collar Workers						
NN (6916; 2529)	5.80	5.85	.05	5.82	5.88	.06
UU (3987; 937)	6.17	6.22	.05	6.13	6.19	.06
NU (644; 231)	5.94	6.05	.11	5.89	6.02	.13
UN (599; 207)	6.02	5.98	−.04	6.01	5.99	−.02
NU–NN	.14	.20	.06	.07	.14	.07
UU–UN	.15	.24	.09	.12	.20	.08
Full-Time White-Collar Workers						
NN (9231; 2672)	6.31	6.36	.05	6.18	6.25	.07
UU (1303; 205)	6.30	6.35	.05	6.18	6.24	.06
NU (399; 86)	6.25	6.32	.07	6.04	6.16	.12
UN (343; 74)	6.29	6.32	.03	6.11	6.12	.01
NU–NN	−.06	−.04	.02	−.14	−.09	.05
UU–UN	.01	.03	.02	.07	.12	−.05
High-School Graduates						
NN (5998; 2501)	5.91	5.95	.04	5.79	5.85	.06
UU (2682; 703)	6.17	6.21	.04	6.04	6.15	.09
NU (515; 210)	5.98	6.07	.09	5.86	5.99	.13
UN (460; 187)	6.06	6.00	−.06	5.95	5.93	−.02
NU–NN	.07	.12	.05	.07	.14	.07
UU–UN	.11	.21	.10	.09	.18	.09
College Graduates						
NN (6008; 1968)	6.38	6.44	.06	6.16	6.26	.10
UU (900; 162)	6.33	6.40	.07	6.19	6.26	.07
NU (309; 82)	6.25	6.38	.13	6.00	6.14	.14
UN (301; 92)	6.32	6.39	.07	6.11	6.22	.11
NU–NN	−.13	−.06	.07	−.16	−.12	.04
UU–UN	.01	.01	.00	.08	.04	−.04

Sources: Tabulated from a matched file of the Annual Merged files of the Current Population Surveys for 1987 and 1988. Blue-collar and white-collar workers are those who remain in their respective collar class in both years; education is based on 1988 reported education. Sample sizes as in Table 4.4.

The implication of such a comparison is that the percentage of the contribution of the drop in density from consistent longitudinal calculations would be considerably higher than that obtained by comparing the union wage effects of Table 4.4 with the trends in differentials of Table 4.2. The same considerations apply to the contribution of the change in density to the trend in the college/high-school differential. Hence, while I interpret the longitudinal calculations as indicating that there is a real (but smaller) effect of unionism on differentials than in cross sections, I use the cross-section calculations to infer the percentage effect of changes in union density on changes in wage differentials. This is valid as long as the "biases" inherent in the cross-section analyses are roughly constant over time.

Table 4.5 turns to longitudinal estimates of the effects of unionism on the standard deviation of the logarithm of weekly earnings, the most widely used indicator of overall earnings inequality. Each line shows the standard deviation for a given group defined by its union status in 1987 and 1988, and the change in standard deviation. The numbers under full-time blue-collar workers NN show, for example, that the standard deviation in ln earnings for workers who were nonunion in both periods were 0.53 in 1987 and 0.54 in 1988, for a 0.01-point gain. Consistent with the claim that unionism reduces dispersion of earnings, workers who shifted from nonunion to union status (NU) had, by contrast, a 0.09-point drop in inequality. The implication is that unionism lowered dispersion by 0.10 points. Comparing union workers who become nonunion (UN) with workers who remain union (UU), the table shows a smaller 0.04 increase in dispersion, again implying that unionization reduces dispersion. Throughout the table, the same pattern is evident: workers who become union experience a drop in dispersion when compared with those who remain nonunion, and those who become nonunion experience an increase in dispersion when compared with those who remain union. Similarly, the magnitude of the differences is almost always larger for the NU versus NN group than for the UN versus UU group.

Comparing the results of the longitudinal comparisons of Table 4.5 with those given in the comparable cross-section contrasts (Figure 4.2) or, alternatively, with the difference between the variances for the UU and NN groups in Table 4.5, we see that the longitudinally based estimates of the reduction in the variance of ln earnings due to unionism are roughly half as large as the cross-section–based estimates. This implies that the estimated effect of unionism on the dispersion of ln earnings is more robust to measurement error and selectivity factors than estimated effects of unionism on mean earnings. For this reason, estimates of the quantitative contribution of declining density to the upward trend in the standard deviation of ln earnings may be more reliable than estimates of the contribution of declining density to the trend in skill differentials.

Table 4.5 Estimates of the Standard Deviation of Ln Weekly Earnings and Changes in the Standard Deviations, by Change in Union Status: 1987–1988

Group	Men Aged 25–64			Men Aged 25–34		
	1987	1988	Change	1987	1988	Change
Full-Time Blue-Collar Workers						
NN	.53	.54	.01	.42	.42	.00
UU	.36	.35	−.01	.36	.34	−.02
NU	.50	.41	−.09	.41	.36	−.05
UN	.45	.48	.03	.39	.42	.03
NU–NN	−.03	−.13	−.10	−.01	−.06	−.05
UU–UN	−.09	−.13	−.04	−.03	−.08	−.05
Full-Time White-Collar Workers						
NN	.52	.51	−.01	.44	.43	−.01
UU	.35	.34	−.01	.31	.30	−.01
NU	.50	.39	−.11	.39	.35	−.04
UN	.44	.50	.06	.38	.49	.11
NU–NN	−.02	−.12	−.10	−.05	−.08	−.03
UU–UN	−.09	−.16	−.07	−.07	−.49	−.12
High-School Graduates						
NN	.53	.52	−.01	.51	.49	−.02
UU	.33	.34	.01	.35	.34	−.01
NU	.52	.39	−.13	.52	.35	−.17
UN	.41	.47	.06	.41	.46	.05
NU–NN	−.01	−.13	−.12	.01	−.14	−.15
UU–UN	−.08	−.13	−.05	−.06	−.12	−.06
College Graduates						
NN	.52	.50	−.02	.56	.54	−.02
UU	.38	.35	−.03	.41	.36	−.05
NU	.55	.40	−.15	.55	.44	−.11
UN	.41	.51	.10	.49	.48	−.08
NU–NN	.03	−.10	.13	−.01	−.10	−.09
UU–UN	−.03	−.16	−.13	−.08	−.12	−.04

Sources: Tabulated from a matched file of Annual Merged Current Population Surveys for 1987 and 1988. Blue-collar and white-collar workers are those in the same collar class in both years; education is based on 1988 education. Sample sizes as in Table 4.4.

Declining Unionism and Overall Dispersion

Thus far I have analyzed the effect of unionism on earnings differentials and on within-group dispersions of earnings separately. To bring the two sets of calculations together and assess the effect of unionism on the overall dispersion of earnings, I use the variance (v) of ln earnings as my measure of dispersion and exploit the variance decomposition detailed in Appendix 4A, which decomposes the change in the variance of ln earnings associated with a change in union density into three terms: (1) the dispersion-reducing effect of unionism on the variance of ln earnings among blue-collar union workers; (2) the dispersion-increasing effect of unionism on the earnings of blue-collar workers due to the union differential; and (3) the dispersion-reducing effect of unionism due to the union-induced reduction in the collar differential.

Table 4.6 presents the results of my decomposition analysis for male workers divided by collar. In the table I transform the standard deviations of the ln earnings on which I have focused thus far (because they are the usual metric for measures of dispersion) into the variances that enter the decomposition equation (see Appendix 4A Equations (4A.6) and (4A.7)) and then transform the statistics back into standard deviations. To be conservative, I exclude the effect of declining density of white-collar workers on the variance in earnings of white-collar workers; this has little effect on the calculations. I limit my analysis to cross-section–based estimates of union effects.

Line 1 of the table records the standard deviations of ln earnings in 1978 and 1988 and the change in standard deviations that represents the phenomenon to be explained. Line 2 transforms the standard deviations into variances and also gives the change in the variances. The next three lines record the estimated contribution of the fall in density on the overall variance of ln earnings due to the difference in the variance between union and nonunion blue-collar workers; the effect of the union wage differential on the earnings of otherwise similar blue- and white-collar workers; and the effect of the union wage differential on the white-collar/blue-collar earnings differential. Line 6 gives the sum of these figures: the estimated change in variance due to the three sets of factors. Note that the largest component is due to the lower variance of ln earnings from Line 3, which was the estimate least affected by the longitudinal calculations.

The next three lines present the final results. Line 7 adds the estimated change in variance to the observed variance in 1978 from Line 2 to obtain a predicted variance for 1988 had union density remained constant. Line 8 transforms this into a predicted standard deviation. Line 9 gives the percentage of the change in the standard deviation of ln earnings attributable to the fall in union density; it is simply the difference between the 1978 standard

Table 4.6 Sources of Change Estimates of the Effect of Declining Union Density on Male Earnings Inequality in the CPS: 1978–1988

Item	Ages 25–64	Ages 25–34
(1) Standard Deviations in ln earnings		
1978	.485	.438
1988	.519	.498
change	.034	.060
(2) Variances of ln earnings		
1978	.235	.191
1988	.269	.248
change	.034	.057
(3) Change due to decline in density and lower variance of wages among blue-collar unionists	.005	.008
(4) Change due to decline in density and wage differential between union and non-union blue-collar workers	−.000	−.001
(5) Change due to decline in density and union-induced reduction in white-collar/blue-collar differential	.002	.004
(6) Total change in variance due to decline in union density	.007	.011
(7) Predicted variance, at 1978 blue-collar union density	.262	.237
(8) Predicted standard deviation, at 1978 blue-collar union density	.512	.487
(9) Percentage of the change in standard deviation of ln earnings due to decline in union density	21%	21%

Sources: Calculated using formulas described in the text from data in the May 1978 and Annual Merged 1988 CPS files.

deviation from Line 1 and the predicted 1988 standard deviation from Line 8 divided by the actual change in standard deviations. As best I can tell, roughly 20 percent of the rise in the standard deviation of ln earnings among men is attributable to the fall in density.

Unionism and Earnings Inequality Across OECD Countries

A complementary way to study the effect of unionism on inequality in the 1980s is to contrast earnings differentials and dispersion within and across countries that have differing union densities and types of union movements. In this section I show that unions reduce dispersion in other countries as well as in the United States. Furthermore, differentials are smaller and rose less in those countries with greater union densities.

Unionism and Dispersion in Other OECD Countries

To estimate how unionism affects the dispersion of earnings in OECD countries beyond the United States, I use microdata files available from the International Social Survey Programme (ISSP). These files contain information on union status and earnings for 500 to 2,000 workers in several OECD countries and the United States.[10] The surveys are comparable to the General Social Survey conducted by the National Opinion Research Center of the University of Chicago. I tabulate coefficients of variation of earnings of union and nonunion workers in total, and for manual and nonmanual workers where possible from the ISSP files.

The results, given in Table 4.7, show that compression of earnings among union members is not unique to the United States. In each country in the ISSP, the variation in earnings is markedly lower among unionists. The difference is greatest among all workers, because the data combine manual and nonmanual workers. However, the difference is still substantial when manual and nonmanual workers are taken separately. Perhaps most strikingly, the union/nonunion differences in variation are about the same magnitude in the other OECD countries (save for Australian manual workers) as they are in the United States, despite differences in the nature of union movements. Given that union density averages some 26 percentage points higher in the other five countries in the ISSP than it does in the United

[10] I include Switzerland in this analysis, and refer to it as an ISSP country although it is not one of those countries actually participating in the survey. The Soziologisches Institut der Universität Zürich conducted a separate survey using the 1987 ISSP module. This is the source of the data for Switzerland.

Table 4.7 Coefficients of Variation in Earnings Union and Nonunion Manual and Nonmanual Workers by Country

	All Workers			Manual Workers			Nonmanual Workers		
Country	Union	Nonunion	Differential	Union	Nonunion	Differential	Union	Nonunion	Differential
U.S.	58	81	−23	52	69	−17	63	83	−19
U.K.	53	74	−21	51	77	−16	52	71	−19
W. Germany	43	64	−21	38	52	−14	47	66	−19
Austria	43	60	−17	31	46	−15	47	68	−21
Australia	56	65	−9	44	50	−6	48	63	−15
Switzerland	46	85	−39	. . .	. . .		. . .	. . .	

Sources: Calculated from ISSP Data Set. See Blanchflower and Freeman (1992) for details.

States (see Blanchflower and Freeman, 1992), this implies that the dispersion-reducing effect of unionism on organized workers holds over a wide range of density, and does not diminish as the heterogeneity of organized labor increases because of greater density.

Dispersion of Industrial Earnings Among Countries

I next examine the relation between unionism and the most readily available statistic on earnings inequality among countries—the dispersion of average earnings by industry. I calculated variances in the logarithm of earnings among industries from three sources: the ILO's *Yearbook of Labor Statistics*, which contains hourly earnings for approximately 20 two-digit and three-digit manufacturing and mining industries; the reports on wages overseas of the Bureau of Labor Statistics' Office of International Affairs, which gives hourly earnings in manufacturing industries from countries that compete with the United States in world markets; and the United Nations' *Yearbook of Industrial Statistics*, which reports labor compensation and numbers of employees. The latter can be used to estimate earnings per worker in a wider set of industries, but lacks data on hours and neglects the service sector. As there is no reason to prefer one of these sources to another (they cover different industries and each has its own serious data problems), I use them all, in the hope that each will serve as a check on the others.[11]

Table 4.8 presents the measures of dispersion of industry earnings from the three sources by country ordered by union density. There is a strong pattern in the data, with highly unionized Sweden having the lowest dispersion and the least unionized United States having the highest dispersion. The correlation coefficients between the densities in Column 1 and the variances in Columns 2, 3, and 4, given at the bottom of the table, are all significantly negative, implying that higher degrees of union organization are indeed associated with a narrower industry wage structure.

Finally, I turn to the related question of whether more highly unionized countries had a slower increase in earnings inequality, as reflected in industry wage differentials, than less highly unionized countries. The evidence that dispersion is lower in unionized countries, although consistent with such a relation, does not provide the answer. Unions overseas, like those in

[11] While dispersion of earnings across industries reflects some of the same factors that earnings differentials between skill groups reflect—it will change in the same way that skill differentials change, as long as the skill mix within industries is roughly constant—it also reflects factors such as product market conditions that are unlikely to affect skill differentials—and may change differently from those differentials or from overall inequality.

Table 4.8 The Relation Between Union Density and Dispersion of Earnings Across Industries Among OECD Countries

Country, by Union Density	Density 1979	Variance of Ln Earnings (X100) in 1980s by Source		
		UN	ILO	BLS
1 Sweden	89	13	9	10
2 Denmark	86	14	12	10
3 Finland	84	15	14	. . .
4 Belgium	77	24	16	20
5 Norway	60	25	12	. . .
6 Austria	59	27	22	25
7 Australia	58	24	. . .	. . .
8 U.K.	58	27	17	19
9 Italy	51	19	10	13
10 Ireland	49	21	22	20
11 New Zealand	46	21	20	. . .
12 Netherlands	43	. . .	14	16
13 W. Germany	42	. . .	14	19
14 Canada	36	25	26	26
15 Switzerland	34	. . .	. . .	17
16 Japan	32	26	25	29
17 France	28	. . .	14	14
18 U.S.	25	28	26	28

Correlations with Union Density
UN measure of dispersion, −.73
ILO measure of dispersion, −.59
BLS measure of dispersion, −.80

Sources: Basic data are from Freeman (1988). Percent union based on U.S. Department of Labor figures; variance of earnings from UN, based on earnings estimated by dividing labor compensation by employment; variance of earnings from ILO, based on published hourly earnings figures. Both the French and Italian union densities are questionable estimates.

the United States, could lower the level of dispersion but fail to slow the market trend toward inequality.

Table 4.9 presents data from the ILO *Yearbook of Labor Statistics* that indicates that the movement toward increased inequality in the industry wage structure was in fact less pronounced in the more unionized countries than in the less unionized ones. The table measures inequality by the ratio of the earnings in the third top-paying industry in a country (roughly the upper decile or quintile in the data) to the earnings in the third lowest-paying

Table 4.9 Earnings Ratios and Changes in Earnings Ratios Between High-Paying/Low-Paying Industries Across Countries, by Union Density

Country, by Union Density	Ratios of Earnings in Third Highest-Paying Industry to Third Lowest-Paying Industry 1978	1987	Change
1 Sweden	1.20	1.27	.07
2 Denmark	1.18	1.24	.06
3 Finland	1.44	1.41	−.03
4 Belgium	1.59	1.53	−.06
5 Norway	1.25	1.33	.08
6 Austria	1.59	1.65	.06
7 U. K.	1.27	1.34	.07
8 Ireland	1.59	1.74	.15
9 New Zealand	1.41	1.58	.17
10 Netherlands	1.32	1.31	−.01
11 Germany	1.53	1.54	.01
12 Canada	1.82	2.08	.26
13 Switzerland	1.15	1.25	.10
14 Japan	1.70	1.76	.06
15 France	1.39	1.54	.15
16 U.S.	2.08	.2231	. . .

Correlations with Union Density
Change in Ratio of Third Highest-Paying Industry to Third Lowest-Paying Industry: −.61

Note: Norway, United Kingdom and Switzerland data refer to males only.
Sources: For union density used in correlations, see Table 4.7. Earnings in industries, from ILO, *Yearbook of Labor Statistics*, 1981 and 1991.

industry in that country (roughly the lowest decile or quintile).[12] The particular top or bottom three industries can change across the years, and the number of industries varies by country.

There are other ways to organize these data, but no organization is likely to change the basic pattern shown in the table—that the increase in industrial earnings inequality is inversely associated with unionization. The greatest increases in the ratio of earnings of high- to low-paying industries occurs in the United States, Japan, and Canada—all countries with relatively low (and

[12] The results are similar when one looks at the same industries in each country, though the presence of some industries, or data for those industries in some countries but not in others, limits the number of comparisons.

for the United States and Japan, declining) union density. The smallest increases are in Sweden, Denmark, and Belgium. While the table does not prove that unionism is responsible for the more modest increase in inequality in those countries (they may have simply faced different market pressures for inequality), the fact that the increase in inequality was less where unions were strongest clearly supports the main conclusion of this study—that declines in unionization contribute to increases in inequality.

Summary and Interpretation

This chapter has presented three different types of evidence that show that unionism reduces inequality of earnings and that the changing level of union density played a role in the increases in inequality that characterized the 1980s. These types of evidence are microdata comparisons of organized and unorganized workers, longitudinal comparisons of workers who changed union status, and comparisons of the level and changes in the spread of industry wage structures between more- and less-unionized countries. That unionism was inversely related to levels and changes in dispersion in all of these data suggests that reduction in dispersion should be taken as one of the primary outcomes of unionism, on a par with union-induced increases in wages that dominated much historical discussion of what unions do.

In terms of explaining the rise in earnings inequality of the 1980s, the statistical calculations indicate that, had U.S. union density been stable, inequality would have risen less than it did, though it still would have increased substantially. The fall in union density in the United States contributed to the rise in inequality on a par with most other measurable factors, such as changes in the industrial mix of employment (see Blackburn, Bloom, and Freeman, 1990) save possibly for the deceleration in the growth of relative supplies of skilled labor (Blackburn, Bloom, and Freeman, 1990; Katz and Revenga, 1989; and Katz and Murphy, 1992).[13] Overall, declining unionization was a supporting player in the story of the increase in inequality—not the main character: Rosencrantz or Guildenstern, not Hamlet. For the future, continued decline in union density in the United States is likely to place additional downward pressure on the relative wages of blue-collar and less-educated workers, and thus make it more difficult for the nation to reverse the trend toward greater inequality.

[13] Declining union density helps explain the increase in skill differentials and inequality in the 1980s, but by itself cannot tell us why differentials rose in the 1980s compared with the 1970s. This is because union density fell in the 1970s as well as in the 1980s, albeit more slowly. On the other hand, the decline in density may help account for the longer-run increase in inequality within skill groups that occurred in both the 1970s and 1980s as density fell.

APPENDIX 4A

The basic equation I use to add the effects of unionism on the variance of ln earnings and on skill differentials is:

$$V(\ln W) = a\,V(\ln W_b) + (1 - a)\,V(\ln W_w) + a(1 - a)(CD)^2, \quad (4A.1)$$

where W refers to the earnings of all workers; W_b to the earnings of blue-collar workers; W_w to the earnings of white-collar workers; CD is the mean of the differential in log earnings between white-collar and blue-collar workers; and a is the proportion of workers who are blue collar.

If u percent of blue-collar workers are unionized, the mean earnings of those workers can be written as

$$\overline{\ln W_b} = u\overline{\ln W_u} + (1 - u)\overline{\ln W_n} = \overline{\ln W_n} + u\,UD, \quad (4A.2)$$

where W_u refers to the earnings of union blue-collar workers; W_n to the earnings of nonunion blue-collar workers; and UD is the traditional union ln earnings differential. Bars above variables are means.

Let CD_n be the white-collar/blue-collar differential among nonunion workers. Then, assuming no spillovers of union wage gains to white-collar workers in union settings, the effect of the union differential on the collar differential is

$$CD = \overline{\ln W_w} - \overline{\ln W_n} - u\,UD = CD_n - u\,UD. \quad (4A.3)$$

Turning to the effect of unionism on the dispersion of wages among blue-collar workers, I decompose $V(\ln W_b)$ as follows:

$$V(\ln W_b) = u\,V(\ln W_u) + (1 - u)\,V(\ln W_n) + u(1 - u)(UD)^2. \quad (4A.4)$$

Holding fixed other differences between union and nonunion workers,[14] $V(\ln W_u) - V(\ln W_n)$ will measure the union-induced compression of earnings within the organized group.

Finally, substituting Equations (4A.2), (4A.3), and (4A.4) into Equation (4A.1) yields an identity linking the three union effects on dispersion to the variance of ln earnings for all workers:

[14] Freeman (1980) presents variance-covariance formulas from a log earnings equation that provides the appropriate calculation to compare variances, controlling for the variance of characteristics among groups of workers.

$$\begin{aligned} V(\ln W) = {} & au\,[V(\ln W_u) - V(\ln W_n)] \\ & + a(1-a)\,[CD_n - uUD]^2 + au(1-u)(UD)^2 \\ & + aV(\ln W_n) + (1-a)\,V(\ln W_w). \end{aligned} \tag{4A.5}$$

Here $au\,[V(\ln W_u) - V(\ln W_n)]$ is the union-induced reduction in the variance of ln earnings among union members; $a(1-a)\,[CD_n - uUD]^2$ is the contribution to the variance of the union-altered white-collar/blue-collar differential; $au(1-u)\,[UD]^2$ is the increase in variance due to the traditional union wage differential; and the remaining terms refer to the variance of earnings among nonunion white-collar and blue-collar workers.

Differentiating Equation (4A.5) with respect to u shows the effect of small changes in union density on overall dispersion yields:

$$\begin{aligned} \frac{dV(\ln W)}{du} = {} & a\,[V(\ln W_u) - V(\ln W_n) \\ & + (1-2u)(UD)^2 - (1-a)\,2\,(CD_n - UD)\,UD]. \end{aligned} \tag{4A.6}$$

When, as in the period under study, union density undergoes large changes, say from u to u', the differentials in (4A.6) must be replaced with differences, yielding the following expression:

$$\begin{aligned} & a(u' - u)\,[V(\ln W_u) - V(\ln W_w)] \\ & + a\,[u'(1-u') - u(1-u)]\,(UD)^2 \\ & - a(1-a)\,[(CD_n - u'\,UD)^2 - (CD_n - uUD)^2]. \end{aligned} \tag{4A.7}$$

Summing the last two terms in (4A.6) and substituting reasonable values of parameters shows why unionism on net reduces dispersion: in the 1970s both the union share of blue-collar male workers and the white-collar share of the male workforce were on the order of .5; hence the sum of the last two terms is negative when the union differential is less than twice the collar differential, which is empirically true.

Equations (4A.6) and (4A.7) are, it should be stressed, more than accounting identities. This is because in taking derivatives (differences), I assumed that changes in density have no effect on underlying wage differences or variances. This rules out potential "second-order effects" of declining density on the union premium, the dispersion of union wages, the dispersion of nonunion wages, and the nonunion collar differential.[15] The cross-country

[15] In addition, we ignored the possible union effects on employment. Union-induced reductions in employment that raise joblessness could, for instance, be viewed as adding a group of workers with zero wages, thus contributing to inequality.

comparisons can be viewed as a way of examining the relation between unionism and dispersion that allows for such broader effects of changing density.

References

Bell, Linda, and Richard Freeman. 1991. "The Causes of Rising Inter-Industry Wage Dispersion in the U.S." *Industrial and Labor Relations Review* 44(2) (January):275–287.

Blackburn, McKinley, David Bloom, and Richard Freeman. 1990. "The Declining Economic Position of Less Skilled American Men." In Burtless, Gary, ed. *A Future of Lousy Jobs?* Washington, D.C.: Brookings Institution.

Blanchflower, David, and Richard Freeman. 1992. "Unionism in the U.S. and Other Advanced OECD Countries." *Industrial Relations* 31 (1):56–79.

Bronars, Steven, and Donald Deere. 1989. "Union Organizing Activity and Union Coverage 1973–1988." NBER Conference on Labor.

Burtless, Gary. 1990. "Earnings Inequality Over the Business and Demographic Cycles." In Burtless, Gary, ed. *A Future of Lousy Jobs?* Washington, D.C.: Brookings Institution.

Farber, Henry. 1990. "The Decline in Unionization in the United States: What Can Be Learned from Recent Experience?" *Journal of Labor Economics* 8(1) (part 2, January):75–105.

Freeman, Richard. 1976. *The Overeducated American.* New York: Academic Press.

———. 1980. "Unionism and the Dispersion of Wages." *Industrial and Labor Relations Review* 34 (1) (October):3–23.

———. 1982. "Union Wage Practices and Dispersion Within Establishments." *Industrial and Labor Relations Review* 36 (1) (October): 3–21.

———. 1984. "Longitudinal Estimates of the Effects of Unionism." *Journal of Labor Economics* 2 (1) (January): 1–26.

———. 1985. "Why Are Unions Faring Poorly in NLRB Representations Elections?" In Kochan, Tom, ed. *Challenges and Choices Facing American Labor.* Cambridge, MA: MIT Press.

———. 1988. "Labour Market Institutions and Economic Performance." *Economic Policy* (April):64–80.

Freeman, Richard, and James Medoff. 1984. *What Do Unions Do?* New York: Basic Books.

Friedman, Milton. 1962. *Capitalism and Freedom.* Chicago: University of Chicago Press.

Goldfield, Michael. 1987. *The Decline of Organized Labor in the United States.* Chicago: University of Chicago Press.

Juhn, Chinhui, Kevin M. Murphy, and Brooks Pierce. 1989. "Wage Inequality and the Rise in the Returns to Skill." NBER Conference on Labor.

Katz, Lawrence, and Kevin M. Murphy. 1992. "Changes in Relative Wages, 1963–1987: Supply and Demand Factors." *Quarterly Journal of Economics* 107:35–78.

Katz, Lawrence, and Ana Revenga. 1989. "Changes in the Structure of Wages: The United States vs. Japan." *Journal of the Japanese and International Economies* 3:522–553.

Lewis, H. Gregg. 1963. *Unionism and Relative Wages in the United States*. Chicago: University of Chicago Press.

———. 1986. *Union Relative Wage Effects: A Survey*. Chicago: University of Chicago Press.

Murphy, Kevin M., and Finis Welch. 1992. "The Structure of Wages." *Quarterly Journal of Economics* 107(1) (February):285–326.

Troy, Leo, and Neil Sheffrin. 1985. *Union Sourcebook*. New Jersey: IRDIS.

U.S. Bureau of the Census. 1991 and other years. *Statistical Abstract*. Various editors. Washington, D.C.: U.S. Government Printing Office.

U.S. Department of Labor. 1991 and other years. *Monthly Labor Review*. Various editors.

Webb, Sidney, and Beatrice Webb. 1902. *Industrial Democracy*. London: Longmans Green & Co.

PART THREE

Demographic Changes and the Distribution of Family Income

5

Family Structure, Family Size, and Family Income: Accounting for Changes in the Economic Well-Being of Children, 1968–1986

Peter Gottschalk / Sheldon Danziger

The percentage of children living in families with incomes below the official poverty line increased moderately between 1969 and 1979, from 13.8 to 16.0 percent, then rose sharply to 21.8 percent in 1983. During the recent economic recovery these figures declined somewhat, to 19.0 percent in 1989 (U.S. Bureau of the Census, 1989, Table 19). As a result, poverty rates for children in 1989 were at about the same level as in 1965, shortly after the War on Poverty was launched.

Not only are poverty rates among children higher today than they were in the late 1960s, but the poverty rate is now much higher among children than among the elderly. Whereas poverty rates were 64 percent higher for the elderly than for children in 1966 (28.5 versus 17.4 percent), they were 40 percent lower in 1989 (11.4 versus 19.0 percent).

Families with children have experienced a lower-than-average growth in mean income and rising economic inequality in recent years (U.S. House of Representatives, 1989). Between 1973 and 1987, the mean income of families with children, adjusted for family size and inflation, increased by 13.2 percent, whereas the mean for all families increased by 17.2 percent. The adjusted income of the poorest 20 percent of families with children declined by 22 percent, while that of the richest 20 percent increased by 24.7 percent (U.S. House of Representatives, 1989, p. 989).

Some early studies (e.g., Preston, 1984; Danziger and Gottschalk, 1986) presumed the rise in child poverty over the past twenty years reflected deteriorating economic circumstances among families with children. This assumption, however, ignores a variety of demographic and other economic factors that affect both the mean and the dispersion of income for families with children.

Four economic, demographic, and public policy factors have a potential impact. First, as a result of slow productivity growth, economic growth has been, at best, sluggish since the early 1970s. Robert Lawrence (1988) reports that the output per worker grew by 1.9 percent annually between 1950 and 1973, fell by 0.2 percent annually between 1973 and 1979, and then increased by 0.8 percent annually between 1979 and 1987. As a result, real mean earnings per worker have increased little, and the probability that a family relying primarily on earnings would be poor has not declined as it did in the two decades following World War II.

Second, the proportion of all children living in single-parent families has increased dramatically. With only one parent to raise the children and earn a living, the heads of single-parent households work fewer hours. Furthermore, because the single parent is usually a woman, and because the average wages of women are lower than those of men, the shift to single-parent families has reduced the pay per hour as well as the number of hours worked. Thus, even if the probability of being poor had remained constant for two-parent and single-parent families, the child poverty rate would have risen as the percentage of children living in mother-only families increased.

Third, the distribution of earnings of males has become more unequal (Dooley and Gottschalk, 1984; Henle and Ryscavage, 1980; Burtless, 1990; Moffitt, 1990). This increased inequality, *ceteris paribus*, has contributed to the rising rate of poverty (Gottschalk and Danziger, 1985).

The fourth factor reducing the resources available to children has been the reduction in government income transfers, particularly unemployment compensation and cash welfare benefits. As program rules were changed, and as states failed to adjust benefits sufficiently to match increases in the cost of living, the antipoverty impacts of cash transfers declined for both two-parent and single-parent families (Danziger, 1989).

Slow increases in the mean and the rising inequality of family income have been accompanied by two additional demographic factors that can affect measured poverty and family income inequality among children: changes in the number of children per family and the characteristics of the women having children.

A reduction in the mean number of children per family will, *ceteris paribus*, reduce measured poverty, as family income is shared among a smaller number of persons. Such a demographic change lowers poverty rates by reducing a family's needs relative to its income. The normative implications of reduced needs are, however, ambiguous. While increases in productivity raise the income-to-needs ratio with no offsetting costs, reductions in family size involve an offsetting cost. If families reduce their size in order to protect themselves against deteriorating economic circumstances, then parents are trading off a desired family size against desired living standards. In this case, the costs associated with raising the income-to-needs ratio are not reflected in standard measures of poverty and economic well-being. The normative implications become even more ambiguous if an increased labor supply of wives and a reduced family size are a joint response to declining male earnings. In this case, the measured increase in family income does not reflect the additional costs associated with reduced home production or forgone leisure.

The second demographic factor that may affect child poverty is the changes in the characteristics of women having children. For example, in recent years families with high earnings potentials have experienced an above-average reduction in births (Connelly and Gottschalk, 1991). A decline in fertility among high-income women would increase the incidence of child poverty, defined as the ratio of the number of poor children to all children, by reducing the denominator of the poverty rate. As the following example makes clear, this is not, however, a necessary outcome. Consider a world of only two married-couple families. In the initial year, the first family earns \$30,000 and has three children; the second family earns \$15,000 and has four children. Because the official poverty lines are roughly \$14,000 for a family of five and \$16,000 for a family of six, the second family is poor. The child poverty rate is thus 4/7. In a later year, there are also two families with children. They also have incomes of \$30,000 and \$15,000, but their sizes are smaller. The first family has one child, the second has three. With an income of \$15,000, the second family is not poor. There are now four children, but none are poor. Given the way the child poverty rate is measured, one cannot know a priori how changes in family size and composition affect the child poverty rate. Even though the reduction in the number of children was greater for the higher-income family, the child poverty rate fell.

The objective of this chapter is to determine the quantitative importance of the various economic and demographic factors on three summary measures of the resources available to families with children: the mean family income, the variance of the logarithm of family income, and the child poverty rate.[1] We develop a decomposition that allows us to answer counterfactual questions, such as "What would poverty rates have been if family size had decreased and no other economic or demographic change had taken place?" Although the answers to such questions quantify which factors are

[1]We examine changes in total family income, but do not separate out changes in mean incomes due to productivity changes, earnings of other family members, or income transfer policy changes.

relatively important, the answers fall far short of a structural explanation of the changes in poverty. To the extent that the observed changes in family size, family structure, and family income are exogenous, then our decomposition measures the causal impact of each factor. But if they are endogenous, then our decomposition measures the direct impact (lower income increases poverty), but not the indirect impact (lower income lowers fertility, which in turn reduces poverty across children). In the absence of a structural model of labor supply, family size, and family income, it is impossible to do more than decompose the changes.

Our approach is to estimate a reduced-form model that describes how marital status, the number of children, and family income vary with a set of exogenous characteristics. The results are used to calculate how much of the changes in child poverty and the log variance reflect changes in the demographic structure of women (the propensity to marry, the propensity to have children, and the number of children they have) and the economic structure of families (economic stagnation and increased inequality of family income), holding the demographic structure of women constant.

Changes in Family Structure, the Characteristics of Women Having Children, and Family Size: 1968–1986

We use the March 1969 and March 1987 Current Population Survey (CPS) computer tapes to account for changes in the distribution of well-being of children between 1968 and 1986. These are the earliest and latest years for which comparable data were available when we conducted our empirical work. Our sample consists of women under the age of 55 who were the head of a household or the spouse of the household head.[2] Separate analyses are conducted for blacks and whites.[3]

[2]The 1969 CPS reports incomes for 1968; the 1987 CPS reports incomes for 1986. We refer to the year for which we have income data. It would be technically correct to say that we have income information for 1968 and demographic information for 1969.

In 1968 all female household heads were unmarried. In 1986, 4.9 percent of all white female heads reported themselves as married with their spouses present; the corresponding figure for blacks was 6.7 percent.

A small number of households were excluded because they reported nonpositive incomes or persons in the family or negative numbers of their own children under 18 years of age. We excluded women who were neither the head nor the spouse because subfamilies were not consistently coded in the two years.

[3]Persons who reported their race as neither white nor black were excluded from the study. A separate analysis could not be done for this eighteen-year period for white non-Hispanics, black non-Hispanics, and Hispanics, as information on Spanish origin has only been asked in the CPS since 1974.

Since the CPS is a stratified random sample, means are calculated using appropriate sample weights. Our focus on the proportion of children who were poor requires that each observation be weighted by the product of the number of children in a given family and that family's sample weight. The characteristics of a mother, however, are weighted by her own person weight to yield estimates of the population of mothers.

Changes in Family Structure

Table 5.1 classifies all of the women in our sample by whether they are a household head or a spouse and whether or not a child resides with them (four mutually exclusive categories).[4] The proportion of women in our sample who were spouses with children present declined for both blacks and whites between 1968 and 1986. As is well known, this was partially the result of an increase in the proportion of women raising children in families where the father was not present. Table 5.1, however, shows that the decline in the percentage of women raising children in two-parent families also resulted from an increase in the percentage of women living without a spouse or a child.

The shift toward female household headship was much more rapid among black than white women. By 1986, about half of the black women in our sample headed their own households; the corresponding fraction for whites was less than one-fifth. The percentage of black women living with a husband and child declined by about 22 percentage points, from 53.2 to 31.6 percent; there was also a small decline in the percentage living with a husband but without children. The other two categories increased substantially—the percentage living with children but without a husband increased by 18 points (from 24.3 to 41.9 percent), while the percentage of women living on their own, without a husband or children, increased by 7.5 points (from 3.7 to 11.2 percent). This reflects the fact that in 1986 black women were less likely to be married, whether they had children or not.

In 1986, a majority of the white women in our sample lived with children and a husband. The percentage living in this category, however, was 14.5 points lower than in 1968 (66.6 versus 52.1 percent). Each of the other three

[4]The CPS gathers data not on whether or not the woman has ever had children, but whether or not a child under the age of 18 now lives with her. Thus, a woman who had her only child when she was 20 and who is now 40 will appear in our sample as childless. Similarly, a divorced woman who has a 15-year-old child living in a different household with his or her father will also be classified as childless. Since our focus is not on fertility but on the child poverty rate and the characteristics of the mothers who have children living with them, this does not pose a serious problem for our analysis. Our child poverty rate, however, does not include children who live in single-parent families headed by men.

Table 5.1 Distribution of Women, by Household Headship and Presence of Children

	Black Women		White Women	
	1968	1986	1968	1986
Female Household Head	27.94%	53.06%	6.93%	18.25%
Children present	24.28	41.85	5.32	12.95
No children present	3.66	11.21	1.61	5.30
Spouse of Household Head	72.06	46.94	93.07	81.75
Children present	53.24	31.62	66.63	52.05
No children present	18.82	15.32	26.44	29.70
All Women	100.00	100.00	100.00	100.00
Total Number of Women (millions)	3.61	5.27	34.05	39.20

Source: Computations by authors using March 1969 and March 1987 Current Population Survey computer tapes.

Notes: Each woman is counted once in Tables 5.1 and 5.2. The data are weighted to reflect the population of women who are heads or spouses under the age of 55. Unrelated individuals (women living alone) are counted as single-person households. The number of observations for 1968 and 1987, respectively, are 26,318 and 26,041 for white women, and 2,711 and 2,986 for black women.

categories increased somewhat. A 7.6 point increase in the percentage living with children but without a husband accounts for about half of the change in living arrangements. Of the remaining 6.9 point decline, the increase in the percentage living on their own accounts for 3.7 points and the increase in the percentage living with a husband but without children accounts for 3.3 points.

The number of women under 55 increased from 3.6 to 5.3 million, or by 45 percent, for blacks, and from 34.1 to 39.2 million, or by 15 percent, for whites. If there had been no change in the probability that a woman had a child and in the number of children per woman, this large increase in the number of women would have led to a corresponding increase in the total number of children. However, as we show below, there was a decline both in the propensity to have children and in the number of children among women who have them.

One goal of the model we estimate is to measure how the decline in the propensity to have children affected measured poverty. As suggested above, if most of these women were in nonpoor households, then the decline in the number of children would be poverty-increasing for children, in the same way that the trend toward female headship among the mothers of children increases child poverty.[5]

Changes in the Characteristics of Women

Although it is not possible with descriptive statistics to determine whether these childless women would have been poor had they had children, Table 5.2 is suggestive. It classifies all women by race, education, household headship, and the presence of children. For those with children, it shows the mean number of children.

A comparison of Columns 1 and 2 for female heads and Columns 4 and 5 for spouses shows that the educational attainment of women without children tends to be somewhat higher than that of women with children for both blacks and whites in each year. For example, in 1968, 5.1 percent of black female household heads without children had completed college (16+ years), compared with only 1.9 percent of those with children. Because women without children have above-average education, the increased percentage of women without children over the period, as shown in Table 5.1, may have tended to raise the child poverty rate.

Among women with children there were declines in the mean number of children for women in each education category. Higher education is associated with both higher income and fewer children. As a result, the rising educational attainment and falling number of children, *ceteris paribus*, are poverty-decreasing and will tend to offset somewhat the poverty-increasing effect of the trend toward female headship, shown in Table 5.1.

The largest changes in educational attainment occurred for blacks, especially for female heads. For example, in 1968, 68.6 percent of female heads with children had not completed high school; these women had an average of 3.3 children living with them. By 1986, the modal category for black female heads was that of high-school graduates, averaging 1.9 children per woman. Even among those who had not graduated from high school, the mean number of children had declined by about 1 child per woman, to 2.4. A similar pattern occurred for black married women with children. The percentage without a high-school degree declined from 54.3 to 15.7 percent, and the mean number of children for this group declined by about 0.8 (from 3.3 to 2.4). For both female heads and spouses, there were substantial increases in the percentage with some college and with college degrees.

For whites, the percentage of women who were high-school graduates was

[5]The low family income that is associated with out-of-wedlock birth or the decline that normally accompanies marital disruption are some of the main mechanisms by which the trend toward female headship has affected childhood poverty (see Smith, 1989).

Table 5.2 Distribution of Women by Household Headship, Presence of Children, and Education

	Female Household Head			Spouse of Household Head		
Years of Schooling Completed	No Children Present (%) (1)	Children Present (%) (2)	Mean Number of Children (3)	No Children Present (%) (4)	Children Present (%) (5)	Mean Number of Children (6)
Black Women						
1968						
<12	58.26	68.56	3.26	55.29	54.27	3.25
12	27.80	26.59	2.61	28.58	33.55	2.65
13–15	8.80	2.97	2.47	9.46	6.79	2.41
16+	5.14	1.87	2.55	6.67	5.39	1.83
1986						
<12	30.14	29.24	2.37	27.44	15.65	2.44
12	37.72	48.24	1.94	43.14	46.50	1.93
13–15	21.30	16.32	1.69	14.47	23.15	1.96
16+	10.84	6.20	1.38	15.25	14.70	1.67
White Women						
1968						
<12	33.54	42.18	2.41	32.28	30.97	2.52
12	44.11	42.20	2.08	46.58	49.41	2.31
13–15	12.00	10.94	2.02	11.85	11.15	2.23
16+	10.35	4.68	2.11	9.29	8.47	2.27
1986						
<12	19.56	23.36	1.94	13.67	13.80	2.06
12	40.56	43.38	1.65	47.66	47.45	1.86
13–15	19.96	19.65	1.61	19.71	20.27	1.88
16+	19.92	13.61	1.56	18.96	18.47	1.81

Source: Computations by authors using March 1969 and March 1987 Current Population Survey computer tapes.
Note: "Mean Number of Children" refers only to those with children.

very similar for female heads and spouses in the two years. The educational upgrading that took place is reflected in the large decline in the percentages of women without a high-school degree and the large increase in the percentages with some college and with college degrees. On its own, this educational upgrading would have led to fewer children. In addition, all of the groups show a decline of about 0.5 children on average.

Changes in Family Size and Structure for Children

Table 5.3 shows the distribution of children by family structure and size. It shows the net result of the changes in family structure, the educational characteristics of women, the presence of children, and the mean number of children per woman documented in Tables 5.1 and 5.2. Between 1968 and 1986, the percentage of black children living with two parents declined from 67.8 to 42.8 percent; the percentage of white children, from 93.1 to

Table 5.3 Distribution of Children, by Family Type and Number of Children per Family

Family Structure/ Number of Children per Family	Black Children 1968 (1)	Black Children 1986 (2)	White Children 1968 (3)	White Children 1986 (4)
Husband-Wife Family	67.8%	42.8%	93.1%	81.4%
One	6.4	8.6	12.3	17.3
Two	11.6	15.4	24.9	34.6
Three	11.9	10.3	23.3	19.5
Four or more	37.9	8.5	32.6	10.0
Female-Headed Family	32.3%	57.2%	7.1%	18.3%
One	2.7	12.0	1.3	5.5
Two	4.7	19.0	1.8	7.3
Three	5.2	12.7	1.5	3.6
Four or more	19.7	13.5	2.5	1.9
All Children	100.0	100.0	100.0	100.0
Weighted Number, millions	8.3	7.7	57.6	47.0

Source: Computations by authors using March 1969 and March 1987 Current Population Survey computer tapes.

Notes: Totals may not equal 100.0 because of rounding. Each child is counted once in Tables 5.3 and 5.4. The data are weighted to reflect the population of children living in families in which a woman under the age of 55 was a head or a spouse.

Table 5.4 Official Child Poverty Rate and Variance of the Log of Family Income for All Children, by Family Type and Number of Children per Family

Family Structure/ Number of Children Per Family	Black Children 1968 (1)	Black Children 1986 (2)	White Children 1968 (3)	White Children 1986 (4)
Husband-Wife Family				
One	8.4%	5.5%	3.1%	4.2%
Two	12.9	8.8	3.6	5.8
Three	18.9	16.9	5.5	11.0
Four or more	38.0	25.1	13.2	23.9
Female-Headed Family				
One	43.3%	38.4%	21.6%	27.5%
Two	54.2	58.5	29.1	35.1
Three	66.1	72.0	47.1	51.9
Four or more	82.6	82.9	62.0	73.5
All Children	42.1	41.7	9.9	14.7
Variance of the Log of Family Income for All Children	0.689	1.100	0.499	0.796

Source: Computations by authors using March 1969 and March 1987 Current Population Survey computer tapes.

81.4 percent. Table 5.3 also shows a shift toward fewer children per family, for both races and for both types of families. For example, the percentage of all black children living in families with four or more children decreased from 57.6 to 22.0 percent; the percentage of all white children living in such families decreased from 35.1 to 11.9 percent.

Table 5.4 shows the official child poverty rate for children, classified as in Table 5.3. The official poverty rate is derived by comparing a household's total money income (from all sources) with a poverty line that varies with family size. In 1986, the official poverty line ranged from $5,701 for a single person to $11,203 for a family of four to $22,497 for a family of nine or more.[6]

The variance of the logarithm of family income is a widely used measure of inequality. Like mean family income, but unlike the child poverty mea-

[6]The poverty line is increased each year by the Consumer Price Index (CPI), so that it remains constant in real terms. We inflate all incomes to 1986 constant dollars using the CPI, so the same thresholds can be used for both years.

sure, it does not vary with family size. In other words, two families with equal incomes but different family sizes may differ in terms of their poverty status, but will be considered equivalent by conventional measures of family inequality.

As Table 5.4 shows, poverty declined slightly for black children, but increased substantially for white children. The official poverty rates for children living in two-parent families are much lower than those for children living in female-headed families in each year. In fact, a husband-wife family with four or more children is less likely to be poor than a female-headed family with only one child. Thus, the shift in family structure away from married-couple families was poverty-increasing.

Note, however, that for whites the group-specific rate shown for each of the eight groups in the table increased between 1968 and 1986. Thus, the white child poverty rate would have increased even if there had been no demographic changes. On the other hand, the group-specific rates for black husband-wife families declined.

Poverty rates for families of four or more are much higher than those for smaller families. Thus, the reduction in the number of children per woman and the trend toward smaller families, shown in Table 5.3, were poverty-decreasing. The model we present in the next section systematically evaluates the net effects of these and other demographic and economic changes on the child poverty rate.[7]

Table 5.4 also shows rising family income inequality. In each year, inequality among blacks is much higher than among whites. But over the period, the log variance of family income for each group increased by about 60 percent.

Methodology

By how much have each of the demographic and economic changes described above affected the child poverty rate? The essence of the estimation problem is that the number of children in a family, the family's income, and whether

[7] In our empirical work, we examine the poverty rate separately for blacks and whites, as their family structure and economic situations differ dramatically. Note from Table 5.3, however, that the number of black children declined from 8.3 to 7.7 million, or by 7.2 percent, whereas the number of white children declined by 18.4 percent, from 57.6 to 47.0 million. Thus, the percentage of children in our sample who are black increased from 12.6 to 14.0 percent. Because minorities have poverty rates that exceed those of white non-Hispanics, the rising percentage of all children who are minorities is poverty-increasing. This is particularly evident in the published census data on child poverty for all children. In this chapter we do not account for the effect on child poverty of changes in the racial-ethnic characteristics of children.

or not the family is headed by a woman are jointly determined. What we ideally would like to estimate is the impact of exogenous changes in family structure, family size, and family income on child poverty rates. However, if the weak economic conditions of the 1970s or changes in women's and men's earnings opportunities affected headship and childbearing decisions, then the observed changes in family size and structure partially reflect the induced effects of economic conditions. Likewise, part of the observed changes in family income may have been caused by exogenous demographic changes (changes in headship and childbearing decisions caused by the women's movement or other changes in societal attitudes toward women's roles). As female headship increased, a greater percentage of all families had to rely on only one breadwinner.

Because estimating a full structural model would require implausible identifying assumptions, we limit our objective to estimating a reduced-form model that is consistent with a linearized version of the underlying structural model. This approach does not isolate the degree to which demographic and economic changes were exogenous. It does, however, describe the relative importance of the observed changes in female headship, family size, and the distribution of family income on the child poverty rate. We believe that this reduced-form approach addresses many questions of interest to policymakers, who are interested in the result of economic and demographic changes, regardless of their source.

In Appendix 5A we provide details on the method and the implicit assumptions behind the regression approach we use to decompose changes in child poverty. These procedures are conceptually similar to a decomposition based on a set of cross-tabulations. Because the latter are more easily understood, we describe our procedure in these terms. In essence, we create a set of cross-tabulations for both black and white women in 1968 and 1986. Each cell is defined by age, education, region, and marital status of the woman. For example, a cell might include black families with a female head, aged 16 to 19, with less than twelve years of education, living in the Northeast.

The entries in this cross-tabulation are used to decompose the change in the aggregate poverty rate into two broad categories: (1) the change that would have occurred if the cell-specific poverty rates had reached their 1986 levels, but the distribution of families across cells had been the same as in 1968 (e.g., if there had been fewer female-headed families, but those female-headed families had experienced the 1986 poverty rates); and (2) the change that would have occurred if the cell-specific poverty rates had remained at their 1968 levels, but the distribution of families across cells had changed (e.g., if the poverty rate among female-headed households had changed).

If this were the limit of our decomposition, the cross-tabulation and regression methodologies would be identical—that is, each aspect of a cell would be identified by a dummy variable. However, we further decompose the change in the cell-specific poverty rates. This requires a regression framework. Appendix 5A explains how we calculate four hypothetical poverty rates and decompose the observed change in cell-specific poverty rates into changes associated with two economic and two demographic factors:

- Mean family income—If all families within a cell had experienced the same growth in family income, the mean of the cell-specific income distribution would have increased, but the shape of the distribution would not have changed. The resulting increase in mean income, with no change in inequality or family size, would have been poverty-reducing.
- Inequality of family income—Families did not all experience the same growth in family income. As we will show, families at the bottom of the (cell-specific) distribution experienced a below-average growth in family income. The resulting increase in inequality is poverty-increasing (holding the mean constant).
- Mean family size—If all families (across all cells) had experienced the same decline in the number of children, then needs would have declined for all families. This would have resulted in a decline in poverty.
- Who has children—Families, however, did not all experience the same reduction in family size. As we will show, the changing composition of those having children would have reduced poverty, even if family size and income had not declined.

The basic data in the cross-tabulations are the proportion of children falling in each cell in each year, the actual poverty rates in 1968 and 1986, and the four hypothetical poverty rates associated with changes in mean income, income inequality, the number of children per family, and who has children. The aggregate poverty rate is calculated as a weighted average of the cell-specific poverty rates.

By proceeding in a set of intermediate steps, we isolate the separate effects of changes in family structure, family size, and the mean and variance of family income. To do so, we estimate regressions for black and white women in each of the two years that predict the probability that a woman is a household head or a spouse, the income her family would have if she were a head (or a spouse), and the number of children she would have if she were a head (or a spouse).[8] The coefficients from these regressions are used to produce a set of seven scenarios for whites and blacks.

[8]Family income is summed over all sources of money income and all persons in the family.

Each scenario makes one successive change to the prior scenario. The first six scenarios are based on the women in the sample in 1986. For each scenario, the equations estimate the probability that children will live in a two-parent family, the mean and variance of the logarithm of family income if the child lives in a one- or two-parent family, the mean number of children per family, and the child poverty rate.[9]

- Scenario 1 reflects all of the economic and demographic conditions in 1986. It uses the 1986 estimated coefficients in all five equations.
- Scenario 2 assumes that the probability of being a female household head (conditional on observed characteristics) was the same in 1986 as in 1968. It uses the 1968 coefficients from the headship equation. A comparison of the outcomes from Scenarios 1 and 2, therefore, illustrates the impact of changes in family structure on the number of children, the mean and variance of family income, and the child poverty rate.
- Scenario 3 further assumes that the mean of the distribution of family income (conditional on observed characteristics) was at its 1968 level, but that the shape of the conditional distribution of income was the same as in Scenario 2.[10] A comparison of Scenarios 2 and 3 shows the impact of changes between 1968 and 1986 in average economic circumstances, while holding the distribution of income at its 1986 value.
- Scenario 4 further allows the shape of the distribution of family income (conditional on observed characteristics) to revert to its 1968 value.[11] Since the mean of the income distribution is the same as in Scenario 3, this scenario measures the impact on child poverty and the log variance of increased within-cell inequality of family income.
- Scenario 5 holds the mean number of children per family constant at its 1986 level, but allows for changes in the characteristics of women

[9]We estimate the income equations using the logarithm of family income as the dependent variable rather than family income, since the distribution of income is better approximated by the lognormal than the normal.

[10]The conditional variance in Scenario 2 is calculated by squaring and summing the difference between each observation's actual log income and its predicted log income, as given in Equation (5A.9) in Appendix 5A (with $\hat{\beta}_{86}$ replacing $\hat{\beta}_{68}$). This residual variance is added to the variance of the predicted log incomes in Scenario 3 (where the $\hat{\Lambda}$'s also take their 1986 values).

[11]The conditional variance of log income now takes on its 1968 value, which is calculated by summing and squaring the difference between actual 1968 income and the predicted 1968 income (using the 1968 values of $\hat{\beta}$ and $\hat{\Lambda}$).

who have children. It uses the coefficients from the 1986 equation determining who has children.[12]

- Scenario 6 allows family size as well as who has children to change to the 1968 values.[13] It therefore isolates the poverty-reducing impact of the reduction in family size.
- Scenario 7 allows the characteristics of women to revert to their 1968 values. It uses the observations from the 1968 data tape and the estimated coefficients in all equations for 1968. A comparison of Scenarios 6 and 7, therefore, measures the impact of educational upgrading and all other observed changes in the characteristics of women that were included as exogenous variables.

Results

Tables 5.5 and 5.6 report the results of using the regression coefficients to calculate the relevant outcomes for the seven scenarios for black and white children, respectively. Each row shows, for a specific scenario, the percentage of children living in two-parent families, the mean and the variance of the log of family income, the number of children per family, and the child poverty rate. The last column shows the aggregate number of children, in millions.[14] Table 5.7 uses the data from Tables 5.5 and 5.6 to show the sign and magnitude of each demographic and economic effect on child poverty and the mean and variance of family income for blacks and whites.

[12]The 1968 coefficients and standard errors in the children's equation are used, but the predicted number of children per family is scaled down by a constant factor across all families in order to keep the average number of children at the 1986 mean. The aggregate number of children increases between Scenarios 4 and 5 even though the number per family is unchanged. This results because using the 1968 coefficients changes the women who are predicted to have children, which in turn changes the weights.

[13]The 1968 coefficients in the children's equation are used and the scaling is eliminated. Hence, the mean number of children per family as well as family composition is changed to the 1968 level.

[14]Each entry in Tables 5.5 and 5.6 is weighted by the family weight times the predicted number of children from the respective equations used for each scenario. To deal with discontinuities in predicted family size, we interpolate between the actual values for families of different sizes. For example, consider the following hypothetical output from one of the scenarios. We predict that a woman has an 80 percent chance of being a spouse and a 20 percent chance of being a female family head, and that she will have 2.6 children if married and 1.8 children if a female family head. Then her expected family size is .8 (2 parents + 2.6 children) + .2 (1 parent + 1.8 children) = 4.24. The poverty line we use for this case then is one that is equal to the poverty line for a family of four plus 24 percent of the dollar value of the difference between the lines for families of four and five persons.

Table 5.5 The Impact of Changes in Family Structure, Family Size, and Family Income on Child Poverty and the Variance of Log Income for Black Children

Scenario	Percentage in Two-Parent Families (1)	Log Family Income (2)	Children Per Family (3)	Percentage Children Poor (4)	Log Variance (5)	Millions of Children (6)
1. 1986 economic and demographic conditions	44.7	9.586	1.59	38.7	1.156	8.40
2. Same as 1, but 1968 headship probability	75.9	9.903	1.56	25.8	1.078	8.20
3. Same as 2, but 1968 economic returns (mean income)	75.9	9.840	1.56	28.2	1.092	8.20
4. Same as 3, but 1968 income inequality	75.9	9.840	1.56	27.7	0.727	8.20
5. Same as 4, but 1968 propensity of women to have children	75.8	9.827	1.61	28.7	0.724	8.49
6. Same as 5, but 1968 mean family size	75.8	9.827	2.44	35.7	0.724	12.86
7. Same as 6, but 1968 characteristics of women	70.8	9.675	2.53	42.6	0.704	9.03

Source: Computations by authors using March 1969 and March 1987 Current Population Survey computer tapes and estimated regression coefficients.

Table 5.6 The Impact of Changes in Family Structure, Family Size, and Family Income on Child Poverty and the Variance of Log Income for White Children

Scenario	Percentage in Two-Parent Families (1)	Log Family Income (2)	Children Per Family (3)	Percentage Children Poor (4)	Log Variance (5)	Millions of Children (6)
1. 1986 economic and demographic conditions	81.2	10.234	1.41	15.1	0.768	55.1
2. Same as 1, but 1968 headship probability	93.2	10.345	1.42	12.1	0.736	55.5
3. Same as 2, but 1968 economic returns (mean income)	93.2	10.333	1.42	11.0	0.709	55.5
4. Same as 3, but 1968 income inequality	93.2	10.333	1.42	9.1	0.518	55.5
5. Same as 4, but 1968 propensity of women to have children	93.2	10.338	1.37	8.1	0.516	53.6
6. Same as 5, but 1968 mean family size	93.2	10.338	1.92	11.1	0.516	75.3
7. Same as 6, but 1968 characteristics of women	92.8	10.241	1.90	13.7	0.516	64.4

Source: Computations by authors using March 1969 and March 1987 Current Population Survey computer tapes and estimated regression coefficients.

Table 5.7 Decomposition of the Effects of Changes in Family Structure, Family Size, and Family Income on the Well-Being of Children

	Black Children			White Children		
	Percentage Point Change in Poverty	Unit Change in Log Family Income:		Percentage Point Change in Poverty	Unit Change in Log Family Income:	
	(1)	Mean (2)	Variance (3)	(4)	Mean (5)	Variance (6)
Total Change (Scenarios 1–7)	−3.9	−0.089	+0.452	+1.4	−0.007	+0.252
Reason						
Increased female headship (1–2)	+12.9	−0.317	+0.078	+3.0	−0.111	+0.032
Changing economic returns (mean income) (2–3)	−2.4	+0.063	−0.014	+1.1	+0.012	+0.027
Rising inequality within group (3–4)	+0.5	0.000	+0.365	+1.9	0.000	+0.191
Changing propensity to have children (4–5)	−1.0	+0.013	+0.003	+1.0	−0.005	+0.002
Declining number of children per woman (5–6)	−7.0	0.000	0.000	−3.0	0.000	0.000
Changing characteristics of women (6–7)	−6.9	+0.152	+0.020	−2.6	+0.097	0.000

Source: Tables 5.5 and 5.6.

A comparison of Rows 1 and 7 in Table 5.5 shows the estimated changes in these economic and demographic outcomes between 1968 and 1986. Row 1 uses all of the 1986 estimated coefficients and the 1986 data on our sample of women; Row 7, all of the 1968 coefficients and the data for that year. While the means of predicted income and predicted number of children (shown in Columns 2 and 3 of Tables 5.5 and 5.6) are very close to the observed means, the predicted poverty rates in Rows 1 and 7 differ somewhat from the actual poverty rates reported earlier.[15]

Between 1968 and 1986, the percentage of black children living in two-parent families declined from 70.8 to 44.7 percent (Table 5.5, Column 1, Rows 7 and 1), and their mean log income fell by about 7 percent, from 9.675 to 9.586 (Column 2). The mean number of children per family, however, fell by about a third, from 2.53 to 1.59 (Column 3). As a result of these changes in family structure, family size, and family income, mean per capita income rose and the child poverty rate fell from 42.6 to 38.7 percent (Column 4). Income inequality (Column 5) increased substantially—the log variance increased from 0.704 to 1.156.

Scenarios 2 through 6 decompose this total change between 1968 and 1986 into the following components: the increased propensity of children to live in single-parent families; changes in economic returns; changes in the inequality of family income; changes in who has children; changes in the number of children per woman; and changes in the characteristics of women.

The scenario in Row 2 shows what would have resulted if family size and family income had remained at their 1986 levels and the probability that a woman in 1986 resided with a spouse was the same as it had been in 1968. In other words, we use the coefficients from the 1968 marital status equations, *ceteris paribus*, and find that the proportion of children living in two-parent families would have risen to 75.9 percent, mean log income would have risen to 9.903, and child poverty would have fallen from 42.6 percent in 1968 to 25.8 percent in 1986, instead of only falling to 38.7 percent. The log variance would have increased less, to 1.078, rather than to 1.156.

Row 3 shows what the situation would have been if the returns to characteristics had been translated into family incomes at the 1968 rates—what the mean and variance of the log of family income and poverty would have

[15] Our estimates are that child poverty fell from 42.6 to 38.7 percent for blacks and rose from 13.7 to 15.1 percent for whites. The actual sample means (Table 5.4) show a decline from 42.1 to 41.7 percent for blacks and a rise, from 9.9 to 14.7 percent, for whites. These differences arise because some of the regressions are not linear and because we account for variance in our predictions only in the income and children's regressions, but not in the headship regression. Furthermore, our calculations assume that the stochastic elements from the children's equation and the income equation are uncorrelated.

been, given the characteristics in our 1986 sample and the income equation coefficients of 1968. By keeping characteristics constant and not allowing the variance of income within these fixed groups to change, we account for the change that would have resulted if everyone within a group had experienced the average growth for persons within this group. The groups are defined by the characteristics in the income equations. For example, this scenario assumes that all high-school graduates of the same age in the same region experienced the same change in family income, but that persons with other characteristics had incomes that grew at their group-specific rates. In this sense, Row 3 keeps the within-group variance constant, but allows between-group variance to change. A comparison of Rows 2 and 3 shows that the changes in the income coefficients were income-increasing (the mean of the log income increased from 9.840 to 9.903, or by about 6 percent), inequality-reducing (the log variance fell slightly), and poverty-decreasing (from 28.2 to 25.8 percent) for black children.[16]

Row 4 shows the impact of using the 1968 residual variance and the 1968 coefficients of the income equations. This holds the groups' means constant at the levels shown in Row 3, but allows within-group variances to change. Note that the effects of increased inequality include only the effects of changes in inequality among women of the same age and education who live in the same region. For example, if the gap in income between women aged 16 to 19 with a high-school degree and living in the West declined relative to older women with more education, this would not show up as an increase in inequality, even though the gap in average incomes between the two groups had increased. In this example, it is only the increased inequality among women aged 16 to 19 with a high-school degree and living in the West (or within other groups) that is indicated in this row.

Increases in inequality between 1968 and 1986 raised the log variance substantially (from 0.727 to 1.092) and raised the poverty rate for black children by about 0.5 percentage points (from 27.7 to 28.2 percent). This relatively small increase in poverty from a substantial increase in inequality reflects the high poverty rate for black children. For example, if half the children were poor (and the distribution was symmetric), increases in inequality would have no effect on poverty. As we shall see, increases in inequality have a larger impact on white poverty rates, which are lower.

As discussed above, it is not possible to know a priori the size or the direction of the impact on child poverty of the declining number of children

[16]Because each higher-numbered row in the table differs from the row above it in only one dimension, the values for some columns in successive rows will remain unchanged. Thus, there is no difference between Rows 2 and 3 in the percentage of children living in two-parent families or the number of children per family.

per woman. We decompose this demographic change into two components: the impact of changes in the probability that a woman of given characteristics has a child, and the impact of changes in the number of children per woman for those who have children.[17]

Our results show that the net effect of changes in those who had children and in the mean number of children per woman was poverty-reducing for black children. A comparison of Rows 4 and 5 shows that the shift in the composition of those who had children reduced the child poverty rate among black children by 1.0 percentage points (from 28.7 to 27.7 percent).

A comparison of Rows 5 and 6 shows the dramatic effects of the reduction in the number of children per woman. If each mother had resided with as many children as observationally identical women had in 1968, then the mean number of children per woman would have been 2.44 instead of 1.61, and the total number of children would have been 12.86 million instead of 8.49 million. The decline in mean family size reduced the child poverty rate by 7.0 percentage points (from 35.7 to 28.7 percent).[18]

Thus far, we have held the characteristics of women at their 1986 values. As shown above, there was a substantial upgrading of educational attainment between 1968 and 1986. The last row shows that changes in the characteristics of women were associated with rising incomes, somewhat smaller numbers of children per family, and a rise in the percentage of children living in two-parent families. Changes in characteristics were as important a factor in reducing child poverty as was the decline in the number of children per woman, accounting for a decline in the poverty rate of 6.9 percentage points, but a small increase in the log variance from 0.704 to 0.724 (Rows 6 and 7).

Table 5.6 presents the same scenarios for white children. In general, the directions of the effects are the same as for blacks, but the magnitudes of the changes are smaller (except for inequality, which has a larger impact). And, whereas the net impact of these changes was a decline in poverty for black children, poverty for whites rose by 1.4 percentage points (from 13.7 to 15.1 percent). As was the case for blacks, the trend toward female head-

[17]Because no research has been done on the labor supply of *remarried* women, we are not sure if their labor supply responses are more like those of married women or single women. Row 5 uses the 1968 coefficients from the children's equation to impute how many children would have lived in the 1986 sample member's family. This changes both the probability that a woman has a child, and the mean number of children per woman. We then scale back each woman's predicted number of children so that the mean number of children per woman remains at its 1986 value. Row 6 then allows the number of children to increase back to the 1968 level.

As a result, the mean number of children per woman is approximately the same in Rows 4 and 5. The difference arises because the variance in the children's equation is added back separately for each scenario.

[18]The log variance is the same in Rows 5 and 6 because we measure the inequality of family income and not the inequality of family income adjusted for family size.

ship was a large factor, raising child poverty by 3.0 percentage points (from 12.1 to 15.1 percent).

White women with given characteristics, holding marital status and family size constant (compare Rows 2 and 3), had lower family incomes in 1986, and hence child poverty was higher by 1.1 percentage points. Poverty also increased by 1.9 percentage points because of the increased variance within groups (compare Rows 3 and 4). Because higher-income women increased their probability of residing without children more than lower-income women, mean income for children fell slightly and child poverty rose by 1.0 points (compare Rows 4 and 5).

These four poverty-increasing factors were offset by two other factors. The predicted number of children declined by more than 20 million, from 75.3 to 53.6 million (compare Rows 5 and 6), reducing poverty by 3.0 percentage points. Finally, changes in the characteristics of women were poverty-reducing, accounting for a 2.6 point decline (compare Rows 6 and 7).

Summary and Conclusions

The 1968–1986 period was one of significant changes in family size, family structure, and family income. The first conclusion we draw is that the relatively small changes in poverty observed over these eighteen years reflect large, but offsetting, demographic and economic changes. Poverty fell (by 3.9 percentage points) for black children and rose by a small amount (1.4 points) for white children. As Table 5.7 shows, however, two of the six factors in our analysis were poverty-increasing for black children (Column 1) and four were poverty-increasing for white children (Column 4).

A second, and related, conclusion is that an exclusive focus on increased female headship neglects another important demographic trend that has prevented the poverty rate from being higher than it already is—namely, decreases in the number of children per family. To argue that poverty would be lower today if fewer children lived in female-headed families is undoubtedly correct.[19] Increases in female headship, *ceteris paribus*, would have raised the poverty rates of black and white children by 12.9 and 3.0 percentage points, respectively. However, it is just as true that poverty rates would be higher today by 7.0 and 3.0 points, respectively, if women had not reduced their number of children. Changes in the characteristics of women were also associated with large reductions in poverty and large increases in mean incomes.

[19] Smith (1989) also finds that increased female headship has a large impact on the poverty rate. In fact, he concludes that the increase in female headship completely explains the rise in the child poverty rate. Our framework shows that although this factor is important, there are several counteracting factors that also must be considered.

A third conclusion is that economic stagnation and increasing inequality are important factors accounting for the disappointing trends in child poverty. As Columns 2 and 5 in the top row of Table 5.7 show, mean family incomes were lower and, as Columns 3 and 6 show, the log variance of family income was higher for both black and white children in 1986 than they were in 1968. The income declines (about 9 percent for blacks and 0.7 percent for whites) are primarily due to the shift toward female household headship, which was large enough to more than offset the substantial income-increasing impact of changes in the characteristics of women. The log variance increased substantially for blacks and whites, with most of the increase attributable to rising inequality within age/education cells.

The overall picture that emerges is one of offsetting changes in the effects of both economic and demographic factors. It is certainly true that if female headship had not increased, or if incomes had not become more unequal, we would have experienced substantial reductions in poverty. However, it is also true that without the decline in family size and the increased educational attainment of women, child poverty rates would have been substantially higher.

APPENDIX 5A

Our reduced-form model consists of the five following equations for black women and white women in 1968 and 1986.

$$\begin{aligned} H^* &= X\beta_t + \epsilon_h, \\ Pr(H = 1 \mid X) &= PR\,(H^* > 0), \\ &= PR\,(\epsilon_h > -X\beta_t). \end{aligned} \tag{5A.1}$$

$$\begin{aligned} C^* &= X\Gamma_{0t} + \epsilon_{c0} \quad \text{if } H = 0. \\ C^* &= X\Gamma_{1t} + \epsilon_{c1} \quad \text{if } H = 1, \end{aligned} \tag{5A.2}$$

where

$$C = C^* \quad \text{if } C^* \geq 0,$$

and

$$C = 0 \quad \text{if } C^* < 0. \tag{5A.3}$$

$$I = X\Lambda_{0t} + \epsilon_{I0} \quad \text{if } H = 0. \tag{5A.4}$$

$$I = X\Lambda_{1t} + \epsilon_{I1} \quad \text{if } H = 1, \tag{5A.5}$$

where $H = 1$ if the woman is the head of a household, 0 if she is a spouse;

C = the number of own children who reside in the household; and
I = the total family income from all sources and all persons in the household.

Equations (5A.1), (5A.2), and (5A.3) define two latent variables, H^* and C^*, which describe the propensity of a woman to be the head of a household and the latent number of children in her family. Equation (5A.1) gives the probability that a woman is the head of a household in year t as the probability that the latent variable H^* exceeds 0. This probability is given by the cumulative density function (cdf) of ϵ_h evaluated at $-X\beta_t$, which is denoted as Φ_h. Equations (5A.2) and (5A.3), respectively, describe the number of children who would be in two-parent and single-parent households if the number of children were not a truncated variable. Instead, the latent variable C^* is set equal to the actual number of children, C, in two-parent and female-headed families in year t if C^* is non-negative, and 0 otherwise. Equations (5A.4) and (5A.5) model the distribution of total family income for married and female-headed families, respectively, conditional on the variables in X.

We assume that all errors in the underlying structural model are normal random variables. This allows us to estimate Equation (5A.1) as a probit equation and Equations (5A.2) and (5A.3) as Tobit equations.

The fact that we start from a general reduced-form model has two implications for estimation. First, all variables appearing in one equation appear in all other equations. Second, since all stochastic terms in the underlying structural model appear in all the reduced-form equations, we cannot assume that the errors are uncorrelated across equations. This implies that, conditional on observables, headship may be correlated with the number of children a woman has and the income she receives. Together, these two implications suggest that selectivity may be present. However, standard corrections for selectivity are severely limited—without exclusionary restrictions to identify the selection mechanism, the selectivity process can only be identified through functional form.

Rather than using weakly identified corrections for selectivity and concluding that we have properly taken into account nonrandom selectivity in the two family headship categories, we accept the fact that the estimated coefficients may partially reflect selectivity. For example, the coefficient on education in the family income equation for female heads may have increased because the returns to education increased or because unobserved characteristics correlated with education (such as ability) became more important in determining headship. In either case, the structure changed in such a way as to raise the relative income of educated women.

This is consistent with the reduced-form approach, which describes observed changes without trying to identify structural coefficients. When we did estimate income as a switching regression to account for selectivity, we were not able to reject the null hypothesis that there was no selection. Furthermore, the correction had imperceptible effects on the predicted income in the two states. We also tested whether ϵ_c and ϵ_h were correlated by estimating a bivariate probit model. Again, we could not reject the null hypothesis that the errors were uncorrelated.

Equation (5A.1) was estimated over our full sample of women under the age of 55 who were heads of households and spouses. The equations for the number of children and family income were then estimated separately for heads and spouses. These five equations were then estimated in 1968 and 1986, yielding 20 sets of coefficients (five equations for each race for two years), which are available on request from the authors.

The 1968 estimated coefficients were then used to impute to each woman in 1986 the expected probability of marriage, the expected number of children, and the expected income she would have experienced if she had had the average experience of observationally identical women in 1968. These probabilities are obtained by substituting the characteristics of each woman in the 1986 sample into the 1968 coefficients estimated from Equations (5A.1) through (5A.5). More precisely, for individual i in 1986 we calculate the following:

The probability of being a female household head if the process determining headship was the same in 1986 as it had been in 1968:

$$Pr(H_i = 1 \mid X_i) = \Phi_h(-X_i\hat{\beta}_{68}); \tag{5A.6}$$

The probability of having a child if a head or a spouse

$$Pr(C_i > 0 \mid X_i, H_i = 1) = \Phi_c(-X_i\hat{\Gamma}_{1,68}), \tag{5A.7A}$$
$$Pr(C_i > 0 \mid X_i, H_i = 0) = \Phi_c(-X_i\hat{\Gamma}_{0,68}); \text{ and} \tag{5A.7B}$$

The expected number of children if a head or a spouse

$$E(C_i \mid X_i, H_i = 1) = \Phi_c(-X_i\hat{\Gamma}_{1,68})X_i\Gamma\hat{}_{1,68}, \tag{5A.8A}$$
$$E(C_i \mid X_i, H_i = 0) = \Phi_c(-X_i\hat{\Gamma}_{0,68})X_i\Gamma\hat{}_{0,68}. \tag{5A.8B}$$

The predicted number of children in each state is equal to the conditional mean plus a random draw from the estimated distribution of $\hat{\epsilon}_{co}$ or $\hat{\epsilon}_{ci}$. The number of children, not conditional on headship, can then be obtained by weighting the predicted number of children by the probability of being in each headship category, as shown in (5A.6):

$$\hat{C}_i = \Phi_b(-X_i\hat{\beta}_{68})[\Phi_c(-X_i\hat{\Gamma}_{1,68})X_i\hat{\Gamma}_{1,68} + \hat{\epsilon}_{ci}] + [1 - \Phi_b(-X_i\hat{\beta}_{68})][\Phi_c(-X_i\hat{\Gamma}_{0,68})X_i\hat{\Gamma}_{0,68} + \hat{\epsilon}_{co}]. \quad (5A.8C)$$

Likewise, the expected family income of the household, not conditional on marital status, is given by

$$E(I_i|X_i) = \Phi_h(-X_i\hat{\beta}_{68})\,X_i\hat{\Lambda}_{68} + [1 - \Phi_h(-X_i\hat{\beta}_{68})]\,X_i\hat{\Lambda}_{0,68}. \quad (5A.9)$$

And the log variance (conditional on X_i but not marital status) is given by

$$\text{VAR}(I|X_i) = [\Phi_h(-X_i\hat{\beta}_{68})]\sigma^2_{1,68} + [1 - \Phi_h(-X_i\hat{\beta}_{68})]\sigma^2_{0,68}, \quad (5A.10)$$

where $\sigma^2_{1,68}$ $\sigma^2_{0,68}$ are the variances of the family income regressions for heads and spouses, respectively, in 1968.

The probability that the household would have had income less than its family-size specific poverty threshold, T_i, is given as

$$Pr(I_i < T_i\,|\,X_i) = \Phi_h(-X_i\hat{\beta}_{68})\,\Phi_I\left[\frac{T_i - X_i\hat{\Gamma}_{1,68})}{\sigma_{1,68}}\right] + [1 - \Phi_b(-X_i\hat{\beta}_{68})]\,\Phi_I\left[\frac{(T_i - X_i\hat{\Gamma}_{0,68})}{\sigma_{0,68}}\right]. \quad (5A.11)$$

By weighting the predicted probability from Equation (5A.10) by the number of children in each household, we obtain estimates of the child poverty rate.

Thus, this set of equations, estimated with the 1968 data and applied to the entire 1986 sample, yields the child poverty rate that would have existed in 1986 if nothing had changed between 1968 and 1986 except the characteristics of the women.

This research was supported in part by grants from the U.S. Department of Health and Human Services, Office of the Assistant Secretary for Planning and Evaluation, and the Russell Sage Foundation. Sanders Korenman and James Smith provided valuable comments on a previous draft; Jon Haveman, research assistance. Any opinions expressed are those of the authors and not of any sponsoring institution or agency.

References

Burtless, Gary. 1990. "Earnings Inequality Over the Business Cycle." In Burtless, Gary, ed. *A Future of Lousy Jobs?* Washington, D.C.: Brookings Institution.

Connelly, Rachel, and Peter Gottschalk. 1991. "The Effect of Cohort Composition on Human Capital Accumulation Across Generations." Boston College, mimeo.

Danziger, Sheldon. 1989. "Fighting Poverty and Reducing Welfare Dependency." In Cottingham, Phoebe, and David Ellwood, eds. *Welfare Policy for the 1990s.* Cambridge, MA: Harvard University Press.

Danziger, Sheldon, and Peter Gottschalk. 1986. "How Have Families with Children Been Faring?" Institute for Research on Poverty Discussion Paper 801–86, University of Wisconsin-Madison.

Dooley, Martin, and Peter Gottschalk. 1984. "Earnings Inequality Among Males in the United States: Trends and the Effect of Labor Force Growth." *Journal of Political Economy* 92 (February): 59–89.

Gottschalk, Peter, and Sheldon Danziger. 1985. "A Framework for Evaluating the Effects of Economic Growth Transfers on Poverty." *American Economic Review* 75: 153–161.

Henle, Peter, and Paul Ryscavage. 1980. "The Distribution of Earned Income Among Men and Women, 1958–77." *Monthly Labor Review* (April): 3–10.

Lawrence, Robert. 1988. "The International Dimension." In Litan, Robert, Robert Lawrence, and Charles Schultze, eds. *American Living Standards.* Washington, D.C.: Brookings Institution.

Moffitt, Robert. 1990. "The Distribution of Earnings and the Welfare State." In Burtless, Gary, ed. *A Future of Lousy Jobs?* Washington, D.C.: Brookings Institution.

Preston, Samuel H. 1984. "Children and the Elderly: Divergent Paths for America's Dependents." *Demography* 21: 435–457.

Smith, James. 1989. "Children Among the Poor." *Demography* 26: 235–248.

U.S. Bureau of the Census. 1989. *Money Income and Poverty Status in the United States: 1988.* Series P–60, No. 16. Washington, D.C.: U.S. Government Printing Office.

U.S. House of Representatives, Committee on Ways and Means. 1989. *Background Material and Data on Programs within the Jurisdiction of the Committee on Ways and Means.* Washington, D.C.: U.S. Government Printing Office.

6

Working Wives and Family Income Inequality Among Married Couples

Maria Cancian / Sheldon Danziger / Peter Gottschalk

The participation of women, particularly married women, in the labor force has risen rapidly since 1950. As wives' earnings have become a more important source of family income, questions have arisen about their impact on family income inequality. In this chapter, we trace the growth of labor-force participation and earnings for married women over the past two decades, and measure the impact of this growth on the distribution of family income of married couples.

Previous studies have generally found that wives' earnings reduce inequality among couples. Two factors, however, suggest that this may have changed in recent years. First, the participation rate of wives whose husbands have the highest earnings has increased disproportionately. Therefore, a traditional explanation of the equalizing impact of wives' earnings—that wives of men with lower earnings work more than the average wife—may have been reversed. Second, returns to a college education have increased substantially for both men and women. Since men tend to marry women with similar educations, this suggests that the correlation of spouses' earnings may have risen.

In addition to examining changes in the contribution of wives' earnings to inequality, this chapter focuses on the differential impact of white and black wives' earnings. Previous research has shown that wives' labor-force participation and wage rates, the correlation of spouses' earnings, and their distributional effects vary substantially by race.

The distributional impact of married women's labor-force participation depends, in part, on what factors have motivated wives to work. It has been suggested that participation has increased in response to increasing real wages for women (Mincer, 1962; see Killingsworth and Heckman, 1986, for a review). However, Claudia Goldin finds that "supply-side" factors such as "reduced numbers of children, increased probability of divorce, reduced barriers to various occupations, and changes in social norms" have also played an important role (Goldin, 1990, p. 137).

Fuchs cites the expansion of the service sector as another key reason that more wives work. He suggests that these jobs are particularly attractive to married women because they generally do not require physical strength, are more likely to allow for part-time employment, and are more likely to be located near residential areas (1983, pp. 132–133).

A traditional explanation for the increase in two-earner families is the need for wives' earnings to help families "make ends meet." However, increases in wives' work in the 1950s and 1960s are unlikely to have resulted from increasing need, because the real earnings of husbands throughout the wage distribution were rising rapidly at that time. This rationale may have become important after 1973, when real growth in male earnings began to stagnate. Since that time, real wages have actually declined for less-skilled and younger men. The increased labor-force participation of wives in recent years may reflect a desire to offset the disappointing performance of their husbands.[1]

We do not develop a causal model to test the importance of these alternative factors. Rather, we follow a number of previous empirical studies in this area and evaluate the effect of wives' earnings on the distribution of family income among married couples. These studies have generally documented that wives' earnings are equalizing. However, there is less agreement on how the impact varies according to race, and whether the equalizing impact has grown or disappeared in the 1980s.

Smith (1979) analyzed Census data on black and white families in 1960 and 1970. He found that wives' earnings were equalizing for whites in both years; they were somewhat less equalizing for blacks in each year, especially in 1960. Danziger (1980) also found that wives' earnings were equalizing for whites, while they had a negligible effect on inequality among nonwhites. Comparing results from the 1968 and 1975 Current Population Surveys (CPS), he found a slight increase in the equalizing effect over time for both groups. Lehrer and Nerlove (1981; 1984) also found white wives' earnings

[1]Bergmann (1986, p. 130) suggests that couples may feel the need for a second income more to "keep up with the Joneses" than to pay for necessities. As more and more wives work, the extra consumption made possible by a second paycheck may begin to seem necessary.

to be more equalizing than the earnings of black wives.[2] Betson and van der Gaag (1984), using data from the 1968 to 1980 CPS, showed that the equalizing impact of black wives' earnings grew substantially over these years.

In parallel work, Blackburn and Bloom (1990) analyzed CPS data for all married-couple families for the past decade. Their results are consistent with ours, reported below, for whites. They do not disaggregate by race.[3]

Trends in the Labor-Force Participation of Married Women

We analyze data from the March Current Population Survey (CPS) computer tapes for income years 1968, 1973, 1978, 1983, and 1988. This provides five observations over the twenty-year period. We find little cyclicality or variation in wives' participation or earnings at various points in the business cycle. The dominant factor appears to follow a secular trend—the work effort of wives increases continuously, as does the share of family income represented by their earnings.

We restrict our sample to married couples with both spouses present and where both spouses are less than 65 years of age. Data are presented separately for white non-Hispanic and black non-Hispanic couples.[4] Working

[2] Lehrer and Nerlove stress the importance of variation across the life cycle. In particular, while black wives' earnings consistently have less of an equalizing effect, in the period between marriage and child-bearing, wives' earnings actually increase income inequality among black families. CPS data do not allow as precise an analysis of life-cycle variation as the National Survey of Family Growth, used by Lehrer and Nerlove. However, we have examined differences in labor-force participation and wages for married couples with children under six and do not find any major differences between this group and all married couples.

[3] See also Cancian, Danziger, and Gottschalk, 1992. They examine the relative changes in the labor-force participation of married women and female heads of household, and analyze the impact of married women's earnings on both the level and the distribution for all families.

[4] Wives are considered to be "working" if they report positive earnings *and* positive weeks worked. Also note that for 1968, all whites and all blacks are included, whereas for 1973 and later, only whites and blacks not of Hispanic origin are included in the sample. Families were considered "white (black), non-Hispanic" when the husband identified himself as white (black), and as not being of Spanish origin. Married couples include all households where the head identified himself as married, spouse present (married couples with absent spouse in the Armed Forces are included in the sample, for all years except 1988).

We did not attempt to include cohabiting couples. Declines in marriage rates over the period discussed here may be related to increases in cohabitation. However, Bumpass and Sweet (1989) demonstrate that cohabitation is a short-lived state, with a median duration of only 1.3 years. Thus, "despite the high levels of lifetime experience, cohabiting couples are a small proportion of all couples" (1989, p. 620). Moreover, given their short duration, it is questionable whether these unions involve the same economic relationships as marriage. For example, one might expect greater labor-force participation of women who are cohabiting, as these women are presumably less dependent on their partners' earnings.

wives affect inequality among married couples, but they also increase the differences *between* married couples and all other income-receiving units. We do not focus on income inequality for all families or households in this chapter (Blackburn and Bloom, 1987; and Cancian, Danziger, and Gottschalk, 1992, do examine wives' earnings in the context of all families).

The mean annual earnings of wives depends on the percentage of wives who are working, the mean weeks worked, and the mean weekly wages of working wives. We examine each component in turn. These descriptive data anticipate the effects of wives' earnings on family income inequality. In a later section, we formally decompose the change in inequality.

Table 6.1 and Figure 6.1 show the percentage of white and black couples with working wives.[5] For each group, couples are ranked by decile of husbands' earnings.[6] Thus, the first number in Table 6.1 shows that in 1968, 50.3 percent of white wives whose husbands' earnings were in the bottom decile worked at some time during the year. In contrast, only 32.1 percent of the wives whose husbands' earnings were in the highest decile worked.[7]

Over the twenty-year period there have been substantial increases in the percentage of wives working among both white and black couples, regardless of their husbands' place in the earnings distribution. The labor-force participation rate of married women increased from about one-half to about three-quarters among whites, and from about two-thirds to almost four-fifths among blacks. The largest increases for white couples occurred among wives of men in the highest deciles. For example, between 1968 and 1988, the percentage of all working wives went up by about 24 points (from 48.6 to 72.5 percent), but by about 30 points for wives whose husbands were in the top three deciles. Thus, the participation of wives of men with high earnings increased disproportionately. By itself, this would lead to greater inequality.

Black wives were more likely to work in 1988 than in 1968 (78.3 versus 63.9 percent). While black wives continued to work more than whites, the gap has narrowed over time. As Figure 6.1 shows, the percentage of black wives who work has not varied much by decile. Even the wives of black men with the highest earnings have a labor-force participation rate that is quite similar to the average in all years.

[5]Tables that present data on the percentage of wives working, mean weeks worked, and mean weekly wages for white and black couples with children under six are available from the authors on request.

[6]The decile cutoffs are computed separately for whites and blacks for each year. All data analyses reported here use the CPS family weights—each couple is counted once regardless of the number of persons residing in the family. All earnings and incomes are expressed in constant 1988 dollars, using the CPI-X1.

[7]Data for the first decile of husbands' earnings should be interpreted with care. In 1988, for example, 7.2 percent of white husbands and 12.1 percent of black husbands reported zero earnings. Thus, wives in this decile primarily have husbands who do not work.

Table 6.1 Percentage of Wives Working Classified by Husbands' Earnings Decile

	1968	1973	1978	1983	1988
		All White Non-Hispanic Married Couples			
Husbands' Decile					
1	50.3	53.6	50.4	48.6	54.9
2	55.6	60.8	67.8	69.4	76.1
3	54.7	61.9	67.4	69.9	78.4
4	55.0	61.2	69.8	72.0	79.6
5	53.1	56.6	66.8	72.1	77.7
6	52.7	57.2	62.6	68.5	76.7
7	48.3	53.4	62.5	67.7	74.5
8	43.8	51.3	57.4	65.2	71.8
9	39.4	46.1	56.0	61.8	70.8
10	32.1	36.6	43.0	55.8	63.8
Mean	48.6	54.0	60.5	65.3	72.5
		All Black Non-Hispanic Married Couples			
Husbands' Decile					
1	50.2	46.6	54.0	56.5	62.8
2	72.9	64.2	73.0	65.0	71.4
3	67.9	63.9	72.6	67.0	81.4
4	65.4	61.9	68.0	73.3	80.5
5	62.8	67.4	71.9	77.0	81.6
6	57.8	64.5	70.7	73.7	82.0
7	68.1	65.5	79.0	78.8	79.1
8	66.1	69.3	75.9	74.9	84.6
9	63.9	62.6	65.8	73.2	81.7
10	61.0	66.3	67.3	77.3	78.2
Mean	63.9	63.2	70.3	71.5	78.3

Table 6.2 and Figure 6.2 use the same format to show how the mean weeks worked of working wives varies with respect to husbands' earnings in each of the five years.[8] Mean weeks worked increased for white and black wives in all deciles between 1968 and 1988. Once a married woman has begun to work, the number of weeks is relatively invariant with respect to husband's earnings, and, *ceteris paribus*, has very little effect on inequality.

[8]From 1976 forward, weeks worked per year are reported in single weeks in the CPS. Before this, however, data were presented only for the categories 1–13, 14–26, 27–39, 40–47, 48–49, and 50–52 weeks. For these years, we used the within-interval means calculated by Smith and Welch (1989, p. 529).

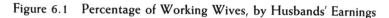

Figure 6.1 Percentage of Working Wives, by Husbands' Earnings

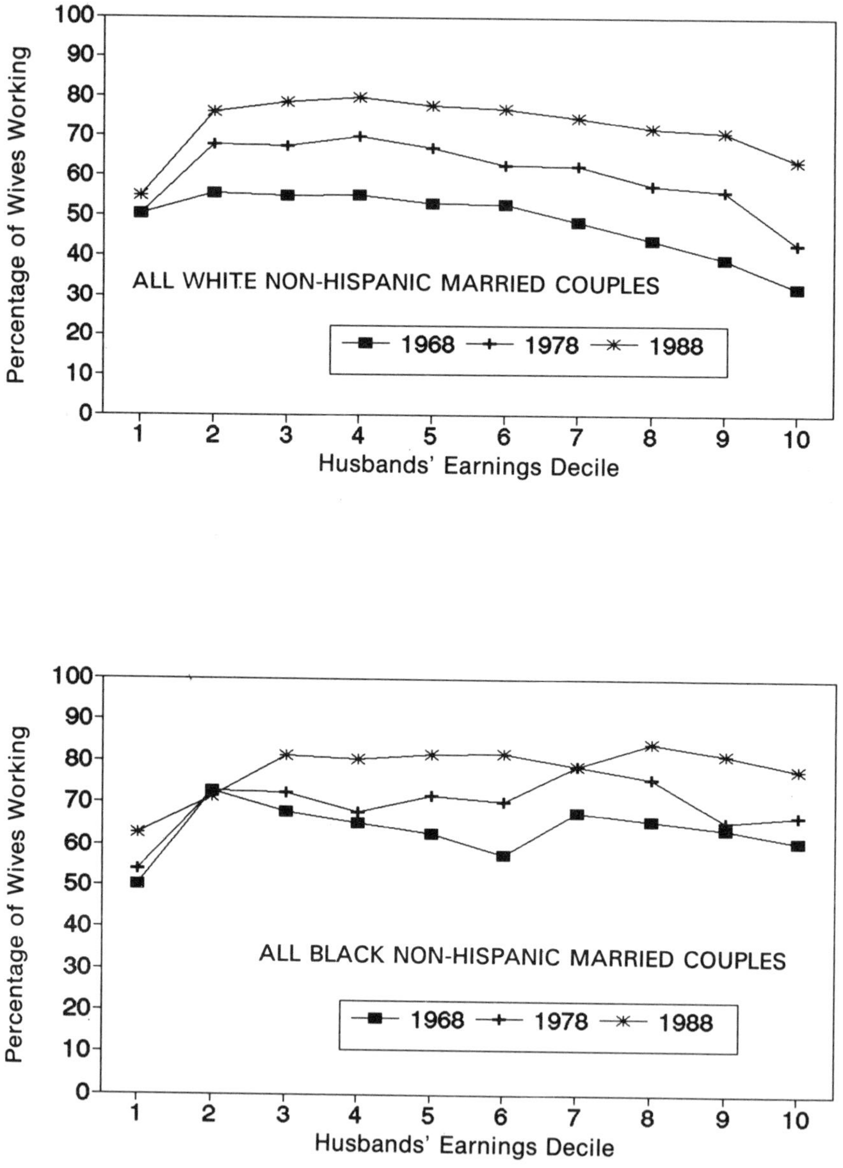

Table 6.2 Mean Weeks Worked by Working Wives Classified by Husbands' Earnings Decile

	1968	1973	1978	1983	1988
	All White Non-Hispanic Married Couples				
Husbands' Decile					
1	39.1	40.0	41.0	43.6	43.3
2	38.4	38.3	38.6	41.0	42.6
3	38.4	39.1	40.7	42.0	43.6
4	39.0	39.5	40.6	42.9	44.3
5	40.3	39.6	42.1	42.9	45.0
6	39.1	38.5	41.1	42.9	45.6
7	38.4	39.5	41.5	43.1	44.8
8	38.7	39.1	40.2	42.6	44.6
9	38.9	38.4	38.8	42.5	44.0
10	39.6	38.4	39.2	42.6	42.5
Mean	39.0	39.0	40.4	42.6	44.1
	All Black Non-Hispanic Married Couples				
Husbands' Decile					
1	38.5	40.9	42.5	45.3	45.5
2	35.8	36.3	39.1	41.4	44.3
3	38.6	36.3	39.9	45.6	42.3
4	38.3	43.6	43.2	41.4	44.3
5	40.1	40.3	42.1	44.7	45.7
6	35.9	39.6	44.1	41.0	45.7
7	41.1	42.1	45.4	46.7	47.4
8	40.4	40.0	44.4	44.9	46.9
9	42.7	44.1	42.3	47.6	46.2
10	42.5	42.2	45.2	45.3	45.2
Mean	39.5	40.4	42.8	44.5	45.4

Table 6.3 and Figure 6.3 present the mean weekly wages of working wives (in constant 1988 dollars), classified by husbands' earnings deciles.[9]

[9]Weekly wages are computed as the ratio of annual earnings to annual weeks worked. Fuchs (1988) found that among married women aged 25 to 64 who worked, 22 percent worked less than 30 hours per week in 1960, while 25 percent worked less than 30 hours per week in 1986. Blank (1989) finds that a similar proportion of all working women worked part-time throughout the 1980s. Thus, the weekly wage figures presented here understate the mean weekly wage for full-time workers. Our analysis of the data presented in Tables 6.1, 6.2, and 6.3 for full-time full-year working wives, however, suggests that the magnitude of this downward bias did not vary substantially over the period considered, and thus should not greatly affect trends in inequality.

Figure 6.2 Mean Weeks Worked by Working Wives

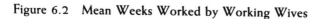

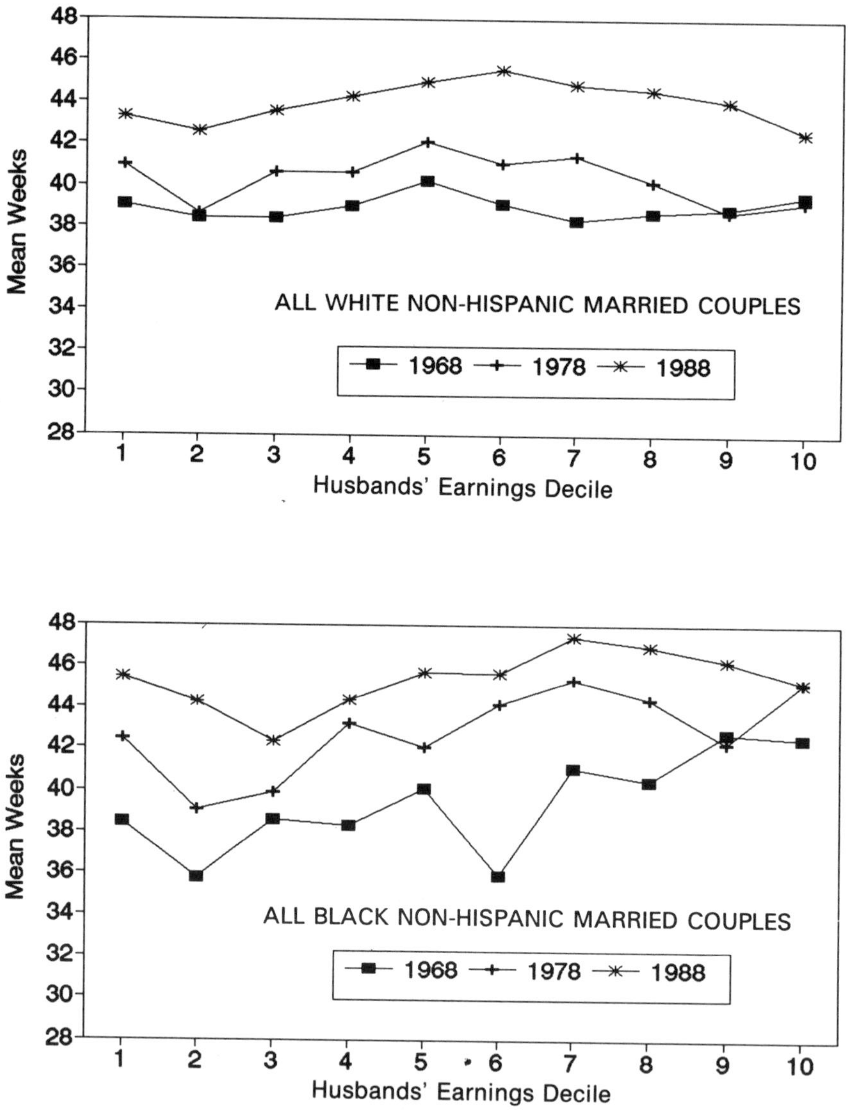

Table 6.3 Mean Weekly Wages of Working Wives[a] Classified by Husbands' Earnings Decile

	1968	1973	1978	1983	1988
	All White Non-Hispanic Married Couples				
Husbands' Decile					
1	231.1	261.7	270.9	282.3	298.7
2	221.7	232.5	236.2	246.0	264.4
3	227.7	243.5	245.7	246.1	270.3
4	234.1	257.7	263.7	254.4	303.1
5	243.1	269.1	272.9	283.3	306.7
6	255.9	269.0	275.1	287.0	330.1
7	254.4	282.4	283.5	299.1	336.0
8	263.6	289.6	278.7	303.8	359.1
9	268.3	294.9	301.0	317.2	374.0
10	304.4	318.5	333.5	379.7	428.8
Mean	246.9	268.3	273.1	287.3	324.6
	All Black Non-Hispanic Married Couples				
Husbands' Decile					
1	160.3	193.8	265.3	257.2	267.8
2	121.4	190.1	221.1	274.6	230.5
3	137.8	177.2	225.8	232.4	235.8
4	145.3	206.1	241.5	235.2	284.8
5	196.0	243.9	239.2	272.0	316.7
6	216.9	269.7	298.1	256.5	320.7
7	218.8	267.6	318.2	318.3	339.9
8	260.2	273.1	320.6	319.9	372.6
9	278.4	343.2	347.1	332.0	417.6
10	325.6	357.3	396.8	402.7	448.2
Mean	205.9	254.2	287.5	293.0	325.8

[a] All dollar figures are in constant 1988 dollars using the CPI-XI.

The wives of higher-earning men have higher wages in every year, but the range of mean wages for wives by husbands' deciles is rather narrow. For whites, the slope has increased over time, as the wages of wives of higher-earning men have risen more rapidly than average. In 1968, the wives of men in the top decile earned about 20 percent more than average; by 1988, they earned about 30 percent more.

Among black couples, there has always been a higher correlation of spouses' earnings than there has for whites, as can be seen by comparing

Figure 6.3 Mean Weekly Wages of Working Wives

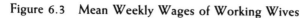

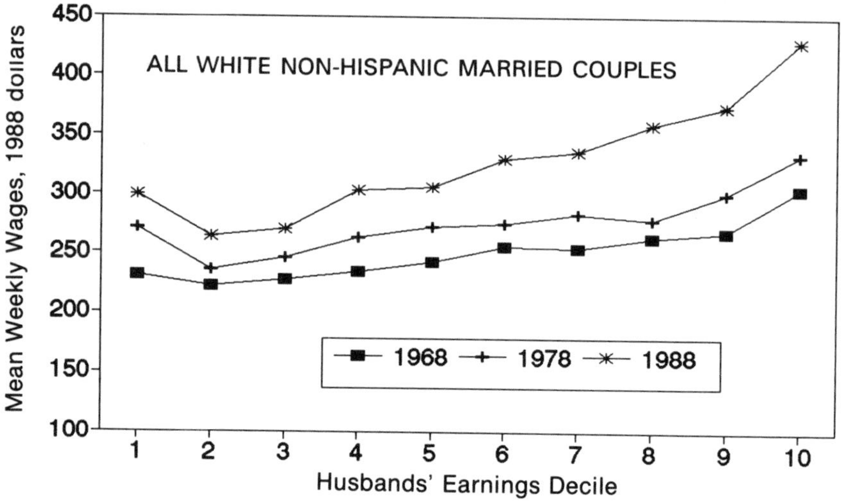

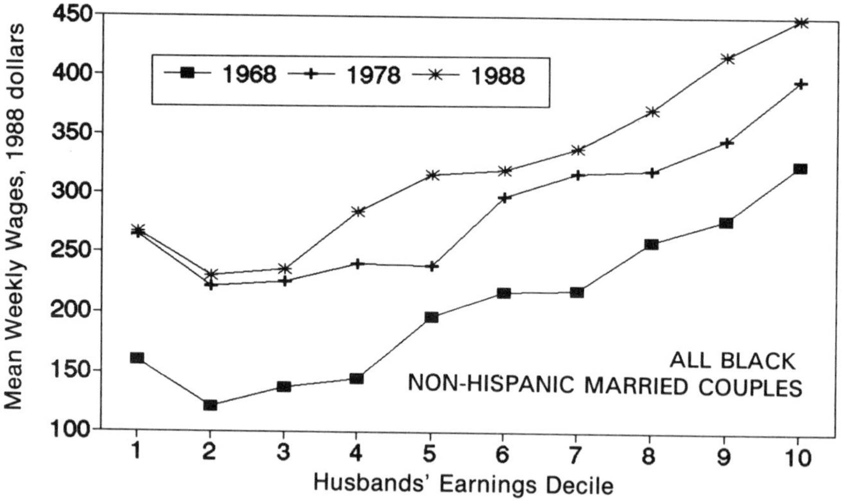

the slopes of the lines in the top and bottom panels of Figure 6.3. But, over time, this positive relationship has weakened. The wives of blacks in the top decile earned about 60 percent above average in 1968, but only about 38 percent above average in 1988.

The Contribution of Wives' Earnings to the Level and Distribution of Family Income

Effects on Mean Family Income

Married women's labor-force participation has increased substantially over the past twenty years, both in terms of the percentage of wives who work, and the mean weeks worked by those who work. At the same time, married women's real weekly earnings have also risen. These factors have combined to make wives' earnings an increasingly important source of family income.

Table 6.4 shows mean family income (in constant 1988 dollars) for all married couples and for those with working wives in 1968, 1978, and 1988. Total family income is divided into three mutually exclusive categories—husbands' earnings, wives' earnings, and a residual category that includes all other income sources (mainly property income, government cash transfers, and the earnings of other family members).[10]

The contribution of wives' earnings to total family income increased for both whites and blacks over the two decades. In 1968, wives' earnings constituted about 14 percent of total family income for white couples; by 1988, this was up to about 22 percent. Black wives' contribution also increased, from about 22 percent to about 31 percent over the same period.

In 1968, the mean earnings of white husbands whose wives worked was about $2,000 lower ($23,560 versus $25,726) than the mean for all husbands. But, by the 1980s, this was no longer the case. Black husbands with working wives had mean earnings similar to those of all black husbands in each of the years shown.

Total family income growth and growth in husbands' earnings were greater in the 1968 to 1978 period than in the following decade. For white couples, total family income grew by 20 and 14 percent in the successive decades; for blacks, by 35 and 13 percent. For white husbands, earnings grew by 11 and 4 percent; for black husbands, by 23 and 4 percent.

The last two columns of Table 6.4 allocate the total change in family income (the absolute difference between 1968 and 1978 and between 1978

[10] Negative incomes reported for any income source were set equal to zero.

Table 6.4 Mean Family Income of Married Couples, by Source[a]

	1968	1978	1988	Percentage of Change in Total Family Income Due to Each Income Source 1968–1978	1978–1988
All White Married Couples					
Total family income	$34,014	$40,725	$46,490	100	100
Husbands' earnings	25,726	28,496	29,625	41	20
Wife's earnings	4,719	6,692	10,382	29	64
Other income	3,569	5,537	6,483	29	16
Percentage due to wives' earnings	13.9	16.4	22.3	—	—
White Couples, Wife Works					
Total family income	36,232	42,844	49,267	100	100
Husbands' earnings	23,560	27,025	29,282	52	35
Wife's earnings	9,435	11,047	14,311	24	51
Other income	3,237	4,772	5,673	23	14
Percentage due to wives' earnings	26.0	25.8	29.0	—	—
All Black Married Couples					
Total family income	24,306	32,789	37,093	100	100
Husbands' earnings	16,060	19,732	20,560	43	19
Wife's earnings	5,260	8,665	11,658	40	70
Other income	2,987	4,392	4,875	17	11
Percentage due to wives' earnings	21.6	26.4	31.4	—	—
Black Couples, Wife Works					
Total family income	26,696	36,386	40,671	100	100
Husbands' earnings	16,014	20,065	21,316	42	29
Wife's earnings	8,039	12,305	14,778	44	58
Other income	2,642	4,016	4,577	14	13
Percentage due to wives' earnings	30.1	33.8	36.3	—	—

[a] All dollar figures are in constant 1988 dollars using the CPI-XI. The percentage due to wives' earnings is defined as (mean wives' earnings/mean total family income) × 100.

and 1988) into changes attributable to each of the three income sources. For both white and black couples, growth in husbands' earnings was the most important factor in the 1968 to 1978 decade, accounting for 41 and 43 percent of the growth in family income. White wives accounted for 29 percent; black wives, for 40 percent. In the 1978 to 1988 period, however, the situation was reversed. Wives' earnings were, by far, the most important factor, accounting for 64 percent and 70 percent of family income growth for white and black couples, respectively.

Married women experienced substantial wage growth between 1968 and 1988, as mean weekly wages grew by about 30 percent for white wives and 60 percent for black wives. Over the same period, the percentage of wives working increased by about 25 percentage points for whites, and 15 percentage points for blacks; mean weeks worked by working wives rose five to six weeks for both whites and blacks. Thus, the more than doubling of mean annual earnings of married women over the twenty-year period is a result of substantial increases in participation and wages, with increased participation a more important factor for whites, and wage gains more important for blacks.

Effects on Inequality of Family Income

The increased labor-force participation and earnings of wives raised the mean income of married couples. What were their effects on income inequality? To answer this question, we follow several recent studies (for example, Lehrer and Nerlove, 1981; Schrim, 1988; and Blackburn and Bloom, 1990), and adopt as our summary measure of inequality the squared coefficient of variation (CV^2). Given three income sources, the CV^2 can be expressed:

$$C_f^2 = a^2C_h^2 + b^2C_w^2 + c^2C_r^2 + 2p_{hw}abC_hC_w + 2p_{hr}acC_hC_r + 2p_{wr}bcC_wC_r, \text{ where}$$

C_f, C_h, C_w, C_r = coefficient of variation of family income, husbands' earnings, wives' earnings, and residual income.

p_{hw}, p_{hr}, p_{wr} = correlation coefficient between spouses' earnings, between husbands' earnings and residual income, and between wives' earnings and residual income.

$a = \mu_h/\mu_f$ (mean husbands' earnings as a proportion of mean family income).

$b = \mu_w/\mu_f$.

$c = \mu_r/\mu_f$.[11]

[11] The squared coefficient of variation is defined as the variance divided by the squared

Inequality of total family income can thus be expressed as a weighted average of the inequality of each income source and the correlations among the sources. The weights correspond to the proportion of total income from each source.

The data presented thus far suggest that wives' earnings have become an increasingly important source of family income, and that changes in wives' labor-force participation and wages have varied substantially by race and husbands' earnings. In order to gauge the impact of these changes on the distribution of income among married couples, we describe changes in the dispersion of each income source and the correlations among the sources. We then present a decomposition of the trend in inequality.

Table 6.5 shows the squared coefficient of variation (CV^2) of total income and of each of the three income sources for white and black couples from 1968 to 1988.[12] Inequality of family income declined between 1968 and 1978, and then increased by a greater amount between 1978 and 1988. The trends for the three income sources vary both among themselves and over time.

For all white married couples, the CV^2 of wives' earnings fell by more than 20 percent during each decade, from 2.300 in 1968 to 1.347 in 1988. This drop is primarily attributable to increased labor-force participation, rather than a more equal distribution of earnings among working wives. That is, many fewer wives had zero earnings in 1988 than 1968. In fact, the CV^2 of wives' earnings for working wives (which excludes the zero earners) actually rose over this period, from 0.645 to 0.702.

For blacks, the large decline in the CV^2 of wives' earnings among all couples in each decade reflects both an increased percentage of wives working, and a more equal distribution of earnings among working wives. The CV^2 of wives' earnings for all black couples fell from 1.633 to 0.893, while the CV^2 among working wives declined from 0.724 to 0.488.

---

arithmetic mean. It is preferable to variance as an inequality measure because it is scale independent. And, unlike the variance of the logarithm of income, another inequality measure that is scale independent, the coefficient of variation is equally sensitive to transfers at all income levels (Kakwani, 1980, p. 87). For a discussion of the relative merits of these and other measures of income distribution see Kakwani (1980), especially Chapter 5.

[12] Between 1968 and 1988 the percentage of all white households categorized as "married, spouse present" fell from 76 to 57 percent. For black households, the percentage was much lower to begin with, and it fell further, from 54 to 33 percent. Thus, our analysis of the effects of wives' earnings on the distribution of income among married couples captures only part of the effect of changes in women's earnings. For example, the increasing earnings of women may have encouraged later marriages or higher divorce rates. If so, the married couples from our 1968 sample would not represent the same population as our 1988 sample's married couples. For further discussion of trends in labor-force participation of married and unmarried women, and the implications of selection for trends among married women, see Cancian, Danziger, and Gottschalk (1992).

Table 6.5 Squared Coefficient of Variation of Total Family Income and Each Source

				Percentage of Change	
	1968	1978	1988	1968–1978	1978–1988
All White Married Couples					
Total family income	0.372	0.321	0.377	−13.7	17.4
Husbands' earnings	0.451	0.437	0.528	−3.1	20.7
Wives' earnings	2.300	1.793	1.347	−22.0	−24.9
Other income	5.447	3.661	3.647	−32.8	−0.4
White Couples, Wife Works					
Total family income	0.273	0.266	0.331	−2.8	24.5
Husbands' earnings	0.373	0.376	0.472	0.8	25.6
Wives' earnings	0.645	0.691	0.702	7.1	1.7
Other income	4.529	3.853	4.032	−14.9	4.7
All Black Married Couples					
Total family income	0.356	0.355	0.379	−0.3	7.0
Husbands' earnings	0.406	0.435	0.615	7.2	41.3
Wives' earnings	1.633	1.159	0.893	−29.0	−22.9
Other income	4.502	3.926	3.098	−12.8	−21.1
Black Couples, Wife Works					
Total family income	0.306	0.304	0.311	−0.7	2.3
Husbands' earnings	0.351	0.389	0.560	10.9	43.9
Wives' earnings	0.724	0.522	0.488	−27.9	−6.4
Other income	4.973	4.459	3.317	−10.3	−25.6

Table 6.5 also shows an increase in the CV^2 of husbands' earnings. For whites, the CV^2 of earnings rose from 0.451 to 0.528 between 1968 and 1988, with all of the increase coming after 1978. For blacks, the total percentage of increase was much larger, and inequality grew during each decade. The CV^2 of husbands' earnings rose from 0.406 to 0.615 between 1968 and 1988.

The CV^2 of the residual income category is very high for both blacks and whites in each year because many couples received no income from these other sources. However, inequality in this source, like that of wives' earnings, declined substantially over the period.

Table 6.6 shows that over the past twenty years there has been a substantial increase in the correlation of spouses' earnings for whites. This has been driven by increased labor-force participation and substantial wage increases, especially among women with high-earning husbands. The correlation of spouses' earnings rose from −0.044 to 0.091 for all white married couples.

Table 6.6 Correlation of Spouses' Earnings

	1968	1978	1988
White Couples			
All married couples	−0.044	−0.012	0.091
Couples with working wives	0.101	0.085	0.155
Black Couples			
All married couples	0.221	0.210	0.247
Couples with working wives	0.393	0.308	0.259

This increase reflects the increased labor-force participation of white wives, as well as an increase in the correlation of spousal earnings for couples with a wife who works, from 0.101 to 0.155.[13]

A somewhat different picture emerges for black couples. The correlation of black spouses' earnings is considerably higher than that of white spouses, for all couples and for the subset with working wives. However, while the correlation of earnings increased sharply for whites, it rose only modestly among all black couples, from 0.221 to 0.247. The correlation among black couples with working wives fell substantially, from 0.393 to 0.259.

The correlations of spouses' earnings shown in Table 6.6 are, however, still small compared to other measures of assortative mating. For example, the correlation of spouses' years of education is more than 0.60 for blacks and whites and has been relatively stable over these two decades (data not shown, but available from the authors).

One common measure of the impact of wives' earnings on family income inequality is the percentage of change in income inequality due to wives' earnings. Table 6.7 shows the percentage of change in the CV^2 and the Gini coefficient due to the inclusion of wives' earnings; that is, the distribution of family income is compared to what it would have been if the earnings of

[13] Smith (1979) analyzes differences in the correlation coefficient by race and work status; Lehrer and Nerlove (1981) discuss differences by life-cycle stage as well. These authors find that white spouses' earnings are less correlated than those of black spouses, though the gap narrows when the analysis is limited to families with working wives. In addition, Lehrer and Nerlove find considerable variation in correlation coefficients over the life cycle, especially for whites. Blackburn and Bloom (1990) discuss changes over time in the correlation coefficient for all married couples, and analyze the causes of these changes. See Shaw (1992) for a discussion of the implications of life-cycle variation. See Schrim (1988) for a detailed analysis of the role of the correlation coefficient in determining the CV^2, and a review of empirical estimates of the correlation coefficient.

Table 6.7 Percentage Change in the CV^2 and Gini Coefficient of Total Family Income Due to Wives' Earnings

	1968	1978	1988
	All White Couples		
CV^2 of			
Total family income	0.372	0.321	0.377
Total less wives' earnings	0.455	0.398	0.485
Percentage change	−18.1	−19.5	−22.1
Gini coefficient of			
Total family income	0.300	0.301	0.324
Total less wives' earnings	0.320	0.329	0.357
Percentage change	−6.2	−8.5	−9.4
	All Black Couples		
CV^2 of			
Total family income	0.356	0.355	0.379
Total less wives' earnings	0.374	0.395	0.482
Percentage change	−4.8	−10.2	−21.2
Gini coefficient of			
Total family income	0.322	0.308	0.337
Total less wives' earnings	0.320	0.320	0.367
Percentage change	0.8	−3.8	−8.2

all wives had been zero, and husbands' earnings did not respond to wives' labor-force participation or earnings.[14]

According to this measure, white wives have had a relatively stable impact on family income inequality, reducing the CV^2 by about 20 percent and the Gini coefficient by about 9 percent over the two decades. This suggests that the increased correlation coefficient of spouses' earnings has been offset by the fall in the CV^2 of wives' earnings and the increased share of total income earned by wives. Thus, there is little support for the view that wives' earnings are responsible for the increase in inequality of family income.

For blacks, the equalizing impact of wives' earnings has risen substantially. The earnings of black wives reduced the CV^2 by only about 4 percent in 1968, but by about 21 percent in 1988. Their earnings had a negligible impact on the Gini coefficient in 1968, but reduced it by about 8 percent in

[14]The percentage change in CV^2 (Gini) due to wives' earnings is calculated by computing the CV^2 (Gini) of total income less wives' earnings, and comparing this with the CV^2 (Gini) of total income.

1988. The increased equalizing impact of black wives' earnings reflects the modest increase in the correlation coefficient being offset by the fall in the CV^2 of wives' earnings.

The calculations in Table 6.7 represent a rather crude measure of the impact of wives on the distribution of total family income in any year, because the implicit counterfactual is a world in which wives do not work and their husbands' earnings are not responsive to changes in wives' labor-force participation or earnings. A more realistic scenario measures the impact of *changes* in wives' earnings, by comparing inequality of family income measured at the current level and distribution of wives' earnings with the inequality that would have existed had the level and distribution of wives' earnings remained at levels from an earlier year. Again, the assumption is that husbands' earnings do not respond to the changes in wives' earnings, but the changes in wives' earnings are less extreme.[15]

Because the CV^2 of total family income can be readily decomposed, as shown above, we can measure the impact of changes between any two years in the level and distribution of any income source on inequality. We focus on three groups of income components:[16]

- Group (1) changes in the level and distribution of income sources other than wives' earnings (the sum of the effects of mean husbands' earnings, CV^2 of husbands' earnings, mean residual income, CV^2 of residual income, and correlation of husbands' earnings and residual income);
- Group (2) changes in the level and distribution of wives' earnings (the sum of the effects of mean wives' earnings and CV^2 of wives' earnings); and
- Group (3) changes in the correlation of wives' earnings and other income sources (the sum of the effects of correlation of wives' earnings with husbands' earnings and with the residual income source).

The first group contains changes in the level and distribution of income sources other than wives' earnings, and the correlation across these sources; the second group includes the effects of changes in the level and distribution of wives' earnings; the third includes the correlation of wives' earnings and the other sources.

We begin our decomposition by substituting the 1988 value for one of the groups of components, leaving all other components at their 1968 values.

[15]These two alternative counterfactuals give different decompositions, since the impact of changes in other sources of income depends on the level of earnings of the wife.

[16]The contributions of each of the individual components are shown in Appendix 6A.

Table 6.8 Changes in the Squared Coefficient of Variation of Total Family Income Due to Changes in:

	(1) The Level and Distribution of Income Sources Other than Wives' Earnings	(2) The Level and Distribution of Wives' Earnings	(3) The Correlation of Wives' Earnings and Other Income Sources	(4) Actual Change in Inequality (1) + (2) + (3)
White Married Couples				
1968–1978	−0.039	−0.016	0.003	−0.052
1978–1988	0.062	−0.030	0.025	0.057
1968–1988	0.029	−0.053	0.028	0.005
Black Married Couples				
1968–1978	0.006	−0.019	0.012	−0.001
1978–1988	0.054	−0.028	−0.001	0.025
1968–1988	0.072	−0.058	0.009	0.024

The difference between the CV^2 in 1968 and the CV^2 with the first set of components changed is the impact attributed to the change in that group of components. We then change the second set of components, calculating the CV^2 with the first and second sets at their 1988 values, and all other components at their 1968 values. The difference between the CV^2 with just the first set of components changed and the CV^2 with the components of both the first and second groups changed is the impact attributed to the change in the second group. We continue this process, each time changing one additional set of components.

The advantage of this method is that the sum of changes attributed to the individual components equals the total change over time. The principle disadvantage of the approach is that order matters.[17] For example, the estimated impact of the change in the distribution of wives' earnings will differ depending on whether it is the first, second, or later component that is changed.

Table 6.8 presents the results of the decomposition in which all the components in Group 1 are changed first, then those in Group 2, and finally

[17] Blackburn and Bloom (1990) use an alternative approach, attributing to each factor the change caused by changing that factor alone, while leaving all others at their base-year values. In this case, order is irrelevant. The disadvantage of their approach is that the sum of changes over all factors does not equal the total change. Over the period they analyzed, the discrepancy is relatively minor. However, in some cases, including the period analyzed here, the sum of individual changes will be many times the actual total change. See Appendix 6B.

those in Group 3. Alternative orders are shown in Appendix 6A, Table 6A.1, with the order indicated in the first column.[18]

For both white and black married couples, we decompose the change in the CV^2 between 1968 and 1978, between 1978 and 1988, and over the entire twenty-year period. For whites, changes in the level and distribution of wives' earnings (Group 2) were equalizing in both periods, primarily due to the decline in the CV^2 of wives' earnings. However, as can be seen in the third column, the increased correlation of wives' earnings and other income sources (Group 3) was inequality increasing, especially in the second period. This increase is entirely due to the increased correlation of spouses' earnings. This factor alone accounted for a 0.025 increase in the CV^2 compared to a 0.045 impact of inequality of husbands' earnings between 1978 and 1988 (see Table 6A.1).

Changes in the level and distribution of the other sources of income (Group 1) were equalizing between 1968 and 1978. However, changes in these income sources increased inequality of total family income substantially between 1978 and 1988. In the first period, the equalizing impact can be attributed primarily to a fall in the CV^2 of residual income and a declining correlation of husbands' earnings and residual income. In the second period, the increased inequality is driven by the substantial rise in the CV^2 of husbands' earnings.

For black married couples, changes in the level and distribution of wives' earnings were equalizing in both periods, due to the falling CV^2 of wives' earnings. Changes in the other income sources (Column 1 of Table 6.8) had relatively little impact in the earlier period. However, between 1978 and 1988, they accounted for a substantial increase in income inequality. This increase was almost completely due to the rise in the CV^2 of husbands' earnings. The change in the correlation between husbands' earnings and wives' earnings (Column 3) had almost no impact.

Table 6.8 shows how recent actual changes in the level and distribution of wives' earnings have affected the distribution of family income for couples. Together with the results of Table 6.7, this documents that working wives continue to equalize the distribution of income for couples. But will further increases in labor-force participation and further increases in the correlation between husbands' and wives' earnings reverse these results?

[18] Within each group, components are changed in the same order each time, as indicated in the first column in Table 6A.1. The impact of each component within the group depends in part on the order of change. However, the impact attributed to the group as a whole will be the same, regardless of the order in which components *within* the group are changed.

There is some variation in the estimates of impact due to each group of components, depending on the order in which they are changed. Nevertheless, the overall pattern of effects is consistent with our interpretations of the descriptive tables presented above.

We attempt to estimate the impact of further increases in married women's labor-force participation and further increases in the correlation of spouses' earnings using a methodology similar to that used in Table 6.8. We first ask, "How would the distribution of family income change if all wives worked?" Obviously, any such simulation is dependent on the assumptions made. We assume that the additional wives entering the labor force would have the same level and distribution of earnings as wives who worked in 1988. Further we assume that the mean and CV^2 of husbands' earnings and residual income would equal that of all families (those with working and nonworking wives) in 1988. Finally, we assume that the correlation coefficients for wives' earnings and husbands' earnings, and for wives' earnings and residual income, would have their 1988 values for the subsample of couples with working wives.

When we simulate the CV^2 of total family income based on these assumptions, we estimate that if all wives worked, the CV^2 of total family income would fall from 0.377 to 0.342 for whites, and from 0.380 to 0.319 for blacks. This suggests that further increases in labor-force participation of married women are unlikely to become inequality increasing.

The preceding simulation assumed that the correlation between the earnings of husbands and working wives stayed constant at its 1988 value. As we saw earlier, however, there has been an upward drift of this correlation for whites. We now simulate the following. We assume that as wives' participation increases to 100 percent, the correlation increases as well. We now ask, "How high must the correlation rise to offset the inequality reduction shown in the prior simulation?" That is, what would the correlation have to be for the simulated CV^2 to remain at the current 1988 values of 0.377 for whites and 0.380 for blacks? We find that the correlation would have to more than double (from 0.155 to 0.334 for whites, and from 0.259 to 0.556 for blacks) before the increased participation of wives would become disequalizing. Changes of this magnitude are unlikely since, over the past two decades, the correlation of spouses' earnings for couples with working wives increased only from 0.101 to 0.155 for whites, and actually decreased for blacks (see Table 6.6). Therefore, unless we experience historically large increases in the correlation between husbands' and wives' earnings, we expect that wives' earnings will continue to be an equalizing factor.

Conclusions

Income inequality among couples increased over the past twenty years and would have increased to an even greater extent were it not for the increased earnings of wives. For white wives, the disproportionate increase in labor-force participation of "rich" wives has contributed to an increased correlation of spouses' earnings. However, the general increase in labor-force participation has substantially reduced the CV^2 of wives' earnings and raised the share of total income earned by wives. The net effect is that white wives' earnings continue to equalize the distribution of family income.

Black wives' earnings have become increasingly important in equalizing family income during a period of sharp rises in the inequality of husbands' earnings. Over the period when the CV^2 of black husbands' earnings rose from 0.406 to 0.615, the CV^2 of wives' earnings fell from 1.622 to 0.893. At the same time, the correlation of spouses' earnings rose relatively little. These factors, combined with the increasing share of total income derived from wives' earnings, caused the equalizing impact of wives' earnings to grow dramatically.

There has been concern that recent changes in the pattern of labor-force participation and wages of married women would cause wives' earnings to be less equalizing or even to increase inequality. We find no evidence for such a concern. The data discussed above suggest that the equalizing impact of wives' earnings has grown slightly for whites and substantially for blacks. Our analysis is consistent with previous studies, which suggested that black wives' earnings were less equalizing than white wives' earnings in the 1960s and early 1970s. However, our results indicate that in the 1980s the difference between the equalizing impact of black and white wives' earnings disappeared.

While the net effect of wives' earnings continues to be equalizing, it is important to recognize that other factors have contributed to offsetting the increased correlation between the earnings of husbands and wives. By itself, the increased correlation would have had an impact about half as large as that of the increased inequality of husbands' earnings. Substantial effort has been directed toward understanding the causes of increased inequality of male earnings. Our results suggest that it would be appropriate to focus additional effort toward understanding the causes of the increased correlation between husbands' and wives' earnings.

APPENDIX 6A

The following table gives a full breakdown of the summary measure shown in Table 6.8. Within each group the components are changed in the order listed.

Table 6A.1 Changes in the Squared Coefficient of Variation of Total Family Income Due to Changes in:

Order of Groups	(1) The Level and Distribution of Income Sources Other than Wives' Earnings						(2) The Level and Distribution of Wives' Earnings			(3) The Correlation of Wives' Earnings and Other Income Sources		
	Mean *H*	*CV(H)*	Mean *R*	*CV(R)*	*p(H,R)*	Total	Mean *W*	*CV(W)*	Total	*p(H,W)*	*p(W,R)*	Total
White Married Couples												
1968–1978												
1,2,3	−0.003	−0.009	0.038	−0.041	−0.025	−0.039	−0.003	−0.013	−0.016	0.006	−0.003	0.003
1,3,2	−0.003	−0.009	0.038	−0.041	−0.025	−0.039	−0.002	−0.013	−0.015	0.006	−0.003	0.003
1978–1988												
1,2,3	−0.001	0.045	0.006	−0.000	0.013	0.062	−0.009	−0.021	−0.030	0.025	0.000	0.025
1,3,2	−0.001	0.045	0.006	−0.000	0.013	0.062	−0.002	−0.025	−0.027	0.022	0.000	0.022
1968–1988												
1,2,3	−0.004	0.048	0.052	−0.051	−0.016	0.029	−0.008	−0.044	−0.053	0.032	−0.004	0.028
1,3,2	−0.004	0.048	0.052	−0.051	−0.016	0.029	0.007	−0.053	−0.046	0.025	−0.003	0.022
Black Married Couples												
1968–1978												
1,2,3	−0.013	0.015	0.014	−0.011	0.001	0.006	0.023	−0.042	−0.019	−0.002	0.014	0.012
1,3,2	−0.013	0.015	0.014	−0.011	0.001	0.006	0.027	−0.044	−0.018	−0.002	0.013	0.011
1978–1988												
1,2,3	−0.003	0.074	0.003	−0.016	−0.003	0.054	0.007	−0.036	−0.028	0.010	−0.010	−0.001
1,3,2	−0.003	0.074	0.003	−0.016	−0.003	0.054	0.007	−0.035	−0.028	0.010	−0.010	−0.001
1968–1988												
1,2,3	−0.015	0.114	0.006	−0.031	−0.002	0.072	0.035	−0.093	−0.058	0.007	0.003	0.009
1,3,2	−0.015	0.114	0.006	−0.031	−0.002	0.072	0.039	−0.096	−0.057	0.006	0.002	0.008

APPENDIX 6B

Decomposing the Change Over Time in CV^2

Consider total income from two sources, h and w. The distribution of total income can be characterized by its squared coefficient of variation, C^2, which can be decomposed:

$$C^2 = a^2C_h^2 + b^2C_w^2 + 2abC_hC_w\rho, \tag{6B.1}$$

where C_h = coefficient of variation of source one,
C_w = coefficient of variation of source two,

$$a = \frac{\mu_h}{(\mu_h + \mu_w)},$$

$$b = \frac{\mu_w}{(\mu_h + \mu_w)}, \text{ and}$$

ρ = correlation of income sources.

For two periods, t and $t+1$, we have two income distributions characterized by C_t^2 and C_{t+1}^2. For period $t+1$, the decomposition of Equation (6B.1) may also be represented:

$$\begin{aligned} C_{t+1}^2 = {} & (a + \Delta a)^2(C_h + \Delta C_h)^2 + (b + \Delta b)^2(C_w + \Delta C_w)^2 \\ & + 2(a + \Delta a)(b + \Delta b)(C_h + \Delta C_h)(C_w + \Delta C_w)(\rho + \Delta\rho). \end{aligned} \tag{6B.2}$$

If we expand Equation 6B.2, we get a complex expression, which includes the terms contained in Equation (6B.1) in addition to many other terms. In order to better understand the change in C^2 between t and $t+1$, we would like a decomposition or simulation of that change that organizes all these terms in an intuitive way.

One alternative is to change one component at a time. One can then attribute to each component the change resulting from changing that component while all other components remain unchanged.[1]

If $C_t^2(X_{t+1})$ is the squared coefficient of variation of total income calculated with all components having their time t value except X, then this method suggests:

$$\begin{aligned} C_{t+1}^2 \overset{?}{=} {} & C_t^2 + (C_t^2(C_{h,t+1}) - C_t^2) + (C_t^2(C_{w,t+1}) - C_t^2) \\ & + (C_t^2(a_{t+1},b_{t+1}) - C_t^2) + (C_t^2(\rho_{t+1}) - C_t^2). \end{aligned} \tag{6B.3}$$

[1] See Blackburn and Bloom (1990).

However, the right-hand side of Equation (6B.3) is missing a number of terms. In other words, when the change due to each component is computed as above, the sum of the individual changes will not necessarily equal the total change.[2]

Alternatively, we can change the components sequentially, attributing to each component the change resulting from changing that component in addition to any previous changes.

If $C_t^2(X_{t+1}^1, X_{t+1}^2, \ldots, X_{t+1})$ is the squared coefficient of variation of total income calculated with components $1, \ldots, k$ having their time $t + 1$ value, and all other components have their time t value, this method suggests:

$$\begin{aligned} C_{t+1}^2 &= C_t^2 + [C_t^2(C_{h,t+1}) - C_t^2] \\ &\quad + [C_t^2(C_{h,t+1}, C_{w,t+1}) - C_t^2(C_{h,t+1})] \qquad (6B.4) \\ &\quad + [C_t^2(C_{h,t+1}, C_{w,t+1}, a_{t+1}, b_{t+1}) - C_t^2(C_{h,t+1}, C_{w,t+1})] \\ &\quad + [C_t^2(C_{h,t+1}, C_{w,t+1}, a_{t+1}, b_{t+1}, \rho_{t+1}) - C_t^2(C_{h,t+1}, C_{w,t+1}, a_{t+1}, b_{t+1})], \\ &\qquad \text{where the first } [\ldots] \text{ is due to } \Delta C_h, \text{ the second} \\ &\qquad \text{is due to } \Delta C_w, \text{ and so forth,} \\ &= C_t^2(C_{h,t+1}, C_{w,t+1}, a_{t+1}, b_{t+1}, \rho_{t+1}), \\ &= C_{t+1}^2. \end{aligned}$$

When the change due to each component is computed in this way, the sum of individual changes will equal the total change.

However, a disadvantage of this method is that the change in the squared coefficient of variation of total income attributed to each component will depend on the order in which components are changed. All the terms of the expansion of Equation (6B.2) are captured by the right-hand side of Equation (6B.4). But some of these terms may be attributed to changes in different components, depending on the order in which components are changed.[3]

Jon Haveman and Cathy Sun provided computational assistance; Gregory Acs, Jon Bound, Gary Burtless, Laura Dresser, Sanders Korenman, Robert Schoeni, and Matthew Shapiro provided helpful comments on earlier drafts.

[2] In some cases, including the period examined by Blackburn and Bloom (1990), the discrepancy will be relatively minor. In other cases, including the periods examined in here, the discrepancy will be quite large.

[3] Blackburn and Bloom change components one at a time, but use two alternative "orders": setting all components to time t, and changing one component to time $t+1$; and setting all components to time $t+1$ and changing one component to time t. This is equivalent to changing the component first and last in a sequential simulation. Unfortunately, this approach will not generally yield the upper and lower bounds for the change attributable to the component.

References

Bergmann, Barbara R. 1986. *The Economic Emergence of Women.* New York: Basic Books.

Bergmann, Barbara R., et al. 1980. "The Effect of Wives' Labor Force Participation on Inequality in the Distribution of Family Income." *Journal of Human Resources* 15:452–456.

Betson, David, and Jacques van der Gaag. 1984. "Working Married Women and the Distribution of Income." *Journal of Human Resources* 19:532–543.

Blackburn, McKinley, and David Bloom. 1987. "Earnings and Income Inequality in the United States." *Population and Development Review* 13:575–609.

———. 1990. "Changes in the Structure of Family Income Inequality in the U.S. and Other Industrialized Nations During the 1980s." Unpublished paper.

Blank, Rebecca. 1989. "The Role of Part-Time Work in Women's Labor Market Choices Over Time." *American Economic Review* 79 (2):295–299.

Bumpass, Larry, and James Sweet. 1989. *American Families and Households.* New York: Russell Sage Foundation.

Cancian, Maria, Sheldon Danziger, and Peter Gottschalk. 1992, in press. "The Changing Contributions of Men and Women to the Level and Distribution of Family Income, 1968–1988." In Wolff, E., ed., *Poverty and Prosperity at the Close of the Twentieth Century.* New York: MacMillan.

Danziger, Sheldon. 1980. "Do Working Wives Increase Family Income Inequality?" *Journal of Human Resources* 15:444–451.

Fuchs, Victor. 1983. *How We Live.* Cambridge, MA: Harvard University Press.

———. 1988. *Women's Quest for Economic Equality.* Cambridge, MA: Harvard University Press.

Goldin, Claudia D. 1990. *Understanding the Gender Gap: An Economic History of American Women.* New York: Oxford University Press.

Gronau, Reuben. 1982. "Inequality of Family Income: Do Wives' Earnings Matter?" *Population and Development Review* 8:119–136.

Horvath, Francis W. 1980. "Working Wives Reduce Inequality in the Distribution of Family Earnings." *Monthly Labor Review* 103:51–53.

Kakwani, Nanak C. 1980. *Income Inequality and Poverty: Methods of Estimation and Policy Applications* [esp. Chapter 5, "Measures of Income Inequality"]. Oxford: Oxford University Press.

Karoly, Lynn A. 1992. "The Trend in Inequality among Families, Individuals, and Workers in the United States: A Twenty-Five Year Perspective." In Danziger, Sheldon, and Peter Gottschalk, eds. *Increasing Income Inequality: What Matters and What Doesn't.* New York: Russell Sage Foundation.

Killingsworth, Mark, and James J. Heckman. 1986. "Female Labor Supply: A Survey." In Ashenfelter, O. C., and R. Layard, eds. *Handbook of Labor Economics.* Amsterdam: North Holland.

Layard, Richard, and Antoni Zabalza. 1985. "Family Income Distribution: Explanation and Policy Evaluation." *Journal of Political Economy* 87 (5):S133–161.

Lehrer, Evelyn, and Mark Nerlove. 1981. "The Impact of Female Work on Family

Income Distribution in the United States: Black-White Differentials." *Review of Income and Wealth*, 27 (4):423–431.
———. 1984. "A Lifecycle Analysis of Family Income Distribution." *Economic Inquiry* 22:360–374.
Levy, Frank. 1987. *Dollars and Dreams: The Changing American Income Distribution*. New York: Norton and Company.
Mincer, Jacob. 1962. "Labor Force Participation of Married Women: A Study of Labor Supply." In Gregg Lewis, H., ed. *Aspects of Labor Economics*. Universities-National Bureau Committee for Economic Research. Princeton, NJ: Princeton University Press.
Ryscavage, Paul. 1979. "More Wives in the Labor Force Have Husbands with 'Above Average' Incomes." *Monthly Labor Review* 5:40–42.
Schrim, Allen L. 1988. "Marital Sorting, Wives' Labor Supply, and Family Income Inequality." Unpublished paper, Population Studies Center, University of Michigan.
Shaw, Kathryn L. 1989. "Intertemporal Labor Supply and the Distribution of Family Income." *Review of Economics and Statistics* 71:196–205.
———. 1992. "The Life-Cycle Labor Supply of Married Women and its Implications for Household Income Inequality." *Economic Inquiry* (forthcoming).
Smith, James P. 1979. "The Distribution of Family Income." *Journal of Political Economy* 87:S163–S192.
Smith, James P., and Finis Welch. 1989. "Black Economic Progress after Myrdal." *Journal of Economic Literature* 27:519–564.
Treas, Judith. 1987. "The Effect of Women's Labor Force Participation on the Distribution of Income in the United States." *Annual Review of Sociology* 13:259–288.

PART FOUR

Public Policy Changes and the Distribution of Family Income

7

Growing Inequality in the 1980s: The Role of Federal Taxes and Cash Transfers

Edward M. Gramlich / Richard Kasten / Frank Sammartino

The United States' distribution of income in the 1980s can be likened to Hirschman's (1973) famous tunnel at rush hour. One lane, representing the incomes of highly paid workers and capitalists, is moving ahead rapidly. Another lane, representing the incomes of the majority of families, is barely creeping along.

What should tax and transfer policy do about such a situation? On one side, the official rhetoric of the Reagan Administration seemed to imply that tax and transfer policy should simply get out of the way. Tax rates should be cut, the fast-moving lane would move ahead even more quickly, and, as congestion eased, those in the slow-moving lane would also move more rapidly. On the other side, corresponding to a view that Kaus (1990) terms "money liberalism," is the goal that tax-transfer policy should try to even out the traffic flow, slowing down the fast-moving lane and speeding up the rest of the traffic. It turns out that enormous adjustments in tax and transfer rates would be necessary to do this literally, but policies could still be strongly compensatory.

We do not try to resolve this normative question in this chapter, but we do try to answer an underlying descriptive question—What was the effect of changes in federal taxes and cash transfers on family income inequality in the 1980s? To begin with the proper degree of humility, we start by covering a long list of difficulties in doing any such calculations—what to assume about tax incidence, how to measure family income, what to do about dynamic adjustments to income, life-cycle issues, and state and local taxes. We deal with some of these problems but are not able to treat them all. We list the main policy changes that could have had noticeable impact on the distribution of family incomes over the 1980s. We then use microdata to calculate Gini coefficients and underlying decile data for 1980, 1985, and 1990 for various measures of the income distribution. These calculations yield estimates of the net effect of different policy changes, including especially the phased-in effects of the Social Security Amendments of 1977 and 1983, the Economic Recovery Tax Act of 1981 (ERTA), the Tax Equity and Fiscal Responsibility Act of 1982 (TEFRA), the Tax Reform Act of 1986 (TRA), and the Omnibus Budget Reconciliation Act of 1990 (OBRA).

Problems with Calculations of Tax and Transfer Distributions

Incidence

The first question is that of tax incidence. How should the various taxes be allocated? The standard approach, used by countless authors such as Musgrave, Case, and Leonard (1974) and Pechman (1985), and followed here as well, is to allocate individual income and payroll taxes to income sources (labor and capital income), and to allocate consumption taxes to income uses (consumer expenditures). Atkinson (1990) has recently summarized many of the problems with tax-transfer incidence calculations, giving examples that illustrate how even these generally benign assumptions may be inaccurate.

There still remains the question of how to allocate taxes on corporate income. In a closed economy these taxes would fall on capital, and in a small open economy they would fall on labor. From a macroeconomic standpoint, the U.S. economy seems to behave as a hybrid—call it a large open economy. In such a case both capital and labor should bear some of the corporate tax. For most simulations we therefore assume an intermediate incidence, allocating half of corporate income taxes to capital (split among recipients of dividends, interest, and realized capital gains) and half to labor income (recipients of wage and salary income). In Appendix 7A we show sensitivity calculations for the closed and small open economy cases.[1]

[1]Even in the closed economy case, capital may bear more or less than 100 percent of the corporate tax depending upon assumptions concerning the price elasticity of demand for corporate output, the degree of substitutability between capital and labor in the corporate and noncorporate sectors, and the relative capital intensity of the two sectors. See Shoven (1976) and

Family Income

We construct various measures of family income.[2] The first is pre-tax, pre-transfer income: the sum of labor income (wages, salaries, and self-employment income), capital income (net rents, interest, dividends, and realized capital gains), and other income (pension benefits, alimony, and child support).[3] Family pre-tax, pre-transfer income as measured here excludes accrued but unrealized capital gains, employer contributions to health insurance and pension funds, imputed rents, interest, and other noncash income. Because income is measured before all federal taxes, employer contributions for federal social insurance and federal corporate income taxes are included in pre-tax, pre-transfer family income.

We measure post-transfer, pre-tax income by adding government cash transfers (social security benefits, unemployment insurance benefits (UI), veterans benefits, workers' compensation, Aid to Families with Dependent Children (AFDC), Supplemental Security Income (SSI), and other cash welfare benefits) to pre-tax, pre-transfer family income. In-kind government transfers, such as Medicare, Medicaid, and food stamps, are not included in post-transfer income. We chose not to include in-kind transfers because of the problem of assigning an appropriate value to that income and because similar in-kind income that accrues to higher-income families, such as employer contributions to private health insurance, is not included in pre-transfer income.

We measure post-transfer, post-tax income by subtracting all federal income, corporate, payroll, and excise taxes (except for the windfall profits tax) from post-transfer, pre-tax family income. We do not allocate federal estate and gift taxes, customs duties, and other miscellaneous taxes to family income.

We divide each family's income by the appropriate poverty threshold to adjust for differences in family size. This adjustment assumes that although larger families need more income than smaller families to be equally as well off, the increased need is less than proportional to the number of family members. Persons are then ranked according to their adjusted family income, and percentile distributions computed from the sample of persons.

Ballentine (1980). The incidence of corporate taxes in an open economy is discussed in Harberger (1983). Mutti and Grubert (1985) have shown that even with a modest degree of international capital mobility, the corporate tax is shifted away from capital income.

[2]We use the Census definition of families throughout, except that we treat unrelated individuals as families.

[3]Realized capital gains are those reported on tax returns, averaging about 5 percent of pre-tax, pre-transfer income.

Dynamic Adjustments

Measuring family income before federal cash transfers and taxes is not the same as measuring what family income would have been in the absence of federal tax and transfer policies. Taxes and transfers clearly change not only the level but also the distribution of pre-transfer, pre-tax income. We can identify at least three ways in which policy changes might affect the pre-transfer, pre-tax distribution of income. The first is through changes in the growth rate of the economy. The second is through supply-side effects, such as increased labor supply and increased capital investment. The third is through what might be called portfolio effects, such as the conversion of accrued capital gains into realized gains or the conversion of nonwage compensation such as employer-provided fringe benefits into wage and salary income. Because we measure cash pre-tax, pre-transfer income, these latter conversions will change the observed distribution of income. We have little to say about the effect of tax-transfer policy on overall level of economic activity. In our simulations we take the observed growth in GNP as given, and do not look for distributional changes as a result of that growth. We do explore some dynamic changes in the income distribution based on labor supply and portfolio effects.[4]

Life-Cycle Issues

Following the standard approach in distributional analysis, we rank persons according to their adjusted family income measured in a single year. For many reasons, one year's income may be a poor measure of economic well-being. If it were possible, one would like to rank persons according to adjusted family permanent income or at least this income measured over a number of years.

Neither measure is readily available. One proxy might be to use consumer expenditures, following Friedman's notion that consumption should be proportional to a family's permanent income, although consumer expenditures measured over a limited period are themselves an inexact proxy for permanent consumption. Poterba (1989) and CBO (1990) have shown that, when measured against current consumption, federal indirect taxes are much less regressive than when measured against annual income. We take one small step in the direction of permanent income by allocating federal indirect tax payments to families on the basis of the predicted consumer expenditures for families with a particular income, family size, and age of family head, based on set of subsidiary regressions.

[4]Lindsey (1988; 1990) and CBO (1986) use similar methods to look at the distributional effects of ERTA.

State and Local Taxes

We do not take account of changes in state and local taxes. To do this precisely, of course, would require separate calculations for each state. Both pre- and post-tax income would change if state and local taxes were included. Pre-tax, pre-transfer income would include indirect taxes such as state corporate profits, payroll, and, depending upon the incidence assumption, property taxes. Post-tax income would be reduced by state and local income, sales, and possibly property taxes.

Excluding state and local taxes has an uncertain effect on observed changes in the income distribution over time. State and local taxes, which generally are regressive or at least less progressive than federal taxes, have grown slightly faster than incomes between 1980 and 1989—at a 3.6 percent annual real rate compared with a 3.3 percent rate for real personal income—but much faster than real federal taxes.[5] In 1980, total state and local taxes (excluding contributions for social insurance) were equal to 46 percent of total federal taxes. By 1985 they had reached 51 percent, but fell back to 49 percent by 1989. The increased relative size of state and local taxes would tend to make the change in total taxes more regressive (or less progressive) than changes in federal taxes alone.

Balancing this increase in their relative growth was a small shift toward greater progressivity of state and local taxes as the share of total taxes from individual income taxes grew. This tendency may have been reinforced in the latter half of the 1980s by progressive changes within the state individual income taxes themselves.[6]

Policy Changes in the 1980s

Although nominal federal taxes nearly doubled, from half a trillion dollars in 1980 to just under one trillion in 1989, they grew more slowly than personal income. The growth rate was not even throughout the decade. Between 1980 and 1985 real federal taxes grew at an annual rate of 1.6 percent, compared with a 3.3 percent rate for real personal income. Between 1985 and 1989 real taxes grew at an annual rate of 4.1 percent and real income at a rate of 3.4 percent.

There were major changes in federal tax policy in the 1980s—not always the result of direct legislative action. Some changes reflected legislation en-

[5] In these and all other real calculations we have deflated by the CPI-U for 1985 and by the CPI-U-X1 for 1980.

[6] Galper and Pollack (1988) found evidence of increased progressivity in income taxes for five selected states—California, Colorado, Nebraska, Oklahoma, and Virginia.

acted prior to 1980, and others came about through inaction. Two major pieces of legislation greatly revised the individual income tax. ERTA cut the top marginal tax rate from 70 percent to 50 percent and reduced marginal tax rates in all other tax brackets by 23 percent over a three-year period. ERTA also changed the tax base as well as the rate structure, expanding eligibility and deduction limits for Individual Retirement Accounts (IRA) and introducing a new deduction for married couples when both spouses had earnings, among other changes. Because ERTA made no adjustment to the Earned Income Tax Credit (EITC) and delayed increases in the personal exemption and standard deduction until 1985, low-income families benefitted less than other families. TRA replaced the multibracketed tax structure with a three-bracket formula (15 percent, 28 percent, and the "bubble" rate of 33 percent). TRA targeted many of its benefits to low-income families. It eliminated a number of deductions and income exclusions used mostly by high-income taxpayers, and substantially expanded the personal exemption, standard deduction, and EITC. While marginal tax rates were cut the most for high-income families (from 50 percent to 28 percent), their average tax rates fell the least.

ERTA substantially reduced the corporate income tax in 1981, but subsequent legislation in 1982 (TEFRA), 1984 (the Deficit Reduction Act of 1984), and 1986 (TRA) raised effective rates back to their 1980 level. Social security payroll tax rates rose by 25 percent between 1980 and 1990. Increases enacted by the Social Security Amendments of 1977 raised employer and employee tax rates from 6.1 percent each to 7.7 percent each. The Social Security Amendments of 1983 moved up the effective dates of some of these previously enacted tax increases, amended the income tax code to include some portion of social security benefits in taxable income, and extended coverage to newly hired federal workers. Subsequent legislation extended Social Security Hospital Insurance to state and local government employees.

In 1983, the federal excise tax rates on tobacco were doubled by TEFRA, from $.08 per pack of cigarettes to $.16 per pack. Motor fuels tax rates were more than doubled by the Highway Revenue Act of 1982, from $.04 per gallon of gas to $.09 per gallon. Despite these changes and other small increases in other federal excise tax rates, because most rates are set in nominal terms and are not adjusted for inflation, by 1990 federal excise taxes as a percent of income were at about their 1980 level.

Nominal cash transfers grew from $180 billion in 1980 to $308 billion by 1989, although real growth in transfers lagged behind real income growth. Real transfers per person grew by about 6 percent between 1980 and 1989, while real per capita personal income grew by about 25 percent. As a result, transfers fell from 8.3 to 7.0 percent of per capita personal income. The change in transfers was the result of demographic and economic changes over the decade as well as both active and passive policy changes. Social security cash benefits, by far the largest component of transfers, grew at about the same rate as other incomes. Explicit policy changes in social security tended to lower benefits by delaying the cost-of-living allowance (COLA) by six months in 1983 and all subsequent years, and by eliminating benefits for students and some other dependents. Yet the basic structure of social security, which ties new benefits to the wage level at the time of retirement and then indexes them for inflation, has kept benefits growing roughly in proportion to other incomes. Two other major transfer programs, UI and AFDC, have not kept pace with other incomes. Fewer families were eligible for UI and AFDC benefits because the unemployment rate fell. Federal policy changes in the early 1980s restricted eligibility for both programs, although some of the AFDC changes were subsequently reversed. Benefit levels in both programs, determined by states, have tended to grow more slowly than nominal incomes.

Pre-Tax, Pre-Transfer Incomes

The data we use for the calculations come from the March Current Population Survey—an annual survey of demographic and income information for a sample of about 60,000 families conducted by the Bureau of the Census. We have made statistical imputations from the Statistics of Income microdata files—annual files of approximately 100,000 actual individual income tax returns filed with the Internal Revenue Service—to supply missing or incomplete income information, particularly for high-income families, and to add information on federal income tax deductions and credits. We also have made further statistical imputations from the Consumer Expenditure Survey—an annual survey of quarterly and bimonthly expenditures for a sample of about 5,000 families—to supply family expenditure information used in allocating federal indirect taxes.[7]

To measure the overall impact of tax and transfer changes in the 1980s, we do simulations for three years: 1980, 1985, and 1990. The first year is a natural starting point for examining policy changes in the 1980s. The middle year covers the key tax changes in the early Reagan years, ERTA and TEFRA. And the last is chosen to measure the long-term effects of TRA, most of the changes of which will have taken effect by 1990. We have projected incomes from 1987, the latest year for which complete data were

[7]The major pieces of added information for high-income families were for realized capital gains, for removing the top-coding of other income, and for itemized deductions for IRAs and child care.

Table 7.1 Gini Coefficients for Various Components of Pre-Tax, Pre-Transfer Income: 1980, 1985, and 1990

Year	Wages and Salaries	All Labor Income[a]	Rents, Interest, and Dividends	All Capital Income[b]	All Pre-Tax, Pre-Transfer Income
1980	.493	.486	.890	.906	.473
1985	.523	.529	.878	.907	.513
1990	.537	.540	.882	.912	.523
			Percentage Change		
1980–1985	6.2	8.8	−1.4	0.1	8.4
1985–1990	2.7	2.2	0.5	0.5	2.0
1980–1990	9.0	11.1	−1.0	0.7	10.6

Note: Based on cumulative shares of adjusted pre-tax, pre-transfer family income for persons ranked by adjusted family income.

[a] Wages and salaries plus self-employment income.

[b] Rents, interest, and dividends plus realized capital gains.

available when we began our work, forward to 1990, using observed growth rates of major income categories to make the latter simulations.[8] In doing calculations such as these it is important to standardize income growth. Although the unemployment rate was lower in 1990 than in the other years, the rate of real income growth was very similar in each of the two five-year segments.

Basic summary information is given in Table 7.1. There was a significant shift toward family income inequality in the 1980s, marked by an increase in inequality for most types of income, with the exception that income from rents, interest, and dividends was distributed more equally in 1990 than in 1980. The amount of the shift, measured by the percentage of change in the Gini coefficient, was about 10.6 percent for total pre-tax, pre-transfer income. About 80 percent of the increase in the Gini coefficient occurred in the 1980–1985 period. Part of the early rise could be explained by the occurrence of the 1981 and 1982 recessions. But the trend toward greater inequality of income continued after 1985, during a strong recovery period that typically is characterized by declining income inequality.

Summary measures of inequality, such as Gini coefficients, often over-

[8] By the time the study was published we had evidence that all assumptions were reasonably accurate through 1988. Yet as a result of the economic downturn in 1990, both our aggregate growth rate and our capital gains projections for 1990 are likely to be too high.

simplify a muddled story. In this instance, however, the story is so clear as to be almost astonishing. Table 7.2 shows the shares and growth rates of pre-tax and pre-transfer income for each income decile and for the 5 and 1 percent of persons with the highest incomes. Over the decade, real family income grew by 1.5 percent per annum, less than in earlier decades but still positive. Apart from the first decile, where growth rates can be misleading because there is not much income and where much of the growth is attributable to a reduction in business losses rather than to growth in positive incomes, all deciles up to the ninth showed real income growth less than the average, while the tenth showed much more than the average real income growth. The upper 5 and 1 percent of individuals showed even higher growth.

The same number can be analyzed in income share terms, as is done in the three columns on the left. In these share terms, all deciles but the highest lost ground in both the 1980–1985 and the 1985–1990 periods. The top

Table 7.2 Share and Growth Rate of Pre-Tax, Pre-Transfer Income by Population Decile: 1980, 1985, and 1990

	Share of Each Decile			Annual Real Growth Rate		
Decile	1980	1985	1990	1980–1985	1985–1990	1980–1990
First[a]	0.1	0.1	0.1	−2.4	7.5	2.4
Second	1.9	1.7	1.7	−0.9	2.8	0.9
Third	3.8	3.5	3.4	−1.3	1.7	0.2
Fourth	5.5	5.0	4.9	−1.2	1.4	0.1
Fifth	7.0	6.5	6.3	−1.0	1.5	0.2
Sixth	8.5	8.2	7.8	−0.7	1.4	0.4
Seventh	10.4	10.0	9.7	−0.1	1.3	0.6
Eighth	12.7	12.5	12.3	0.3	1.1	0.7
Ninth	16.6	16.4	15.9	1.2	1.8	1.5
Tenth	33.7	36.9	38.4	3.2	3.2	3.2
Top 5 percent	22.8	25.8	27.7	3.9	3.8	3.8
Top 1 percent	10.1	12.5	14.1	6.4	5.1	5.7
Total[b]	100.0	100.0	100.0			
Mean[c]	33,124	34,865	38,614	1.0	2.1	1.5

Note: For persons ranked by adjusted pre-tax, pre-transfer family income.
[a]Excludes individuals in families with zero or negative incomes.
[b]Includes individuals in families with zero or negative incomes not shown separately.
[c]Mean family income, 1990 dollars.

decile increased its share by 3.2 percentage points from 1980 to 1985 and by 1.5 percentage points from 1985 to 1990. Not only that, the top 5 percent of persons in the pre-tax, pre-transfer income ranking gained 3.0 percentage points from 1980 to 1985 and 1.9 percentage points from 1985 to 1990, indicating that in share terms those in the 91st to 95th percentile essentially just held their own in the 1980s. Persons in the top 1 percent gained 2.4 percentage points in the 1980 to 1985 period and 1.6 percentage points from 1985 to 1990, indicating that those in the 96th to 99th percentile did not gain unduly either. For pre-tax, pre-transfer income, it is only a slight overstatement to characterize the 1980s as a period where 1 percent of the travelers were in a very fast lane, about 19 percent were moving at an average rate, and the rest were barely creeping ahead.

The figures are shown for all pre-tax, pre-transfer income, but the story is the same for both labor and capital income. Labor income (wages, salaries, and self-employment income) plus capital income (rents, interest, dividends, and realized capital gains) together sum to about 95 percent of total pre-tax, pre-transfer income, with pension benefits, alimony, and child support comprising the rest. Table 7.3 shows shares for the two main components of income. Although the top decile increased its share of labor and capital income between 1980 and 1990, all of the increase in the share of capital income was for the top 1 percent. Each of the bottom nine deciles received a smaller share of labor income, and all but one got a smaller share of capital income.

Because labor income accounts for about 80 percent of total pre-tax, pre-transfer income, the increasing inequality of labor income tends to dominate the overall result. That is not the entire story, however. Part of the increase in inequality is attributable to a shift in the composition of total income toward more unequally distributed income sources. The share of total income from wages and salaries declined by 3.9 percentage points between 1980 and 1990, while the share from capital income increased by 2.6 percentage points. The increasing share of capital income was attributable almost entirely to an increase in realized capital gains, as the share from rents, interest, and dividend changed little.

The Impact of Taxes and Transfers: Base Case

Federal taxes and cash transfers not only provided no compensation for the increased inequality of pre-tax, pre-transfer income, they actually worsened the drift. Table 7.4 repeats Gini coefficients for pre-tax and pre-transfer income and shows new Gini coefficients after transfers and taxes are counted. Comparisons of Gini coefficients for pre-tax, pre-transfer income

Table 7.3 Share of Labor and Capital Income, by Population Decile: 1980, 1985, and 1990

Decile	Labor Income[a]			Capital Income[b]		
	1980	1985	1990	1980	1985	1990
First[c]	0.1	0.0	0.1	0.4	0.2	0.3
Second	1.5	1.4	1.5	2.2	1.9	1.6
Third	3.7	3.4	3.4	2.8	2.5	2.3
Fourth	5.8	5.2	5.2	3.1	3.0	2.7
Fifth	7.6	7.0	6.9	3.4	3.2	2.9
Sixth	9.3	8.9	8.6	4.0	4.1	3.7
Seventh	11.5	11.2	10.7	4.8	4.8	4.6
Eighth	14.1	14.0	13.7	6.1	6.1	6.2
Ninth	18.1	18.1	17.3	10.1	9.7	10.0
Tenth	28.9	31.7	33.3	62.9	64.3	65.6
Top 5 percent	17.6	20.0	21.9	53.5	55.7	57.1
Top 1 percent	6.0	7.6	9.2	34.1	37.7	38.8
Total[d]	100.0	100.0	100.0	100.0	100.0	100.0
Percentage of Pre-Tax, Pre-Transfer Income	81.2	78.3	77.3	14.9	17.2	17.5

Note: For persons ranked by adjusted pre-tax, pre-transfer family income.
[a]Wages and salaries plus self-employment income.
[b]Rents, interest, and dividends plus realized capital gains.
[c]Excludes individuals in families with zero or negative incomes.
[d]Includes individuals in families with zero or negative incomes not shown separately.

with those for pre-tax, post-transfer income and post-tax, post-transfer income indicate that both cash transfers and federal taxes continued to redistribute income from higher- to lower-income families throughout the 1980s. The distributional effectiveness of each, however, was less in 1990 than it had been in 1980. When transfers are added (pre-tax, post-transfer income), the percentage increase in the Gini coefficient between 1980 and 1990 is more than for pre-tax, pre-transfer income. When taxes are subtracted (post-tax, post-transfer income), the percentage rise in the Gini is even greater—despite a slightly more redistributive effect of federal taxes between 1985 and 1990. Over the 1980s, then, cash transfers and federal taxes worsened rather than offset the growing inequality in the distribution of pre-tax, pre-transfer incomes.

Another way to look at the role of taxes and transfers is as follows. In 1980, taxes and transfers reduced the Gini by 16.5 percent (the percentage

Table 7.4 Gini Coefficients for Selected Measures of Income: 1980, 1985, and 1990

Year	Pre-Tax Pre-Transfer Income (1)	Pre-Tax Post-Transfer Income (2)	Reduction Due to Transfers (1) − (2)	Post-Tax Post-Transfer Income (3)	Reduction Due to Taxes (2) − (3)
1980	.473	.424	.049	.395	.029
1985	.513	.468	.045	.453	.015
1990	.523	.482	.041	.463	.019
		Percentage Change			
1980–1985	8.4	10.4	. . .	14.7	. . .
1985–1990	2.0	3.2	. . .	2.1	. . .
1980–1990	10.6	13.9	. . .	17.1	. . .

Note: Based on cumulative shares of adjusted pre-tax, pre-transfer family income for persons ranked by adjusted family income.

Table 7.5 Share of Cash Transfers and Federal Taxes, by Population Decile: 1980, 1985, and 1990

	Cash Transfers			Federal Taxes		
Decile	1980	1985	1990	1980	1985	1990
First[a]	27.5	25.0	24.9	0.3	0.3	0.2
Second	19.7	17.4	16.4	0.9	1.0	0.9
Third	11.7	11.8	11.2	2.4	2.5	2.3
Fourth	8.6	9.1	8.8	4.2	4.0	4.0
Fifth	6.5	6.9	7.2	5.9	5.7	5.5
Sixth	5.6	6.8	6.6	7.6	7.6	7.1
Seventh	5.1	5.7	5.9	9.8	9.7	9.2
Eighth	4.2	4.9	5.6	12.6	12.6	12.1
Ninth	4.4	5.0	5.4	17.3	17.2	16.6
Tenth	5.9	6.5	7.1	38.9	39.2	42.0
Top 5 percent	3.3	3.8	4.6	27.3	27.5	30.5
Top 1 percent	0.9	0.9	1.1	12.8	13.3	15.6
Total[b]	100.0	100.0	100.0	100.0	100.0	100.0
Percentage of Pre-Tax, Pre-Transfer Income	8.3	7.8	7.1	25.2	23.5	24.7

Note: For persons ranked by adjusted pre-tax, pre-transfer family income.
[a]Excludes individuals in families with zero or negative incomes.
[b]Includes individuals in families with zero or negative incomes not shown separately.

reduction from .473 to .395). If there had been no change in the inequality-reducing impact of taxes and transfers, and if they had also reduced inequality by this 16.5 percent in 1990, the post-tax, post-transfer Gini for that year would have been .437. Instead the Gini actually increased from .395 to .463 (Table 7.4, Column 3) over the decade. Thus, 62 percent of the increase in post-tax, post-transfer inequality over the decade can be attributed to changes in pre-tax, pre-transfer incomes [(.437 − .395)/(.463 − .395)] and 38 percent to changes in the effectiveness of tax and transfer programs.

Part of the reason for the worsening was the relative decline in total cash transfers, as they fell from 8.3 percent to 7.1 percent of pre-tax, pre-transfer income between 1980 and 1990—shown in Table 7.5. At the same time, the share of transfers received by persons with low incomes fell between 1980 and 1990, while the share received by those with high incomes rose. This is particularly true for persons in elderly families, as illustrated in Table 7.6. Not only have low-income elderly persons received a smaller share of the transfers received by all elderly persons while higher-income elderly have received a larger share, but the share of all transfer payments

Table 7.6 Share of Cash Transfers and Federal Taxes for Families with Persons Age 65 and Over, by Population Decile: 1980, 1985, and 1990

	Cash Transfers			Federal Taxes		
Decile	1980	1985	1990	1980	1985	1990
First[a]	14.7	12.4	11.3	0.6	0.4	0.3
Second	7.1	8.5	9.5	0.3	0.3	0.3
Third	11.1	10.9	10.8	0.8	0.8	0.7
Fourth	10.7	10.8	10.7	1.2	1.3	1.3
Fifth	10.9	10.3	10.3	1.9	2.3	2.5
Sixth	10.1	10.3	10.1	3.3	3.9	4.2
Seventh	9.8	9.7	9.7	5.9	6.1	6.3
Eighth	8.9	9.4	9.0	9.1	9.2	9.3
Ninth	8.0	8.9	8.8	15.3	16.1	15.6
Tenth	8.3	8.6	9.4	61.5	59.6	59.4
Total[b]	100.0	100.0	100.0	100.0	100.0	100.0
Percentage of Total Transfers and Taxes	58.2	65.3	68.4	10.8	11.2	12.3

Note: For persons ranked by adjusted pre-tax, pre-transfer family income for families with persons age 65 and over.

[a]Excludes individuals in families with zero or negative incomes.

[b]Includes individuals in families with zero or negative incomes not shown separately.

received by the elderly has increased. Because the overwhelming part of transfers received by the elderly is for social security, which is not as directly targeted toward low-income recipients as are most other transfer programs, this shift has diminished the overall redistributive effectiveness of cash transfers.

The redistributive effect of federal taxes has also declined over the decade. In the popular press it is common to assess progressivity by looking at the share of taxes paid. Table 7.5 shows how misleading such an approach can be. Just as the top decile has gained more pre-tax, pre-transfer income, it has paid a larger share of the federal tax bill. The top decile share of federal taxes has risen by 3.1 percentage points over the decade; the top 1 percent share has risen by 2.8 percentage points.

But this apparent shift in the tax burden reflects nothing but the rapid rise of pre-tax incomes on the top side, documented fully above. A better way to analyze the numbers is in terms of post-tax, post-transfer income, as in Table 7.7. A comparison of Table 7.2 with Table 7.7 shows that in each

Table 7.7 Share and Growth Rate of Post-Tax, Post-Transfer Income, by Population Decile: 1980, 1985, and 1990

	Share of Each Decile			Annual Real Growth Rate		
Decile	1980	1985	1990	1980–1985	1985–1990	1980–1990
First[a]	2.8	2.4	2.2	−1.0	−0.2	−0.6
Second	4.0	3.3	3.3	−1.7	1.2	−0.2
Third	5.1	4.5	4.4	−1.1	1.1	0.0
Fourth	6.2	5.6	5.5	−0.8	0.9	0.1
Fifth	7.3	6.8	6.6	−0.8	1.2	0.2
Sixth	8.5	8.2	7.9	−0.2	1.1	0.4
Seventh	10.1	9.7	9.5	0.3	1.1	0.7
Eighth	12.0	11.8	11.7	0.7	0.9	0.8
Ninth	15.2	15.1	14.8	1.7	1.5	1.6
Tenth	29.3	33.4	34.7	4.3	2.7	3.5
Top 5 percent	19.5	23.3	24.9	5.3	3.2	4.2
Top 1 percent	8.3	11.2	12.5	8.4	4.5	6.4
Total[b]	100.0	100.0	100.0			
Mean[c]	27518	29422	31840	1.3	1.6	1.5

Note: For persons ranked by adjusted pre-tax, pre-transfer family income.
[a]Excludes individuals in families with zero or negative incomes.
[b]Includes individuals in families with zero or negative incomes not shown separately.
[c]Mean family income, 1990 dollars.

year the distribution of post-tax, post-transfer income is more equal than the pre-tax, pre-transfer distribution, but that the annual real growth rates of post-tax, post-transfer incomes at the top are generally higher than those of pre-tax, pre-transfer incomes. Hence by this test, taxes and transfers have become less progressive over the 1980s, despite the increase in the share of taxes paid by the rich.

Policy Changes in Isolation

Some of the observed changes in the distribution of cash transfers and federal taxes are the result of economic and demographic changes rather than explicit changes in policy. For example, falling unemployment rates and UI have reduced transfer payments to low-income families. The increasing affluence of elderly social security recipients has shifted the distribution of transfer payments higher up in the income distribution. To isolate the effects of policy changes, we hold the distribution of pre-tax, pre-transfer income at its 1990 level but adjust transfers and taxes to reflect what they would have been if the 1980 or 1985 law had remained in effect but benefits and taxes had been adjusted to keep pace with the growth of other incomes.

Table 7.8 shows pre- and post-tax and transfer Gini coefficients for 1990 under three assumptions about transfers and tax law. The first two assumptions are that 1980 and 1985 transfer benefits and tax laws, with their dollar parameters indexed for changes in income, were still in effect in 1990. The third is that actual 1990 benefits and tax law were in effect and hence repeat the 1990 Gini coefficients shown in Table 7.4.

The second column of Table 7.8 shows the effect of changes in transfer benefit levels. Benefits have not kept pace with other incomes since 1980 or 1985. If benefits had been adjusted by income since either 1980 or 1985, the 1990 income distribution would have been slightly more equal.

Comparing the Gini coefficient for post-tax, post-transfer income indicates that the distribution of post-tax, post-transfer income would be only slightly more equal if we went back to 1980 tax law and benefits, indexed for income growth since then. The Gini of .452 (Column 3) suggests that if there had been no tax and transfer policy changes over the decade, 84 percent of the realized increase in post-tax, post-transfer inequality over the decade would have occurred: 16 percent was then due to policy changes.[9] Most of

[9]The post-tax, post-transfer Gini rose by .068, from .375 to .463, over the decade (Table 7.4). Table 7.8 shows that the Gini would have increased by .057, or to .452, even if the 1980 tax/transfer system had remained constant. Thus 84 percent (.057/.068) of the increase was *not* due to changes in the fisc.

Table 7.8 Hypothetical Gini Coefficients for Selected Measures of Income: 1990

Year	Pre-Tax Pre-Transfer Income (1)	Pre-Tax Post-Transfer Income (2)	Reduction Due to Transfers (1) − (2)	Post-Tax Post-Transfer Income (3)	Reduction Due to Taxes (2) − (3)
1980 Benefits and Tax Law	.523	.479	.044	.452	.027
1985 Benefits and Tax Law	.523	.479	.044	.462	.017
1990 Benefits and Tax Law	.523	.482	.041	.463	.019
		Percentage Change			
1980–1985	. . .	0.2	. . .	2.2	. . .
1985–1990	. . .	0.6	. . .	0.1	. . .
1980–1990	. . .	0.8	. . .	2.3	. . .

Note: Based on cumulative shares of adjusted pre-tax, pre-transfer family income for persons ranked by adjusted family income.

these policy changes involved a decrease in the progressivity of federal taxes. Although both the individual income tax and social insurance payroll taxes are now slightly more progressive than in 1980, the federal tax system as a whole is less progressive because social insurance taxes now account for a larger share of the total. The net effect of tax and transfer changes since 1985 is to leave the Gini coefficients almost unchanged.

Table 7.9 provides additional detail about how tax changes since 1980 have changed the post-tax distribution of income. Going back to the 1980 tax and transfer system would lower the share of income of the top 1 percent of the population and raise the share of the bottom 60 percent. Going back to the 1985 tax and transfer system would barely change the distribution.

The picture, then, is of an even greater traffic flow disparity than there was in 1980. In terms of pre-tax, pre-transfer income, the highest-income individuals gained more than others. These gains were augmented by regressive drifts in transfer benefits and taxes, most of which would have occurred even with 1980 policies, but some were due to policy changes occurring through the decade. The most significant of these changes were the fall in the share of transfers going to low-income people and the increased importance of social security taxes.

Table 7.9 Hypothetical Share of Post-Tax, Post-Transfer Income, by Population Decile: 1990

Decile	1980 Benefits and Tax Law	1985 Benefits and Tax Law	1990 Benefits and Tax Law
First[a]	2.4	2.4	2.2
Second	3.4	3.3	3.3
Third	4.6	4.4	4.4
Fourth	5.6	5.5	5.5
Fifth	6.7	6.6	6.6
Sixth	8.0	7.9	7.9
Seventh	9.5	9.5	9.5
Eighth	11.7	11.7	11.7
Ninth	14.8	14.8	14.8
Tenth	33.8	34.6	34.7
Top 5 percent	24.0	24.7	24.9
Top 1 percent	11.7	12.3	12.5
Total[b]	100.0	100.0	100.0
Gini	.452	.462	.463

Note: For persons ranked by adjusted pre-tax, pre-transfer family income.
[a]Excludes individuals in families with zero or negative incomes.
[b]Includes individuals in families with zero or negative incomes not shown separately.

Dynamic Response to Policy

Tax and policy changes are likely to affect the distribution of pre-tax, pre-transfer income. In this section we explore possible effects attributable to changes in the marginal tax rates on earnings and capital gains. Table 7.10 shows marginal tax rates on earnings and capital gains in 1990 under 1990 tax law and under 1980 tax law indexed to 1990. Marginal tax rates on earnings reflect income tax rates, including the EITC, and employee and employer payroll tax rates. The combined effect of the Social Security amendments of 1977, ERTA, and TRA was to lower marginal tax rates on earnings for persons in the top half of the income distribution. In contrast, combined tax changes increased the marginal tax rate on capital gains in all income deciles.

It is reasonable to expect some response by taxpayers to a change in marginal tax rates. To the extent that the distribution of income became more unequal because higher-income families chose to work more, took more

Table 7.10 Average Marginal Tax Rates, by Population Decile: 1990

Decile	Marginal Tax Rate on Earnings		Marginal Tax Rate on Capital Gains	
	1980 Tax Law	1990 Tax Law	1980 Tax Law	1990 Tax Law
First[a]	11.5	14.6	0.0	0.0
Second	19.3	19.3	4.7	13.7
Third	24.8	29.6	2.9	15.5
Fourth	26.2	29.2	3.8	15.1
Fifth	28.3	28.3	5.4	15.1
Sixth	30.3	28.3	6.9	18.0
Seventh	32.3	30.8	8.2	18.7
Eighth	34.7	33.7	9.8	22.6
Ninth	37.5	35.6	11.5	26.0
Tenth	44.3	32.6	22.1	28.5
Top 5 percent	46.6	31.6	22.6	28.5
Top 1 percent	50.1	28.8	23.9	28.0
Total[b]	36.3	31.9	20.4	27.7

Note: For persons ranked by adjusted pre-tax, pre-transfer family income.
[a]Excludes individuals in families with zero or negative incomes.
[b]Includes individuals in families with zero or negative incomes not shown separately.

of their employment compensation in wages rather than fringe benefits, or realized more of their accrued capital gains, the observed growth in income inequality overstates the true growth in inequality.

We show the effect on the distribution of pre-tax, pre-transfer income under a labor supply and capital gains response to changes in tax rates. We use a post-tax wage elasticity of 1.0 for the labor supply of secondary earners and 0.2 for primary earners, and an elasticity of −0.75 for the tax rate on capital gains.[10] We consider these elasticities to be high in a range of possible estimates, particularly the elasticity for the labor supply response of primary workers. We use a high elasticity for this response to reflect not only additional earnings attributable to increased labor supply, but additional mea-

[10]Labor supply elasticity estimates are based on research reported by Killingsworth (1983), while estimates of elasticities for fringe benefits can be found in Long and Scott (1984) and Woodbury (1983). Similar labor supply elasticities have been used by Feenberg and Rosen (1983) and Lindsey (1988, 1990). Estimates of the elasticity of realized capital gains with respect to changes in the marginal tax rate are quite controversial. Summaries of recent studies and the controversy surrounding them can be found in CBO (1988), Auerbach (1988), and Gravelle (1990). The realization elasticity used here is based on equations reported in CBO (1988).

sured money earnings from the conversion of fringe benefits into cash compensation.

If we do not consider the labor supply response, the Gini coefficient in 1990 falls from .523 (Table 7.1) to .516. Thus .007 of the increase in the Gini coefficient could be attributable to higher earnings by upper-income persons in response to a reduction in marginal tax rates. If we take away the capital gains response, the Gini coefficient in 1990 rises to .530. If both the labor supply and capital gains response are removed, the Gini coefficient in 1990 is nearly identical to the actual Gini in 1990, suggesting that the net effect of the labor supply and capital gains response is almost nil.

Compensatory Fiscal Policy

What would it take in the way of tax-transfer policy to undo the increased inequality of pre-tax, pre-transfer income? The changes would have to be enormous. To find these changes, we have simulated a package of progressive changes in federal taxes that includes an increase in the top marginal income tax rate from 28 percent to 50 percent, a 0.5 percent tax on security transactions, elimination of the taxable maximum for Social Security Hospital Insurance taxes, doubling of the EITC, and an increase in SSI benefits—a set of changes that would have reduced the existing federal deficit by about $50 billion in 1991. These changes are far more progressive than almost any of the packages considered in the 101st Congress. Yet even this combination would only lower the post-tax, post-transfer Gini by .01, only about 15 percent of the way back to the post-tax, post-transfer Gini in 1980 (and roughly the same as the Gini given in Table 7.8, which reflects the policy changes of the 1980s).

We can compare these changes to recently enacted legislation designed to reduce the federal budget deficit. Congressional/Administration negotiations culminated in the passage and signing into law of the Omnibus Budget Reconciliation Act of 1990. The Act was expected to reduce the federal deficit by $28 billion in 1991 and by a cumulative $236 billion in 1991–1995. Together with cuts in discretionary spending of $182 billion and anticipated additional savings of $65 billion through reduced debt service, and $9 billion from new IRS enforcement initiatives, total five-year savings are expected to reach $496 billion.

The Act provides for cuts of $99 billion in mandatory and entitlement program spending and revenue increases of $137 billion. Discretionary spending cuts, agreed to in separate appropriations action, were not specified except to provide that all the savings in the first three years come from reductions in defense spending.

Reductions in mandatory spending and entitlement programs include $15 billion from cuts in agricultural programs, Medicare savings of $42 billion (including about $10 billion in increased out-of-pocket cost for Medicare beneficiaries and $32 billion in reduced payments to providers), post office and civil service retirement savings of $14 billion, and newly introduced user fees totaling $14 billion.

Tax increases include $69 billion from increased or extended excise taxes on motor fuels, tobacco, alcoholic beverages, luxury goods, airline travel, telephone communications, and ozone-depleting chemicals; $11 billion from increasing the top statutory tax rate to 31 percent with a maximum tax rate of 28 percent on capital gains; $29 billion from eliminating personal exemptions and limiting the amount of itemized deductions claimed by high income taxpayers; $9 billion from new taxes on insurance companies; $4 billion from other taxes on corporations and businesses; and $41 billion from expanding payroll tax coverage. The tax package includes $27 billion in revenue-losing provisions, including $3 billion increase in the EITC.

Many of the tax provisions in the Act were designed to increase the progressivity of federal taxes. These included much higher refundable credits for low-income families with earnings through the expanded EITC and higher income and payroll taxes for upper-income families. Other provisions of the Act, such as the increases in federal excise taxes and increased out-of-pocket payments for Medicare recipients, should tend to fall more heavily on low-income families.

We have simulated the one-year effect of the major provisions of the Act for 1991. We measure its effects as if all provisions had been fully implemented in 1991. (For example, although tobacco taxes were scheduled to rise by $.04 per pack in 1991 and by an additional $.04 in 1993, we have simulated the full $.08 per pack increase). The results are shown in Table 7.11. The left column (before change) is essentially that given in Table 7.7, moved ahead by one year. The next column is the calculation after OBRA. Although the results are largely progressive, with families in the second and third deciles showing an increase in post-tax, post-transfer income and families in the highest decile showing the largest decrease, the overall effects on post-tax, post-transfer Gini coefficient (not shown in the table) for 1991 are almost nonexistent. It falls from .463 to .460, a change of less than 1 percent.

Conclusions

Given the usual muddle that income distribution statistics often present, the traffic metaphor works remarkably well. There was a major shift in pre-tax, pre-transfer incomes in the 1980s: the top 1 percent of individuals were in

Table 7.11 Share of and Percentage Change in Post-Tax, Post-Transfer Income, by Population Decile, Before and After the Omnibus Budget Reconciliation Act of 1990, 1991

Decile	Share of Each Decile: Before OBRA90	Share of Each Decile: After OBRA90	Percentage Change in Post-Transfer Post-Tax Income
First[a]	2.2	2.3	−0.1
Second	3.3	3.3	0.9
Third	4.4	4.5	0.2
Fourth	5.5	5.6	−0.7
Fifth	6.6	6.6	−0.8
Sixth	7.9	7.9	−0.8
Seventh	9.5	9.5	−0.8
Eighth	11.7	11.7	−0.8
Ninth	14.8	14.8	−0.8
Tenth	34.7	34.6	−1.4
Top 5 percent	25.0	24.8	−1.6
Top 1 percent	12.7	12.5	−2.2
Total[b]	100.0	100.0	100.0

Note: For persons ranked by adjusted pre-tax, pre-transfer family income.
[a]Excludes individuals in families with zero or negative incomes.
[b]Includes individuals in families with zero or negative incomes not shown separately.

a very fast lane, the next 9 percent of individuals were moving reasonably well, and the bottom 80 percent were barely creeping ahead.

While one might expect tax and transfer policies to even out the traffic flow, in fact they did not. Largely because of the decline in the relative importance of transfers, the increase in the share of transfers received by high-income elderly persons, and the rising importance of social security taxes, tax and transfer policies worsened the disparity by a noticeable amount. The majority of these effects are from what could be described as "natural drifts" in tax and transfer policies, though some could be attributed to explicitly antiprogressive measures. Where there was some attempt to redistribute income progressively, as with the Tax Reform Act of 1986 and the Omnibus Budget Reconciliation Act of 1990, the changes, alas, were barely noticeable.

It would have taken enormous tax and transfer policy changes to compensate for the dramatic shift in pre-tax, pre-transfer income over the decade. Not only did actual tax and transfer changes not compensate fully, they were not even in the proper direction.

APPENDIX 7A

Incidence Assumptions

The allocation of corporate taxes is easily the most controversial of any of our incidence assumptions. Should corporate taxes, which are now about 10 percent of total federal tax revenues, be allocated to all capital income, as in the closed economy case, or to labor, as in the small open economy case?

For current purposes, it turns out not to matter very much at all. By construction, the post-tax, post-transfer numbers are the same under either allocation—just the observed distribution of incomes. But the pre-tax distribution should, in principle, depend on the allocation. In practice, it does not. Table 7A.1 compares Gini coefficients for various measures of pre- and post-tax and transfer income, with all corporate taxes allocated to capital income and again with all corporate taxes allocated to labor income. When

Table 7A.1 Gini Coefficients for Alternative Measures of Income: 1980, 1985, and 1990

Year	Pre-Tax Pre-Transfer Income (1)	Pre-Tax Post-Transfer Income (2)	Reduction Due to Transfers (1) − (2)	Post-Tax Post-Transfer Income (3)	Reduction Due to Taxes (2) − (3)
		All Capital Allocation			
1980	.477	.428	.049	.395	.033
1985	.515	.470	.045	.453	.017
1990	.526	.486	.040	.463	.023
		Percentage Change			
1980–1985	7.9	9.8	. . .	14.7	. . .
1985–1990	2.1	3.3	. . .	2.1	. . .
1980–1990	10.2	13.4	. . .	17.1	. . .
		All Labor Allocation			
1980	.470	.419	.051	.395	.024
1985	.511	.465	.046	.453	.012
1990	.521	.479	.042	.463	.016
		Percentage Change			
1980–1985	8.8	10.9	. . .	14.7	. . .
1985–1990	2.0	3.1	. . .	2.1	. . .
1980–1990	10.9	14.2	. . .	17.1	. . .

we make the closed economy assumption that all corporate taxes are allocated to capital, the Gini coefficients for pre-tax, pre-transfer income are indeed slightly higher, but the increase in the Gini coefficient is 10.2 percent over the decade, compared with 10.6 percent for the relevant numbers in Table 7.4. When we make the small open economy assumption that all corporate taxes are allocated to labor income, the Gini coefficients are lower, but they rise by 10.9 percent over the decade. What seems to be true with either assumption is that the corporate tax is a small enough share of total pre-tax, pre-transfer income, and the distribution of capital and labor income overlap enough, that even dramatic changes in assumptions do not change the measure of the trend in inequality by very much at all.

Horizontal Equity

While the effect of federal tax policy between 1980 and 1990 was to worsen the vertical distribution of income, it did improve horizontal equity. Table 7A.2 shows the number of rank reversals between pre-tax and post-tax in-

Table 7A.2 Rank Reversals from Pre-Tax to Post-Tax Income, by Population Decile: 1980 and 1990

	1980[b]			1990[b]		
Decile[a]	Lower	Same	Higher	Lower	Same	Higher
First	. . .	9.6	0.4	. . .	9.6	0.4
Second	0.4	8.6	1.0	0.4	8.7	0.9
Third	1.0	7.5	1.5	0.9	7.8	1.3
Fourth	1.5	6.7	1.8[c]	1.3	7.0	1.7
Fifth	1.7	6.3	1.9[c]	1.7	6.5	1.9[c]
Sixth	2.0	6.3	1.8[c]	1.8	6.5	1.6
Seventh	1.9	6.4	1.7	1.7	6.7	1.6
Eighth	1.8	6.7	1.4	1.6	7.1	1.3
Ninth	1.5	7.6	0.9	1.3	7.9	0.8
Tenth	0.9	7.9	. . .	0.8	8.4	. . .
All Deciles	12.7	75.0	12.0	11.5	76.8	11.5
91st–95th	0.9	3.6	0.5	0.8	3.8	0.3
96th–99th	0.5	3.4	0.1	0.3	3.6	0.0
Top 1 percent	0.1	0.9	. . .	0.0	1.0	. . .

Note: All switches are to the next higher or lower decile except where noted.
[a]Deciles of individuals ranked by adjusted post-transfer, pre-tax family income.
[b]Deciles of individuals ranked by adjusted post-transfer, post-tax family income.
[c]0.1 percent rose by two deciles.

come categories in 1980 and 1990. There was less movement in 1990, with 23.2 percent of persons changing deciles compared with 25.0 percent in 1980. There was also less movement within the highest income decile in 1990. The 1 percent of persons at the top of the pre-tax distribution were still in the top 1 percent once federal taxes were subtracted.

We thank Paul Courant, Robert Plotnick, and the editors for many helpful comments along the way.

References

Atkinson, Anthony B. 1990. "The Distribution of the Tax Burden: 30 Years after *The Theory of Public Finance.*" Essay in honor of Richard Musgrave, University of California, Berkeley.

Auerbach, Alan J. 1988. "Capital Gains Taxation in the United States: Realizations, Revenue, and Rhetoric." *Brooking Papers on Economic Activity* 2.

Ballentine, J. Gregory. 1980. *Equity, Efficiency, and the U.S. Corporation Income Tax.* Washington, D.C.: American Enterprise Institute for Public Policy Research.

Congressional Budget Office. 1986. "Effects of the 1981 Tax Act on the Distribution of Income and Taxes Paid." Staff Working Paper, Washington, D.C., August.

———. 1988. *How Capital Gains Tax Rates Affect Revenues: The Historical Evidence.* A CBO Study, Washington, D.C., March.

———. 1990. *Federal Taxation of Tobacco, Alcoholic Beverages, and Motor Fuels.* A CBO Study, Washington, D.C., August.

Feenberg, Daniel R., and Harvey R. Rosen. 1983. "Alternative Tax Treatments of the Family: Simulation Methodology and Results." In Feldstein, Martin, ed. *Behavioral Simulation Methods in Tax Policy Analysis.* Chicago: University of Chicago Press.

Galper, Harvey, and Stephen H. Pollack. 1988. "Models of State Income Tax Reform." In Gold, Steven D., ed. *The Unfinished Agenda for State Tax Reform.* Denver, CO: National Conference of State Legislatures (November).

Gramlich, Edward, Richard Kasten, and Frank Sammartino. 1989. "Deficit Reduction and Income Distribution." *American Economic Review* 79(2) (May):315–319.

Gravelle, Jane G. 1990. "Can a Capital Gains Tax Cut Pay for Itself?" Congressional Research Service Report, 90-1661 RCO, March 23.

Harberger, Arnold C. 1983. "The State of the Corporate Income Tax: Who Pays It?" In Walker, Charls E., and Mark A. Bloomfield, eds. *New Directions in Federal Tax Policy for the 1980s.* Cambridge, MA: Ballinger.

Hirschman, Albert. 1973. "The Changing Tolerance for Income Inequality in the Course of Economic Development." *Quarterly Journal of Economics* 87(4) (November):545–562.

Kaus, Mickey. 1990. "For a New Equality." *The New Republic* (May 7):18–27.

Killingsworth, Mark R. 1983. *Labor Supply.* New York: Cambridge University Press.

Lindsey, Lawrence B. 1988. "Did ERTA Raise the Share of Taxes Paid by Upper-Income Taxpayers? Will TRA86 Be a Repeat?" In Summers, Lawrence H., ed. *Tax Policy and the Economy*, Volume 2. Cambridge, MA: MIT Press.
———. 1990. *The Growth Experiment: How the New Tax Policy Is Transforming the U.S. Economy*. New York: Basic Books.
Long, James E., and Frank A. Scott. 1984. "The Impact of the 1981 Tax Act on Fringe Benefits and Federal Tax Revenues." *National Tax Journal* 37(2) (June): 185–194.
Musgrave, Richard A., K. E. Case, and H. Leonard. 1974. "The Distribution of Fiscal Burdens and Benefits." *Public Finance Quarterly*, 2(3) (July):259–312.
Mutti, John, and Harry Grubert. 1985. "The Taxation of Capital Income in an Open Economy: The Importance of Resident-Nonresident Tax Treatment." *Journal of Public Economics* 27(3) (August):291–310.
Pechman, Joseph A. 1985. *Who Paid the Taxes, 1966–1985?* Washington, D.C.: Brookings Institution.
Poterba, James M. 1989. "Lifetime Incidence and the Distributional Burden of Excise Taxes." *American Economic Review* 79(2) (May):325–330.
Shoven, John B. 1976. "The Incidence and Efficiency Effect of Taxes on Income from Capital." *Journal of Political Economy* 84(6) (December):1261–1283.
Woodbury, Stephen A. 1983. "Substitution Between Wage and Nonwage Benefits." *American Economic Review* 73(1) (March):166–182.

8

The Minimum Wage and Earnings and Income Inequality

Michael W. Horrigan / Ronald B. Mincy

This chapter examines what would have happened to family income inequality during the 1980s had the minimum wage kept pace with inflation.[1] Two facts suggest that minimum-wage increases could have restrained the increase in family income inequality that occurred during this period. First, earnings at the upper end of the distribution grew much more rapidly than earnings at the lower end (Burtless, 1990). Second, the minimum wage remained unchanged in nominal terms for most of the decade.

Arguments for and against a higher minimum wage are well known. Proponents of the minimum wage often see it as a means of improving the well-being of working poor families and reducing the distance between families in the lower end and those in the remainder of the distribution. The 1980s was the longest period in the history of the minimum wage in which its nominal value remained unchanged. As mean family income increased, families dependent upon minimum-wage income were left behind.

Critics of using the minimum wage as a tool for reducing income inequality argue that the correlation between low-wage earners and their family incomes is weak. Increases in the minimum wage may reach not only targeted low-income families, but also families spread across the entire distribution of incomes. The cost of this target inefficiency is lower demand for labor.

[1] This study uses an extended definition of families. This definition includes married couples, single-parent families, and unrelated individuals. Unrelated individuals may live alone or in households with other persons who are not their family members.

The purpose of this chapter is to help resolve this debate through a careful examination of the effects of simulated increases in the minimum wage on the distribution of family incomes. These simulations take into account disemployment effects, incomplete coverage and compliance, and alternative methods of indexing the minimum wage. After taking these factors into account, we find that simulated minimum-wage increases have virtually no effect on family income inequality.

We then take three further steps. First, we examine the effects of such simulated increases on earnings inequality. Then we examine the target efficiency of the minimum wage in terms of the types of families it affects. Then, using results of recent estimates by Hoffman and Seidman (1990), we compare the target efficiency of the minimum wage to the target efficiency of the Earned Income Tax Credit (EITC). The EITC is an emerging policy for helping the working poor, which some observers view as a substitute for the minimum wage and others view as a complement to it.

Two findings are telling. First, although minimum-wage increases have modest effects on *earnings* inequality, they have virtually no effect on *income* inequality. The lack of effect is due to the low correlation between low wages and low family income. Minimum-wage workers live in families that are more or less evenly placed along the entire distribution of family incomes. What is not known, and what this chapter examines, is the distribution of different types of minimum-wage families across the quintiles of family incomes and the way minimum-wage increases are distributed to different family types across these quintiles. Further, about two thirds of the additional earnings resulting from a minimum-wage increase go to multi-earner families in which a child, spouse, or other relative is the minimum-wage earner. Multiple earners help move these families into the upper tail of the income distribution.

Second, policies such as the EITC are superficially more target efficient than the minimum wage, because they use family income, not wages, as eligibility criteria. But these policies do not dominate the minimum wage as tools for reducing income inequality for two reasons. They do not benefit unrelated individuals, who constitute a large share of low-income households with possible ties to other family members. These policies also may give families in the lower quintiles incentives to reduce work and split up to form multiple households.

In the next section of this chapter we review the literature concerned with the effects of minimum wages on income inequality. Then we discuss the redistributive potential of the minimum wage, its disemployment effects, features of the minimum-wage law, and its target efficiency. These features are incorporated into a model of the effects of minimum-wage increases on family income inequality. We next describe the data used in the simulations and then present and interpret the simulations. In the last section we offer conclusions for policy and research.

Previous Literature

There is a great deal of literature on the effects of minimum wages. Most research has examined the effects of minimum wages on the employment of low-wage workers. (See Brown, Gilroy, and Kohen, 1982, for an excellent review of elasticity estimates.) Although reviewing this literature is not the primary focus of this chapter, we use the research to adjust the amount by which earnings rise following a minimum-wage increase.

The effect of a higher minimum wage on the distribution of family incomes has received less attention. Most studies investigate the correlation between low-wage workers and the income(s) of the families in which they reside. Gramlich (1976) divides low-wage workers into two groups, teenagers and adults. He finds that for both groups, but especially teenagers, significant percentages of low-wage workers are in high-income families. Burkhauser and Finegan (1989b) measure the correlation between the hourly earnings of workers and the income-to-needs ratio of the households in which they reside from 1939 to 1987. They find a strong correlation for unrelated individuals, but weak correlations for household heads and other family members.

Other studies use simulations to examine the effects of a higher minimum wage on the distribution of family incomes. Kelly (1976) studies the effect of a hypothetical increase in the minimum wage on poverty in 1973–1974. He finds that an increase in the minimum wage from $2.00 to $2.65 per hour reduces the poverty gap by 5.8 percent and the number of poor families by 5.8 percent.[2] Kelly's simulations are for an early period (1974) and do not incorporate disemployment effects.

Burkhauser and Finegan (1989a) examine the impact of increasing the 1984 minimum wage of $3.35 to half the average private-sector wage ($4.16). They find that "after the [minimum-wage] increase the share of covered low-wage workers in poverty drops to 11 percent [from 14 percent]. But only $800 million of [the] $7 billion increase goes to poor families." They also find that "nearly one-third of the benefits would go to those with house-

[2] Kelly uses May 1974 data on hourly wages and March 1974 data on incomes. Thus his study matches wage and income data from different surveys, which may have introduced errors in his simulations.

hold incomes at least three times the poverty line. As with Kelly, their simulations do not take into account potential disemployment effects of minimum-wage increases.

Mincy (1990) develops a model to incorporate disemployment effects and simulates the effects of the most recent increase in the minimum wage on both the poverty gap and the number of poor families. Depending on assumptions about compliance and coverage, he finds that the increase reduces the poverty gap by 9 to 11 percent and reduces the number of poor families by 6 to 9 percent.

Using the most sophisticated simulation model to date, Johnson and Browning (1983) examine the effects of a higher minimum wage on the entire distribution of incomes. Their study includes estimates of the effects of a higher minimum wage on tax and transfer payments. They examine the effect of a 22 percent increase in the minimum wage on the distribution of family incomes in 1976 and find that this simulated minimum-wage increase has an equalizing, but very small, impact on the distribution of household incomes.

Johnson and Browning assume universal coverage—that is, anyone earning less than the existing minimum wage benefits from a minimum-wage increase. As in this study, they incorporate disemployment effects in their model. However, their elasticity estimates apply uniformly to all workers. The innovation introduced by Mincy (1990), and repeated here, is to use separate elasticity estimates for different groups of minimum-wage workers.

Notably absent from the minimum-wage literature is a careful description of the types of families that include minimum-wage workers (hereafter, minimum-wage families). In particular, what is missing is a description of families in terms of the relationship of minimum-wage earner(s) to the head of household. The weak correlations between earnings and family income correctly suggest that household heads are a small fraction of all minimum-wage workers.

Modeling the Effects of Minimum-Wage Increases and the Target Efficiency of Minimum Wages

To evaluate the effect of minimum wages on family income inequality, we compare the distributions of family income before and after a minimum-wage increase. To derive these distributions, we specify which workers receive minimum-wage increases and the sizes of those increases. The model adds the increased earnings of eligible workers to family income in order to compute the effect of the increase on family income inequality. We estimated several income inequality statistics, but, given the robustness of findings across different specifications, we report only quintiles of the distribution of family incomes. To explain why the simulations do not affect inequality, we examine the target efficiency of the minimum wage. This examination uses a typology of families based on the relationship of the minimum-wage worker to the household head and on the position of such families in the family income distribution.

Modeling Minimum-Wage Increases

To measure the potential effect of a minimum-wage increase on the overall distribution of family incomes, we first model the factors that determine the workers who are eligible for a minimum-wage increase and the size of the increase for each eligible worker. These factors include potential disemployment effects on teenagers, young adults, and adults; levels of coverage by the minimum wage law and firm noncompliance; and alternative methods for indexing the minimum wage.

INCORPORATING DISEMPLOYMENT EFFECTS A higher minimum wage leads some firms to reduce employment, thereby creating losers and winners among workers who are paid less than the new minimum wage. Thus minimum-wage increases may increase or decrease family income. To account for this possibility we adjust employment using a range of demand elasticities and a methodology described in Appendix 8A. The model uses separate elasticity estimates for teenagers, young adults, and adults, with individual wage data as weights. Brown, Gilroy, and Kohen (1982) provide low and high estimates of employment elasticities for teenagers (16 to 19 years old) and young adults (between 20 and 24 years old). The low estimates of the teenager and young adult elasticities are -0.100 and -0.026. The high estimates are -0.300 and -0.074.

Separate elasticity estimates for adults are not available, so the simulations use elasticities of teenagers and young adults as proxies for elasticities of adults. While there are many possible combinations of elasticity assumptions, we use the four scenarios in Table 8.1. These four scenarios are arranged from lower to higher overall disemployment effects. This order implies a progressively smaller effect of minimum-wage increases on earnings and family income.

Because of the negative correlation between the age of minimum-wage workers and family income, variations in employment elasticities by age may affect the distribution of family incomes. Teenagers who earn the minimum wage are more likely to be members of higher income families than young

Table 8.1 Minimum-Wage Employment Elasticity Scenarios Low to High Overall Disemployment Effects

Scenario	Combination of Employment Elasticities Used for the Simulations: Teens	Young Adults	Adults
Assume Low Teen Elasticity and Teens and Adults are Equal			
(1) Low young adult elasticity	−0.100	−0.026	−0.026
(2) Low teen elasticity	−0.100	−0.026	−0.100
Assume High Teen Elasticity and Young Adults and Adults are Equal			
(3) High young adult elasticity	−0.300	−0.074	−0.026
(4) High teen elasticity	−0.300	−0.074	−0.300

adults or adults who earn the minimum wage. Teenagers also have higher employment elasticities than young adults, and very likely than adults as well. Together these facts suggest that adult and young adult minimum-wage workers will gain more from a minimum-wage increase than teenaged minimum-wage workers. Hence, lower-income families could receive a higher share of the increase than higher-income families, after accounting for disemployment effects. If so, minimum-wage increases adjusted for differential disemployment effects could lower income inequality more than minimum wage increases not so adjusted.

NONCOVERAGE AND NONCOMPLIANCE Although the CPS includes workers who earn less than the minimum wage, it does not distinguish between workers who are not covered and workers whose employers violate the law. Therefore, two sets of simulations are employed. The first set of simulations assumes that all workers earning less than the new minimum wage receive the minimum wage increase. Thus both workers earning at or above the existing minimum, but below the new minimum wage, and workers earning below the existing minimum wage have their hourly earnings increased to the new minimum wage. This scenario allows a higher minimum wage and expanded coverage to occur at the same time, which is consistent with the historical pattern of gradually increasing coverage. The second set of simulations assumes that workers earning below the existing minimum wage, whatever the reason, do not receive the minimum-wage increase. In this scenario, only workers earning at or above the existing minimum, but below the new minimum wage, have their hourly earnings increased to the new minimum wage.

INDEXING THE MINIMUM WAGE Historically, minimum wages have followed an irregular pattern determined by political and economic considerations. Maintaining a decent standard of living for low-wage workers during the late 1930s was a key objective of the original minimum-wage law. Changes in the minimum wage over time reflect attempts to achieve this long-term goal. Each amendment of the Fair Labor Standards Act fixes the minimum wage at some initial level and usually prescribes step changes designed to hit some target over the following two to three years. One such target has been to restore the eroded real value of the minimum wage and to prescribe, in advance, step changes that attempt to maintain its real value. Another target has been to set the minimum wage at 50 percent of the average hourly earnings of production and nonsupervisory workers and prescribe step changes intended to maintain this ratio.

Policymakers rarely hit these targets. When the prescribed step changes are exhausted, the minimum wage declines in real terms because of general price inflation. It also declines in relative terms as productivity increases and wage inflation push average hourly earnings up. Once again, the minimum falls below the long-term target, so that political pressure for an increase begins anew.

Our simulations remove these irregularities by imposing often proposed, but never adopted, yearly indexing. There are two indexing rules. The first rule adjusts for price inflation, using the CPI-U-X1 price index to keep the purchasing power of low-wage workers constant. Such a policy may be politically unacceptable because many workers with higher skills than those of minimum-wage workers have no guarantee that their wages will keep pace with inflation. As a more politically feasible alternative, the second rule maintains the value of the minimum wage at 50 percent of average hourly earnings of production and nonsupervisory workers.

Values of the minimum wage under each indexing rule appear in Table 8.2. In each year, the adjusted minimum wage is higher under the price inflation indexing rule (Column 2) than under the wage inflation indexing rule (Column 4). This reflects declines in the real average hourly wage rate. Note also that, by 1987, both indexing rules would set the minimum wage well above the current law.

Table 8.2 Indexing the Minimum Wage to Reflect Changes in Prices and Average Hourly Earnings

Year	Minimum Wage	Price Inflation Adjusted Minimum Wage[a]	Average Hourly Wage	Wage Inflation Adjusted Minimum Wage[b]	Minimum Wage as a Percentage of Average Hourly Earnings
1979	2.90	. . .	6.16	. . .	0.47
1980	3.10	3.18	6.66	3.08	0.47
1981	3.35	3.54	7.25	3.33	0.46
1982	3.35	3.87	7.68	3.63	0.44
1983	3.35	4.11	8.02	3.84	0.42
1984	3.35	4.28	8.32	4.01	0.40
1985	3.35	4.46	8.57	4.16	0.39
1986	3.35	4.62	5.76	4.29	0.38
1987	3.35	4.71	8.98	4.38	0.37

[a] Values of the minimum wage that would have been observed since January 1, 1980, had the increase in the minimum wage been updated to reflect CPI-U-X1.

[b] Values of the minimum wage that would have been observed since January 1, 1980, had the increase in the minimum wage been updated to preserve the ratio of the minimum wage to average hourly earnings of production or nonsupervisory workers in 1979.

Target Efficiency

The effect of a higher minimum wage on family income inequality depends on the types and relative incomes of minimum-wage families. This study uses both features of the distribution of minimum-wage families to assess the target efficiency of the minimum wage.

First we decompose minimum-wage families into eight exhaustive and mutually exclusive groups.

(1) Unrelated Individuals—A minimum-wage worker living in a single or nonfamily household.
(2) Families Maintained by Women—Families in which the female head of household is a minimum-wage worker.
(3) Families Maintained by Men—Families in which the male head of household is a minimum-wage worker.
(4) Dual-Earner Families—Married-couple families in which both spouses are minimum-wage workers.

(5) Single-Earner Families—Married-couple families in which only one spouse is employed and is a minimum-wage worker.
(6) Mixed-Earner Families—Married-couple families in which both spouses are employed and only one is a minimum-wage worker.
(7) Child-Earner Families—Families in which neither the head of household nor the spouse (if present) is a minimum-wage worker, but where there is at least one child who is a minimum-wage worker.
(8) All Other Families—Families in which there is at least one family member who is the minimum-wage worker, other than the head of household, the spouse (if present), or a child.

This decomposition of broadly defined families emphasizes the characteristics of workers and families most relevant to policies intended to help the working poor. Prominent policies include child-care subsidies, the Earned Income Tax Credit, and mandatory employee benefits, as well as the minimum wage. For example, a family maintained by a woman who earns the minimum wage forms one type of minimum-wage family. This assignment holds even if there are teenagers in the family who are also minimum-wage workers. In fact, each of the minimum-wage family types may contain teenaged minimum-wage workers. However, only two types, the (7) Child-Earner Families and (8) All Other Families, represent families in which neither the head of household nor spouse (if present) is a minimum-wage worker.[3]

Next we examine the distribution of minimum-wage families by quintiles of family income distribution. In particular, this study shows what fraction of minimum-wage families are in each quintile of the family income distribution, what fraction of the total increase in family incomes resulting from a higher minimum wage (hereafter, "the boost") accrues to families in each quintile, and how the boost is distributed across the income quintiles by the different family types.

Data

We use data from both the basic and supplemental files of the March Current Population Survey (CPS). Starting in 1979, the monthly basic CPS collects earnings information from a quarter of the total CPS sample, including

[3]Notice that a family with a minimum-wage worker that is maintained by a woman who is herself not a minimum-wage worker is classified as a Child family.

information on workers paid hourly rates.[4] The March supplemental file records information on the work experience of such individuals during the prior year, including weeks worked, usual weekly hours, and occupation and industry of employment. This file also provides the corresponding family income of these individuals for that prior year.[5]

The universe of families in this study excludes all unrelated subfamilies and families with negative income, but includes unrelated individuals. For a family to be included in the sample, individuals in families must meet certain restrictions. First, individuals cannot be self-employed, government employees, or unpaid family workers. Second, individuals must have the same occupation and industry in March as they had in the prior calendar year. This second restriction minimizes the possible distortions that arise, because the simulations use March hourly earnings as a proxy for hourly earnings over the prior calendar year. The sensitivity of the findings to this latter universe restriction was tested by imposing both restrictions, and then imposing only the first. The results were virtually the same in the two cases.

The CPS data have two important advantages. First, income and earnings data are reported in the same survey, so the simulations produce a nationally representative distribution of both actual family income before, and hypothetical family income after, the boost. Second, because the CPS is a household survey and not an establishment survey, deliberate misreporting of illegal wage payments by firms does not affect the simulations (see Cartensen

[4]The questions from the March CPS asked of the quarter sample include:

25A. How many hours per week does ________ USUALLY work at this job?

25B. Is ________ paid by the hour on this job?

Yes (Go to 25C)

No (Skip to 25D)

25C. How much does ________ earn per hour?

25D. How much does ________ USUALLY earn per week at this job BEFORE deductions? Include any overtime pay, commissions, or tips usually received.

[5]Income is defined by the Census Bureau as the "sum of amounts received from wages and salaries, self-employment income (including losses), Social Security, Supplemental Security Income, public assistance, interest, dividends, rent, royalties, estates or trusts, Veteran's payments, unemployment and workers' compensations, private and government retirement and disability pensions, alimony, child support, and any other source of money income which was regularly received. Capital gains (or losses) and lump-sum or one-time payments such as life insurance settlements are excluded."

Another data source often used in studies of minimum wages is the May supplement to the CPS over the 1973–1978 period. This supplement provided information on hourly earnings. To combine this information with data on both work experience and family income from the prior calendar year, however, it would be necessary to match the responses of individuals to both the March and May supplements to the CPS. These two surveys have different selection probabilities for respondents, making it impossible to determine the appropriate sample weight and derive a nationally representative sample.

and Woltman, 1979). Also, unlike some studies that use the quotient of usual weekly earnings and usual weekly hours to approximate hourly earnings, this study uses reported hourly wage rates. This avoids errors that arise when respondents round off estimates of both usual weekly earnings and usual weekly hours (see Haugen and Mellor, 1990).[6]

There are, however, some disadvantages to using CPS data. First, as already noted, we cannot distinguish between noncoverage and noncompliance for workers earning below the minimum wage.[7] Second, the wage data are from the March survey week, but data on hours and family income refer to the previous year.[8] Third, although respondents report weeks worked part-time and full-time separately, the March survey reports usual weekly hours only for the worker's usual status, either full-time or part-time. Hence, by using usual weekly hours, transitions between full-time and part-time employment are being ignored. The size of the bias caused by these problems is not known. Finally, reported wages exclude tips or commissions

[6]By definition, usual weekly earnings would include tips and commissions. The estimation of "usual" weekly earnings would also solve the problem that, by restricting the universe to workers paid by the hour, the eligible population will exclude any worker paid nonhourly with earnings that, "when translated into hourly rates," would be eligible for a minimum-wage boost. What would be the effect of computing "usual" hourly earnings of workers paid hourly rates? Using the 1988 minimum wage as a benchmark, there were 1.476 million nonhourly paid workers earning an imputed $3.35 per hour or less in that year. When the hourly earnings of all workers are tallied (using either actual or imputed hourly earnings), 5.3 percent of all workers earn $3.35 or less. This compares with 6.5 percent of all hourly paid workers earning $3.35 or less. These results suggest that the provision of supplemental compensation serves to bring many individuals above the minimum-wage threshold. For further information on this point, see Haugen and Mellor (1990).

[7]There are numerous exceptions to the minimum-wage requirement. For example, certain retail establishments may be exempt based on the value of annual reported sales. Since individuals are not asked for—nor could they reliably report—the annual reported sales of their employer, such exemptions are not captured by the CPS.

[8]This makes it impossible to synchronize simulated and actual changes in wages perfectly. While there is no obvious solution to this problem, it occurs only twice with the minimum-wage increases in 1980 and 1981. In 1980 the minimum wage stood at $3.10 an hour. If the CPI-U-X1 had been used to adjust this wage for past inflation, the minimum wage would have been $3.54 throughout 1980. The model in this chapter attempts to capture the disemployment effects that would have occurred throughout 1980 if the minimum wage had increased from $3.10 to $3.54. But to measure this impact it is necessary to use hourly earnings information from the March 1981 survey. However, on January 1, 1981, the minimum wage rose from $3.10 to $3.35 per hour. Hence, the individuals eligible for a minimum-wage increase, those with hourly earnings less than $3.54 in the March survey, are to some extent the survivors of the minimum-wage increase from $3.10 to $3.35 an hour that took place on January 1, 1981. In other words, there may be numerous individuals who were minimum-wage recipients throughout 1980, who were displaced by the increase in the minimum wage on January 1, 1981, and were unemployed or out of the labor force as of the March 1981 survey. Hence, part of the disemployment impact being incorporated into the model has already been observed in the data.

Table 8.3 Percentage of Total Family Income Held by Each Quintile of Families: 1980 and 1987

Quintile	1980	1987	Absolute Change from 1980 to 1987
	Actual		
1	4.288	3.751	−0.5
2	10.063	9.286	−0.8
3	16.572	15.783	−0.8
4	24.919	24.897	−0.0
5	44.158	46.283	2.1
Total	100	100	
	Simulated[a]		
1	4.288	3.785	−0.5
2	10.066	9.318	−0.7
3	16.569	15.867	−0.7
4	24.919	24.819	−0.1
5	44.158	46.211	2.1
Total	100	100	

Source: Tabulations by authors, 1981 and 1988 CPS.

[a] Assumes incomplete compliance and coverage, indexing by CPI-U-X1, and Scenario (3) from Table 8.1.

and thus understate the true hourly earnings of some workers. This means that the count of workers eligible for a boost may be too high.[9]

Results

Family Income Inequality

The top panel of Table 8.3 shows what happened to family income inequality between 1980 and 1987. In 1980, families in the bottom fifth of the family income distribution held 4.3 percent of family income, while families in the top fifth held 44.2 percent. By 1987, all families, except those in the top fifth of family income distribution, had lower shares of family income.

[9] This study did not divide usual hourly earnings data, which does include tips and commissions, by usual weekly hours data to get usual hourly earnings (Johnson and Browning, 1983), because, as mentioned above, this procedure could introduce more serious errors.

The share of family income held by families in the top fifth of the family income distribution rose from 44.2 percent to 46.3 percent.[10] This movement is consistent with the general finding that family incomes have become more unequal since the late 1970s.

The second panel of Table 8.3 shows simulated 1980 and 1987 family income distributions for one of the many simulations we performed. This simulation assumes that the 1987 minimum wage was $4.71 (i.e., that it was adjusted for changes in the CPI-U-X1 price index); assumes employment elasticities in Scenario (3) (−0.300 for teens and −0.074 for all others); and also assumes incomplete coverage and compliance. We find that a higher minimum wage would have almost no impact on family income inequality. Our actual and simulated family income distributions in Table 8.3 are nearly identical, even though the simulated quintile shares assume an increase in the minimum wage. This null effect may have been caused by the small income gains resulting from the minimum-wage increase, which was less than 1 percent of the total family income before the minimum-wage increase. Hence, even if they accrued only to families in the lower quintile, it is doubtful that these income gains could have significantly affected the distribution of family income.

How can we account for the lack of effect of minimum-wage increases on the family income distributions? Why do variations in indexing rules, assumptions about coverage and compliance, and disemployment effects seem to have no effect? We can answer these questions by tracing the effects of minimum-wage increases from the earnings of family members who are eligible to receive those increases to family income.

Earnings Inequality

We begin by looking at earnings effects. Table 8.4 shows the actual and simulated distribution of earnings in 1987 for workers 15 years old or older. Again, the simulations assume incomplete compliance and coverage, increases in the minimum wage using the CPI-U-X1 price index, and disemployment effects defined by Scenario (3) in Table 8.1.[11] Minimum-wage increases have the expected effects on the distribution of male earnings, but these effects are small. In 1987, workers in the bottom fifth of the male earnings distribution held 2.4 percent of male earnings, while workers in the top fifth held 44.3 percent of male earnings. If the minimum wage had

[10] Income inequality among families in our quarter sample of workers paid by the hour grew at a pace similar to that for the entire sample.

[11] Simulated earnings distributions are virtually identical under alternative disemployment effects scenarios.

Table 8.4 Percentage of Aggregate Earnings Held by Each Quintile of Workers: 1987

	Males		Females	
Quintile	Actual	Simulated[a]	Actual	Simulated[a]
1	2.44	2.52	2.10	2.17
2	9.84	9.93	8.54	8.77
3	17.45	17.43	16.82	16.93
4	26.01	25.96	26.13	26.01
5	44.26	44.16	46.40	46.13

Source: Tabulations by authors, 1988 CPS.

[a]Assumes incomplete compliance and coverage, indexing by CPI-U-X1, and Scenario (3) from Table 8.1.

risen to reflect price inflation, there would have been less earnings inequality. Workers in the bottom fifth of the male earnings distribution would have held 2.52 percent of male earnings, a 4 percent increase. Workers in the top fifth would have held 44.2 percent of male earnings, a 0.3 percent reduction.

Minimum-wage increases have somewhat larger effects on the distribution of female earnings. In 1987, workers in the bottom fifth of the female earnings distribution held 2.1 percent of female earnings, while workers in the top fifth held 46.4 percent of female earnings. If the minimum wage had risen to reflect price inflation, workers in the bottom fifth of the female earnings distribution would have held 2.17 percent of female earnings, an increase of 3.3 percent. Workers in the top fifth would have held 46.13 percent of female earnings, a reduction of 0.6 percent. The percentage of female workers who benefit from minimum-wage increases, 17 percent, is larger than the percentage of male workers who benefit, 7 percent. Therefore we expect such increases to have a larger effect on female than male earnings inequality.

Earnings Differences Between Groups

Minimum-wage increases reduce earnings differences between groups of workers in two primary ways. First, such increases reduce differences between the earnings of older and younger workers. Second, such increases reduce differences between the earnings of workers in high- and low-status occupations. Minimum-wage increases have very little effect on earnings differences between workers with more and less education.

In 1987 mean earnings of male workers in the prime age group (35 to 54) were 8.30 times as large as mean earnings of male workers in their teenage years (Table 8.5A). Mean earnings of female workers in the prime age group were 4.98 times as large as the earnings of female workers in their teenage years (Table 8.5A). If the minimum wage had increased to $4.71, these ratios would have been 2 to 3 percent lower, that is 8.06 for males and 4.84 for females. The ratio of the earnings of young adult male and female workers to the earnings of teenagers would also have fallen by 2 to 3 percent, to about 5.98 for males and 4.42 for females.

Gender affects how far occupational wage differentials fall in response to a minimum-wage increase (Table 8.5B).[12] To ease the exposition, we refer to private household and food service workers as workers in minimum-wage occupations. Mean annual earnings of these workers are closest to the annual earnings of a full-time, full-year worker who earns the minimum wage. Male managers and professionals earn more than four times as much as men in minimum-wage occupations. Male operatives, fabricators, and laborers, and male service workers earn about two and a half times as much as men in minimum-wage occupations. The 34 percent increase in the minimum wage from $3.10 in 1980 to $4.71 in 1987 would reduce these ratios by 3 to 4 percent. With the exception of female managers and professionals, women in non–minimum-wage occupations have smaller earnings advantages over women in minimum-wage occupations than do male workers. Further, minimum-wage increases would cause a 2 percent reduction in the ratio of the earnings of female operatives, fabricators, and laborers to the earnings of women in minimum-wage occupations. There would be less than a 2 percent decline in the ratio of the earnings of other female service workers to the earnings of women in minimum-wage occupations.

Minimum-wage increases have even less effect on earnings differentials by education (Table 8.5C). Men with a college education earn twice as much

[12] *Managers and Professionals* include: Administrators and Officials, Public Administration; Managers and Administrators, Except Public Administration, Salaried, Self-Employed; Management-Related Occupations; Accountants and Auditors; Engineers, Architects, and Surveyors; Engineers; Natural Scientists and Mathematicians; Computer Systems Analysts and Scientists; Health Diagnosing Occupations; Physicians and Dentists; Health Assessment and Treating Occupations; Teachers, Librarians, and Counselors; Teachers, Except Postsecondary; and Other Professional Specialty Occupations.

Minimum Wage Occupations include: Private Household Service Occupations and Food Service Occupations.

Operators, Fabricators, and Laborers include: Supervisors and Production Occupations; Precision Production Occupations; Machine Operators and Tenders, Except Precision; Fabricators, Assemblers, and Hand-Working Occupations; and Production Inspectors, Testers, Samplers, and Weighers.

Other Service Occupations include: Health Service Occupations; Cleaning and Building Service Occupations; Personal Service Occupations; and Mechanics and Repairers.

All occupation listings are taken from CPS 1988 rewrite.

Table 8.5A Earnings for Age Groups by Sex, Expressed as a Ratio: 1987

Scenario	Ratio of Prime Adult to Teen	Ratio of Young Adult to Teen	Ratio of Other Youth to Teen	Ratio of Elderly to Teen
Males				
Actual	8.30	6.15	2.97	3.68
Simulated[a]	8.06	5.98	2.91	3.58
Females				
Actual	4.98	4.55	2.83	2.17
Simulated[a]	4.84	4.42	2.77	2.11

Source: Tabulations by authors, 1988 CPS.

Teen → Ages 16–19
Other Youth → Ages 20–24
Young Adult → Ages 25–34
Prime Adult → Ages 35–64
Elderly → Ages 65 +

[a] Assumes incomplete compliance and coverage, indexing by CPI-U-X1, and Scenario (3) from Table 8.1.

Table 8.5B Earnings for Occupation Groups by Sex, Expressed as a Ratio: 1987

Scenario	Ratio of Wages of Other Service Occupations to Minimum Wage Occupations	Ratio of Wages of Operators, Fabricators, and Laborers to Minimum Wage Occupations	Ratio of Wages of Managers and Professionals to Minimum Wage Occupations
Males			
Actual	2.44	2.62	4.34
Simulated[a]	2.35	2.52	4.17
Females			
Actual	1.61	2.05	3.59
Simulated[a]	1.59	2.00	3.45

Source: Tabulations by authors, 1988 CPS.

[a] Assumes incomplete compliance and coverage, indexing by CPI-U-X1, and Scenario (3) from Table 8.1.

Table 8.5C Earnings for Education Groups by Sex, Expressed as a Ratio: 1987

Scenario	Ratio of College to Less Than High School	Ratio of Diploma to Less Than High School	Ratio of College to Diploma
Males			
Actual	2.07	1.24	1.66
Simulated[a]	2.06	1.24	1.66
Females			
Actual	2.26	1.42	1.60
Simulated[a]	2.23	1.40	1.59

Source: Tabulations by authors, 1988 CPS.

College → Completed more than 12 years of education
Diploma → Completed 12 years of education
Less than high school → Completed less than 12 years of education

[a] Assumes incomplete compliance and coverage, indexing by CPI-U-X1, and Scenario (3) from Table 8.1.

as men with less than a high-school diploma. Men with a high-school diploma earn almost 25 percent more than men with less education. Differences between the earnings of more- and less-educated women are slightly larger. Minimum-wage increases would cause almost no change in the ratio of the earnings of men with a high-school diploma to the earnings of men without a high-school diploma. Such increases would barely affect the ratio of the earnings of men with a college education to the earnings of men without a high-school diploma. There would be 1 to 2 percent reductions in the earnings ratios for women with a high-school education to the earnings of women with less than a high-school diploma.

Thus, a partial explanation for the lack of effect of minimum-wage increases on family income distribution is that such increases have modest effects on the distribution of earnings. The low correlation between low income and low earnings is the other part of the explanation. We can see this most clearly by adding the earnings of eligible workers to the incomes of other family members. To do this, we estimated the quintiles of the family income distribution before the minimum-wage increase (Table 8.6). Next, we increased the wages of eligible workers, assuming adjustments according to CPI-U-X1, incomplete coverage and compliance, and Scenario

Table 8.6 Actual Distribution of Minimum-Wage Families Among the Quintiles of the Distribution of Total Family Incomes by Type of Minimum-Wage Family: 1987

		Quintiles				
Type of Family	Total	1	2	3	4	5
Unrelated Individuals	17.37	12.18	4.09	1.00	0.00	0.10
Families Maintained by Women	7.05	3.38	2.53	0.87	0.27	0.00
Families Maintained by Men	1.05	0.32	0.33	0.40	0.00	0.00
Single-Earner Families	4.79	1.19	2.22	1.09	0.19	0.10
Dual-Earner Families	1.70	0.30	0.55	0.34	0.45	0.06
Mixed-Earner Families	30.14	1.43	6.22	9.89	8.06	4.54
Child-Earner Families	30.35	0.52	3.04	4.86	8.87	13.06
All Other Eligible Families	6.72	0.93	1.67	2.15	0.85	1.12
Total Eligible Families	99.90	20.26	20.95	20.62	18.89	19.18

Source: Tabulations by authors, 1988 CPS.

Note: Each family is counted once.

(3) employment elasticities. Finally, we calculated the fraction of the total increase in earnings received by each quintile of our ex-ante family income distribution (Table 8.7).[13]

Why is the small effect of minimum-wage increases on earnings inequality nullified by sorting eligible workers into their respective families? First, families including eligible workers (from now on, minimum-wage families) are evenly spread across quintiles of the distribution of family incomes (Table 8.6, Row 9). For example, 20.26 percent of minimum-wage families are in the bottom quintile of the distribution of family income, but 19.18 percent are in the top quintile. Thus, the poorest and wealthiest families are almost equally likely to benefit from the minimum wage-increase. Second, upper and lower quintiles get sizable shares of the boost (Table 8.7, Row 9). The bottom quintile receives 20.56 percent of the total boost, while the top quintile receives 15.50 percent. Since families in the upper-income brackets share significantly in minimum-wage boosts, families in the lower-income brackets cannot close the gap with the remainder of the distribution.

[13] We produced Tables 8.6 and 8.7 in the following way. First, we established quintiles based on the distribution of income for all families in the sample. Then we distributed minimum-wage families across these quintiles (Table 8.6). Finally, we determined how the boost was distributed across the family type and (ex-ante) quintiles (Table 8.7).

Table 8.7 Simulated Distribution of Minimum-Wage Boosts Among the Quintiles of the Distribution of Total Family Incomes by Type of Minimum-Wage Family: 1987[a]

		Quintiles				
Type of Family	Total	1	2	3	4	5
Unrelated Individuals	17.78	10.74	5.40	1.64	0.00	0.00
Families Maintained by Women	9.44	4.65	3.28	1.20	0.31	0.00
Families Maintained by Men	1.09	0.27	0.36	0.46	0.00	0.00
Single-Earner Families	4.79	1.34	1.82	1.30	0.16	0.17
Dual-Earner Families	4.19	0.88	1.55	0.53	1.11	0.12
Mixed-Earner Families	31.69	1.13	6.76	10.60	8.95	4.25
Child-Earner Families	21.33	0.43	1.83	3.33	3.22	5.40
All Other Eligible Families	8.86	1.14	2.14	2.86	0.95	1.77
Total Eligible Families	99.90	20.56	23.55	21.94	18.35	15.50

Source: Tabulations by authors, 1988 CPS.

[a]Assumes incomplete compliance and coverage, indexing by CPI-U-X1, and Scenario (3) from Table 8.1.

Note: Each family is counted once.

Target Efficiency

The realization that upper- and lower-income families share the benefits of minimum-wage boosts almost equally brings the analysis full circle, to an evaluation of the target efficiency of the minimum wage. How are minimum-wage increases distributed across the quintiles of our family income distribution among different family types? Only 15 percent of minimum-wage families are families that are traditionally targeted by policies to help the working poor. These are families where the head (and the spouse in the case of two earners) receive the minimum wage. If we add the group of unrelated individuals to the target group, the portion of targeted families rises to 32 percent. Further, targeted families and unrelated individuals receive only 37 percent of the boost (Table 8.7). Just over three-fifths of the boost goes to families not traditionally targeted by policies to help the working poor. Mixed-Earner Couples get over 30 percent of the boost, Child-Earner Families get an additional 21 percent of the boost, and the remainder goes to families in which some other family member is the minimum-wage earner. These nontargeted families depend least upon the earnings of minimum-wage workers and are the only families with significant representation in the top three quintiles of our family income distribution.

How does the target efficiency of the minimum wage compare with the target efficiency of other policies to help the working poor? Recent evidence on the redistributive effects of the Earned Income Tax Credit (EITC) suggests that in one respect at least the minimum wage compares very poorly. Hoffman and Seidman (1990) projected the distribution of EITC benefits in 1988 by income classes.[14] Hoffman and Seidman use five groups of families, classified by annual income. The five income groups are: (1) less than $10,000; (2) between $10,000 and $15,000; (3) between $15,000 and $20,000; (4) between $20,000 and $30,000; and (5) over $30,000. Families in the first four income groups roughly correspond to families in the bottom three quintiles of our family income distribution. Hoffman and Seidman find that 41.0 percent of EITC benefits would go to families with incomes of less than $10,000, and 38.9 percent of EITC benefits would go to families with incomes of between $10,000 and $15,000. But only 3.9 percent of EITC benefits would go to families with incomes exceeding $30,000. In other words, about 4 percent would go to families in the top two quintiles of our family income distribution. Thus, by using income, not wages, as the criteria for helping the working poor, the EITC is far more target efficient than the minimum wage.

Nevertheless, the minimum wage substantially benefits one segment of the working-poor population that EITC misses entirely. Unrelated individuals are ineligible for the EITC, because they have no children. But unrelated individuals get almost half the minimum-wage boost going to our expanded version of the group targeted by policies to help the working poor (Table 8.7, Column 1). Thus the foregoing comparison is not enough to assess the target efficiency of the minimum wage, compared with other policies that help the working poor.

Unfortunately the credit and benefit reduction rate structure that makes the EITC target efficient also creates certain disadvantages. Consider what happens to families with one child under current law, which will be fully phased in by 1994. These families get a credit equal to 23 percent of earned income up to $7,089.99 (in 1991 dollars). The maximum credit, $1,631, is available to families whose earned income is between $7,090.00 and $11,169.99. This maximum credit falls by 17.86 percent—the benefit reduction rate—for families with earned income above $11,169.99, and is completely phased out when the family earned income reaches $21,094.00.

These rates create at least two undesirable incentives for families with incomes in the lower quintiles. First, families with incomes in the phase-out

[14]Their projections use data from the Panel Study of Income Dynamics, not the Current Population Survey, but this seems to be a reliable source because estimates of the average EITC benefit and the number of EITC recipients closely match IRS data.

range, $7,090.00 to $21,094.00, face high marginal tax rates, which discourages work (Steuerle and Juffras, 1991). Second, families with incomes above $7,089.99 have incentives to split their incomes so that they continue to receive a credit on earned income. A family could split its income by divorce, separation, or by falsely maintaining a separate household.[15] This incentive would be even stronger if unrelated individuals were covered by EITC.

While a full assessment of the relative target efficiency of the minimum wage is beyond the scope of this chapter, we can suggest a few questions such an assessment would have to answer. Should our society include unrelated individuals in the group targeted by policies to help the working poor? To answer this question, we would have to know more about the composition of unrelated individuals who work. For example, how many working, unrelated individuals are college students, who work part-time; single young men and women, who have completed schooling; and absent parents, with children living in households maintained by a former spouse or partner? Besides knowing more about the composition of working unrelated individuals, we must know more about how policies affect their behavior. For example, if single unrelated individuals received benefits under the EITC, how would marriage rates among such individuals change? If policies to help the working poor included benefits for absent parents, how much would children benefit through the increased capacity of absent parents to pay child support? How much do the current benefit reduction rates in the EITC discourage work?

Answers to these questions are needed to sort out the right mix of policies to reduce income inequality. The minimum wage helps workers without regard to the incomes of other family members. This means that minimum wages benefit upper income families primarily. It also means that minimum wages give workers additional income that affects families in ways that are hard to observe. Other policies, such as the EITC, child tax credits, or child-care allowances help only those workers whose family incomes, as well

[15] For example, suppose a family with two children had two adults who worked for the minimum wage. The husband worked 40 hours per week and the wife worked 20 hours per week. The family's gross income excluding the credit would be $13,260. Because this family's income fell into the phase-out range, the family would have 17.86 percent deducted from the maximum credit ($1,773) for all income above $11,170. Thus, the total benefit from the EITC would be $1,339.73. Now suppose that the couple separated, with each parent taking one child. The household headed by the husband would have a gross income of $8,840 and the household headed by the wife would have a gross income of $4,420. Households with one child receive 23 percent credit up to $7,090 of earned income. Therefore, the household headed by the husband would receive the maximum credit of $1,631 and the household headed by the wife would receive a credit of $1,016. The combined credit of $2,789.60 is nearly double the previous benefit.

as whose own earnings, are low. However, these policies also give families in the lower quintiles incentives to reduce work and split up to form multiple households.

Summary and Conclusions

This chapter examines the effect of a higher minimum wage on family income inequality through the use of a model that simulated minimum-wage increases. We find that these increases have virtually no effect on family income inequality, but that they have modest effects on earnings inequality.

An examination of the target efficiency of the minimum wage shows that about two thirds of minimum-wage increases go to those families that depend least on the earnings of minimum-wage workers. These findings cast doubt on the argument that a higher minimum wage can reduce family income inequality. We then look at the target efficiency of the EITC, and find that the EITC creates work disincentives for working poor families with higher earnings, and provides no benefits to unrelated individuals, who receive a relatively large share of benefits from an increase in the minimum wage. If low income deters individuals from forming families or supporting children, then increasing minimum wages can help where other current policies cannot.

In the future, proponents of higher minimum wages cannot rely on the argument that such increases reduce family income inequality. They can, however, argue that such increases improve labor market equity, the absolute well-being of families, and that they fill a potentially important void left by other policies to help the working poor. Minimum-wage increases reduce earnings inequality, though, as we have shown, the effect is small. Minimum-wage increases also reduce poverty, though in a target-inefficient way. Finally, minimum-wage increases help unrelated individuals, who represent a significant share of the working poor.

APPENDIX 8A

Let F_i denote the income accruing to the ith family before the minimum wage increase (ex-ante). N_i is the number of working members of the ith family who earn less than the new minimum wage ex-ante. $E(dL_j)$ is the expected change in the jth worker's earnings resulting from the minimum-wage increase (ex-post), including the disemployment effect. Thus, the family's expected ex-post income is

$$F_i + \sum_{j=1}^{N_i} E(dL_j).$$

The model ignores changes in hours worked and prices following a higher minimum wage because there is no consensus on the size of these changes. A few studies estimate the effect of a higher minimum wage on hours worked (see Zucker, 1973; Gramlich, 1976; and Linneman, 1982). However, these studies use different samples, different methods, and reach different conclusions. Studies of the effects of a higher minimum wage on prices also lack consensus (see Sellekaerts, 1981). The model also ignores so-called ripple effects; that is, effects that minimum wage increases may have on wages above the statutory minimum. The model only incorporates the widely accepted estimates of the disemployment effect. This implies that the simulations overestimate the effects of minimum-wage increases on family income and family income inequality.

The expected change in earnings for the jth worker is:

$$E(dL_j) = H_j[\lambda_j dw_j - (1-\lambda_j)w_j], \qquad (8A.1)$$

where

λ_j = the probability that the jth worker is employed,
w_j = the jth worker's wage ex-ante,
dw_j = the change in the jth worker's wage, and
H_j = annual hours worked by the jth worker.

To complete the model, we follow Mincy (1990), who derives an estimate of the ex-post employment probability from estimates of the long-run elasticity of employment with respect to minimum-wage changes (hereafter, the employment elasticity). If all workers were identical, the ex-post employment probability would be related to the employment elasticity as follows:

$$\lambda = \frac{J_1}{J_0} = 1 + \left(\frac{dw}{w}\right)\varepsilon, \qquad (8A.2)$$

where

J_0 = the level of ex-ante employment,
J_1 = the level of ex-post employment,

w = the wage,
dw = the wage change, and
ε ($\varepsilon<0$) = the employment elasticity.

The following approximation retains the simple link between the ex-post employment probability and the employment elasticity, but drops the assumption that workers are identical

$$\lambda_j = 1 + \left(\frac{dw_j}{w_j}\right) \varepsilon_k. \tag{8A.3}$$

To complete the approximation, Equation (8A.3) is substituted into Equation (8A.1). Rearranging terms yields

$$E(dL_j) = H_j dw_j \left[1 + \frac{(1 + dw_j)}{w_j} \right]. \tag{8A.4}$$

References

Blackburn, McKinley L., David E. Bloom, and Richard B. Freeman. 1990. "The Declining Economic Position of Less Skilled Men." In Burtless, Gary, ed. *A Future of Lousy Jobs?* Washington, D.C.: Brookings Institution.

Brown, Charles, Curtis Gilroy, and Andrew Kohen. 1982. "The Effect of the Minimum Wage on Employment and Unemployment." *Journal of Economic Literature* 20 (2):487–528.

Burkhauser, Richard V., and T. Aldrich Finegan. 1989a. "The Economics of Minimum Wage Legislation Revisited." Working Paper, June.

———. 1989b. "The Minimum Wage and the Poor: The End of a Relationship." *Journal of Policy Analysis and Management* 8 (1):53–71.

Burtless, Gary. 1990. "Earnings Inequality over the Business and Demographic Cycles." In Burtless, Gary, ed. *A Future of Lousy Jobs?* Washington, D.C.: Brookings Institution.

Cartensen, Larry, and Henry Woltman. 1979. "Comparing Earnings Data from the CPS and Employers' Records." Papers presented at the Annual Meetings of the American Statistical Association Meetings, Washington, D.C.

Ellwood, David T. 1988. *Poor Support: Poverty in the American Family*. New York: Basic Books.

Gramlich, Edward M. 1976. "Impact of Minimum Wages on Other Wages, Employment, and Family Incomes." *Brookings Papers on Economic Activity*, No. 2:409–461.

Haugen, Steven, and Earl Mellor. 1990. "Estimating the Number of Minimum Wage Workers." *Monthly Labor Review* 113 (1)(January):70–74.

Hoffman, Saul D., and Laurence S. Seidman. 1990. "The Earned Income Tax Credit." Kalamazoo, MI: W. E. Upjohn Institute for Employment Research.

Horrigan, Michael, and Steven Haugen. 1988. "The Declining Middle Class Thesis: A Sensitivity Analysis." *Monthly Labor Review* 111 (5)(May):3–15.

Johnson, William R., and Edgar K. Browning. 1983. "The Distributional and Efficiency Effects of Increasing the Minimum Wage: A Simulation." *American Economic Review* 73 (1):204–211.

Kelly, Terrence. 1976. *Two Policy Questions Regarding the Minimum Wage*. Washington, D.C.: The Urban Institute.

Levitan, Sar A., and Issac Shapiro. 1987. *Working Poor: America's Contradiction*. Baltimore, MD: The Johns Hopkins University Press.

Linneman, Peter. 1982. "The Economic Impacts of Minimum Wages: A New Look at an Old Question." *Journal of Political Economy* 90 (June):443–469.

Mincy, Ronald. 1990. "Raising the Minimum Wage: Effects on Family Poverty." *Monthly Labor Review* 113 (7):18–25.

Sellekaerts, Brigette. 1981. "Minimum Wage Indexation." *Report of the Minimum Wage Study Commission*, vol. 7, pp. 145–169.

Steuerle, C. Eugene, and Jason Juffras. 1991. "A $1,000 Tax Credit for Every Child: A Base of Reform for the Nation's Tax, Welfare, and Health Systems." Policy Paper. Washington, D.C.: The Urban Institute.

Zucker, Albert. 1973. "Minimum Wages and the Long Run Elasticity of Demand for Low Wage Labor." *Quarterly Journal of Economics* 87 (May):267–277.

Index

Boldface numbers refer to figures and tables.

G

H

N

O

S

T

Y

Z